LUCIFER BOOK ONE

Mike Carey
Writer

Peter Gross
Ryan Kelly
Dean Ormston
Scott Hampton
Chris Weston
James Hodgkins
Warren Pleece
Artists

Daniel Vozzo
Marguerite Van Cook
Colorists

Todd Klein
Ellie de Ville
Comicraft
Fiona Stephenson
Letterers

Duncan Fegredo
Cover Art

Scott Hampton
Duncan Fegredo
Original Series Covers

Based on characters created by Neil Gaiman,
Sam Kieth and Mike Dringenberg.

LUCIFER BOOK ONE

DC Comics, 2900 W. Alameda Avenue, Burbank, CA 91505
Printed by RR Donnelley, Salem, VA, USA. Fourth Printing.
ISBN: 978-1-4012-4026-4

Library of Congress Cataloging-in-Publication Data

Carey, Mike, 1959-
Lucifer Book One / Mike Carey.
pages cm
"Originally published in single magazine form in Sandman Presents: Lucifer 1-3; Lucifer 1-13."
ISBN 978-1-4012-4026-4
1. Graphic novels. I. Title.
PN6728.L79C38 2013
741.5'973—dc23

2013000124

MIX
Paper from responsible sources
FSC® C101537

Table of Contents

FOREWORD

Writing Lucifer was never hard, not in the way that some other writing was hard. His stories, and his alone, would turn up in my head with beginnings, and middles, and ends. Of all the hundreds of characters in THE SANDMAN, he, above all, had his own agenda from the moment he first came on stage.

I took him, or went with him, on his journey from ruler of Hell in THE SANDMAN #4 (there was a nominal triumvirate in charge at the time, imposed by DC's head office, but you always knew which member of the triumvirate called the shots); to his resignation in the "Season of Mists" story — during the course of which he closed Hell, quit, kissed Mazikeen goodbye, and had his wings cut off; and from there to a nightclub called Lux, where he played cocktail piano and watched everyone else's problems with amused disdain.

He might only have been a supporting character in the SANDMAN story, but there was no doubt in my mind that he was a star.

Lucifer needed his own comic. It seemed obvious, at least to me. He was arrogant, funny, manipulative, cold, brilliant, powerful, and the former Lord of Hell, who resigned because he was done. Heaven wouldn't trust him, Hell would hate him, but anyone who needed a dirty job done would approach Lucifer to do it. (That would have been my approach, anyway.)

Sometime in 1991 I had a meeting in a hotel room with a writer who wanted to write something for Vertigo. He asked me if there was any character I'd suggest pitching to the powers that be at Vertigo as a spinoff series.

"Lucifer," I said.

He looked doubtful. I tried to reassure him by explaining what kind of comic it could be, invoking everything from the Kaballa to Hannibal Heyes and Kid Curry in *Alias Smith and Jones* ("I sure wish the governor would let a few more people in on our secret!"), and at the end of our conversation he looked no less doubtful than he had looked at the start.

"Anybody else?" he said.

It was a question I slowly grew used to as the decade continued. "Who'd make a good spinoff character?"

"Lucifer," I'd say.

And, like the writer in the hotel room, they'd say, "Anyone else?" I think they were mostly worried that a comic starring the Devil (even a Devil who had got bored, and tired, and resigned) might lead somebody to burn down the DC offices. This was particularly true when they were located at 666 Fifth Avenue.

And anyway, to tell good Lucifer stories, we would need a good writer.

In this case, a writer named Mike Carey. Who got it, without needing it to be explained. Mike Carey's Lucifer is even more manipulative, charming and dangerous than I could have hoped. The supporting cast are real people, living and dead, in a real world. Carey's stories are elegantly told, solidly written (for my money, he's easily one of the half-dozen best writers of mainstream comics, and climbing), and they are good comics. Which, like the people in them, are going somewhere.

His collaborators are doing an excellent job of picturing Mike's world.

I still expect the success of Lucifer to prompt someone with more convictions than sense to attempt to burn down the DC offices. Until they do, I shall keep reading.

— Neil Gaiman
The Ice Hotel, Quebec
February 2001

THE STORY SO FAR...

Lucifer has resigned as King of Hell and gone to live on Earth — in Los Angeles, of all places, where he runs a successful piano bar and plans to enjoy a long and peaceful retirement.

This story was told by Neil Gaiman in the SANDMAN arc entitled "Season of Mists," and it's all you need to know before you read this book.

But there are a few other considerations that are worth bearing in mind.

One of them is the Christian doctrine called the *felix culpa*. It means the happy fall, the sin that has good consequences. As a kid, I always had trouble getting my head around that concept, but that probably says a lot more about me than it does about Christian eschatology.

The basic idea is this. Adam and Eve sinned, and were cast out of paradise. After that, all of humanity was forced to live within the legacy of their fatal error. Original sin is something that we're born with. The roots of our family tree were poisoned, so we're all full of poison from the outset, however we conduct ourselves and whatever choices we make.

But God threw us a lifeline, in the form of Jesus Christ. Christ's sacrifice redeemed us, and that was such an astonishing thing, such a miraculous intervention, that it actually made Adam and Eve's sin into a good thing. It was *better* that they sinned, and that humankind fell, so we could be raised again by Christ's ministry.

This is why Milton, in the opening lines of *Paradise Lost*, makes a direct link between the fall of Adam and the incarnation of God in the form of Christ. He promises to talk about

> *Man's First Disobedience, and the Fruit*
> *Of that Forbidden Tree, whose mortal taste*
> *Brought Death into the World, and all our woe*
> *With loss of Eden, till one greater Man*
> *Restore us, and regain the blissful Seat.*

I raise this idea for two reasons: the first is as a way into talking about the genesis of LUCIFER as a monthly book, which (to compare vast things with very, very small ones) had its own "happy fall" built in; the second is because I want to say a word about Jesus of Nazareth, and the reason for his absence from the story you're about to read.

LUCIFER existed as a miniseries before it existed as an ongoing monthly. The first three issues collected in this volume comprise "The Morningstar Option," which came out under the SANDMAN PRESENTS umbrella. It was the first thing I ever wrote for Vertigo, and I can't tell you what a colossal, monumental, towering hugeness of a deal that was for the thirty-year-old me — that I was writing a story set in the SANDMAN continuity, using Neil Gaiman's characters. It was one of the major turning points in my life, and I recognized that fact at the time. Even if I dropped the ball, or scored an own-goal with it, or squeezed it into a shape that wouldn't bounce, nothing could ever take away that moment when the ball had been put into my hands.

Some years later, when the UK inaugurated a national lottery, the television ads showed a whole procession of people getting the news that they'd won. Each time, a giant hand would protrude into the frame with a finger pointing at the lucky winner, and a sepulchral voice would thunder "IT'S YOU!!!!"

That's how I felt. The giant hand had picked me.

It wasn't a giant hand, of course. It was Alisa Kwitney, the first of three brilliant Vertigo editors who've shaped my storytelling to an extent that isn't even funny. But that's by the by.

The truth is that I kind of cheated when I wrote "The Morningstar Option." I disguised it as a complete, self-contained story, but it wasn't. It was conceived as the first installment of a much bigger narrative, and I went on to pitch that overarching story — the LUCIFER monthly — to Vertigo's Shelly Roeberg (now Shelly Bond). The series was commissioned, the art team was assembled, and we got stuck in. We got the first three issues, the first complete story arc, in the can, and we were rolling on towards our launch date with the wind at our backs.

Which was when disaster struck. Our penciller, Chris Weston, and our inker, James Hodgkins, both felt they were in a coalition that wasn't reflecting their work at its best. Citing creative differences, and with no hard feelings (well, none that lasted), they left the book.

We hadn't even hit the stores yet, and we'd just lost our art team. We were on the rocks without ever getting into the water — at least, that was how it felt to me. It was a disaster! The book was fated to undergo a radical change of identity when it was only a few issues old. Given how crucial it is to retain readers in the early days of a new title, and how even tiny wobbles get reflected in sales, this was obviously going to sink us.

But just like Adam and Eve after they accepted that fruit basket from the guy with the forked tongue (Lucifer, according to some accounts, although he denies it), we got saved instead of sunk. We got Dean Ormston in issue #4, and then we got Peter Gross an issue after that. We got a new look that absolutely defined us, only it turned out to be two new looks. For the rest of the run, Peter and Dean alternated — Peter on the long arcs, Dean on the one-offs, with occasional jam sessions in which they shared the art chores for arcs that required radical shifts in tone, like "Mansions of the Silence." It worked so well, and allowed us to accomplish so much, that it's hard to imagine now what LUCIFER might have become if that crisis hadn't happened.

A very different animal, that's for sure, and not just in visual terms. Peter's storytelling instincts saturated LUCIFER, even though he says he held back on some suggestions because he came in late. His genius turned minor characters into core cast members, verbose explanations into transcendent visual moments, themes into leitmotifs. In the first year of our collaboration, we laid down the foundations for everything that followed. It was the partnership that I and the story both needed.

And Dean's dark-adjusted eyes filled the one-offs with a sense of scale and urgency far beyond what I'd thought would be possible. They could have been fripples, distractions, makeweights, but they became something absolutely essential, a way of reflecting on the core story in a host of minor keys.

So, yeah. Sometimes you get what you need, instead of what you want.

Now, coming to that second point. The story you're about to read concerns huge events and high stakes. Universes are made and destroyed, the fate of all that lives is debated and determined, cosmic orders shift and are redefined. But on one level it's a family drama — a story about a father and a son, and their failure to get along. The father is God, the son is Lucifer. And two other brothers, Gabriel and Michael, also make significant appearances (although Gabriel only shows up in flashback).

It was crucial to the way we conceived the story that Lucifer's relationship with God should have that dimension of intimacy — that it should be as close and personal as it was huge and cosmic and eschatological. If Lucifer is just an insubordinate servant, or a treacherous lieutenant, then his story resonates very differently. But for the purposes of this book, that's not what he is at all; he's the child desperately searching for his own autonomy, for a definition of himself that springs entirely from himself, and owes nothing to anyone else.

And in that respect, despite his power and his immortality and all the rest of it, he's Everyman. He's going through something that everyone has to go through — a battle that we all fight and arguably none of us ever win, because the origins of our nature lie outside of ourselves and the boundary between self and world is as porous as a bath sponge.

With that as the conceptual center of the book, we knew going in that if we introduced Jesus as a character we'd be holing our metaphor below the waterline. Lucifer can only be God's son in the absence of that other son, whose story had already been expanded on elsewhere.

Gabriel's absence, by the way, has a very different explanation. It was because he'd already appeared — and been dispatched, horrifically, to Hell — in the pages of HELLBLAZER. Back in those long-gone days, there was a Vertigo-verse of sorts, sustained by the numerous appearances of core characters in each other's books. John Constantine appeared in one of the earliest issues of THE SANDMAN, and his remote ancestor Lady Joanna Constantine was introduced there. Therefore, SANDMAN continuity rubs up against HELLBLAZER continuity. And since THE SANDMAN (as I mentioned earlier) was the book in which Lucifer first handed in his resignation to God, our continuity is part of the same chain. The only time that ever became a problem was when it came to Gabriel. If we showed him alive and well in our narrative's present time, then we were contradicting key events in HELLBLAZER. So we kept him offstage, except in flashback (#50 and #75 were the only issues in which he played a prominent role) and we were coy about his present whereabouts.

So we're canonical as far as HELLBLAZER is concerned, but we exist in a slightly different continuity to the Bible. It's probably best to see this book as an imaginary story, in the sense in which that term used to be used in the DC comics of the 1960s.

Imagine if Superman married Lois Lane.
Imagine if Lex Luthor had superpowers.
Imagine if Lucifer were the son of God...

— Mike Carey
London 2013

scott hampton

The Morningstar Option

Mike Carey
Writer

Scott Hampton
Artist

Todd Klein
Letterer

Jennifer Lee
Assistant Editor

Alisa Kwitney
Editor

Neil Gaiman
Consultant

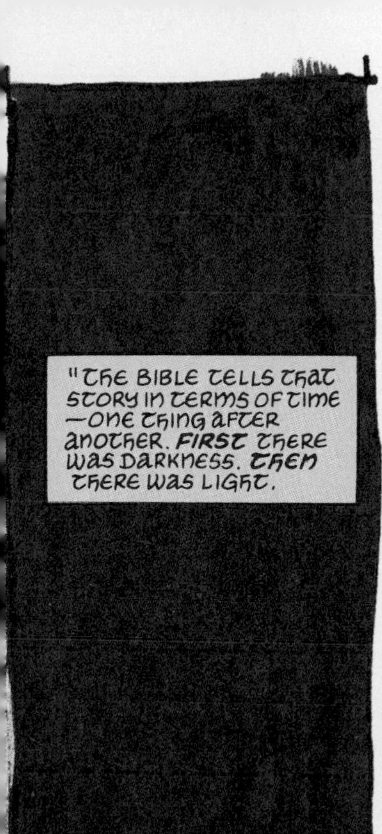
"THE BIBLE TELLS THAT STORY IN TERMS OF TIME —ONE THING AFTER ANOTHER. FIRST THERE WAS DARKNESS. THEN THERE WAS LIGHT.

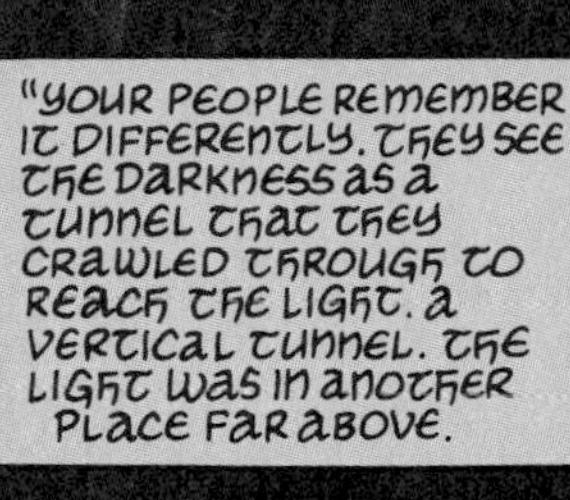
"YOUR PEOPLE REMEMBER IT DIFFERENTLY. THEY SEE THE DARKNESS AS A TUNNEL THAT THEY CRAWLED THROUGH TO REACH THE LIGHT. A VERTICAL TUNNEL. THE LIGHT WAS IN ANOTHER PLACE FAR ABOVE.
"THIS MEANS NOTHING TO YOU, DOES IT?

"IN ANY CASE THEY TELL THE STORY AS A JOURNEY. A HARD AND TERRIBLE JOURNEY. THE PLACE WHERE THEY STARTED FROM WAS FIRST WORLD.
"WHERE THE DARKNESS WAS. WHERE IT STILL IS.

"UNDERSTAND ME. WHATEVER LIVED THERE THEN LIVES THERE STILL, THOUGH YOUR KIND ABANDONED THIS PLACE HALF A MILLION YEARS AGO. THERE ARE FORESTS OF BLACK OAKS, A HUNDRED FEET TALL, STANDING INVISIBLE IN THE DARK. THERE ARE CREATURES... PREDATORS ...THAT HAVE NOT EATEN IN GEOLOGICAL AGES.

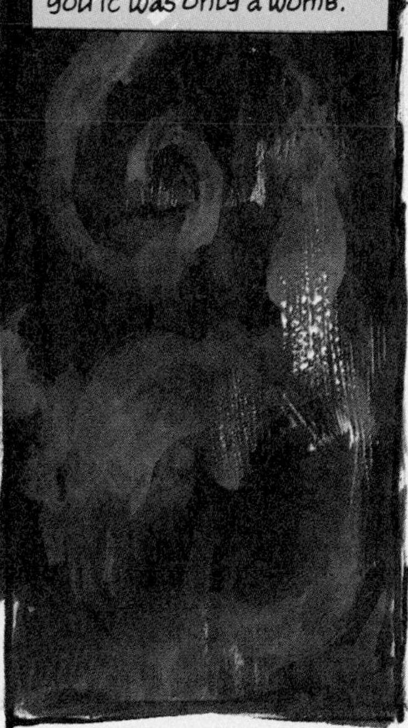
"YOU HAVE FORGOTTEN THE VOICELESS, BUT THEY HAVE NOT FORGOTTEN YOU. THEY WANT YOU TO COME HOME. WANT THE FEEL OF YOUR FEAR AND YOUR WORSHIP. BUT WHILE THE DARKNESS IS A HOME FOR THEM, FOR YOU IT WAS ONLY A WOMB.

"YOU BETRAYED THEM...

"...WHEN YOU WERE BORN INTO THE LIGHT."

NO ASYMMETRY, BUT THE PUPILLARY DILATION IS ON THE SLOW SIDE.
IT'S OKAY, PAUL, THE LIGHT WON'T HURT YOU.

SEE THE PICTURE? THE BOY'S PLAYING WITH A TRUCK, ISN'T HE? CAN YOU POINT TO THE TRUCK? TRY TO POINT TO THE TRUCK, PAUL.
AUL HAS A TRUCK
RY RIDES A

LET'S FEEL THOSE FINGERS. OH, GOOD GRIP, PAUL. NICE GRIP. HE'S LEFT-HANDED, ISN'T HE? LET'S TRY THE OTHER SIDE.

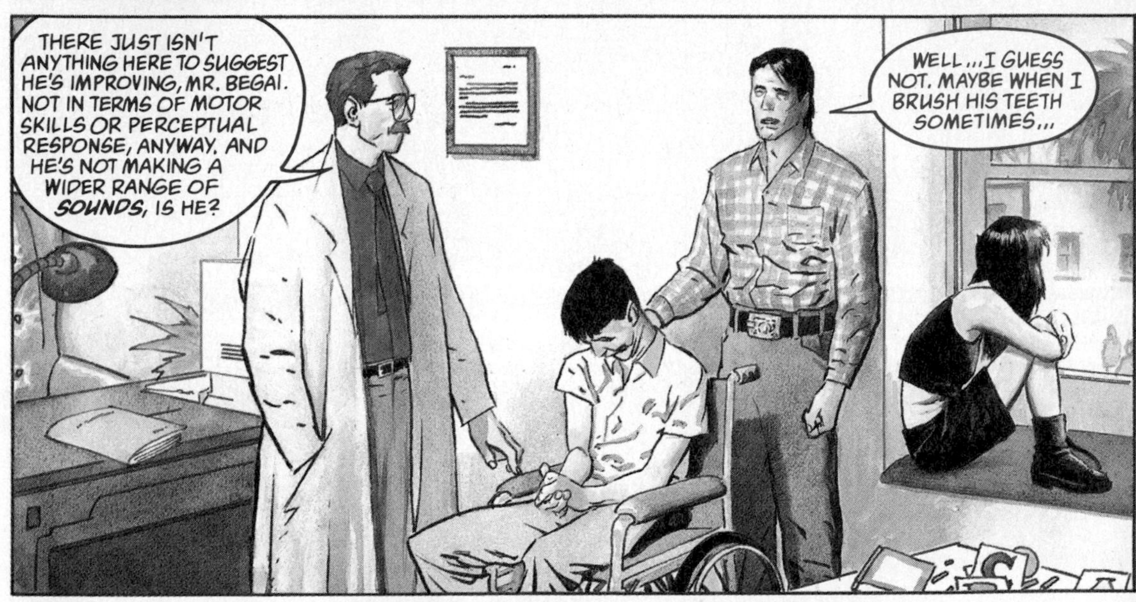
THERE JUST ISN'T ANYTHING HERE TO SUGGEST HE'S IMPROVING, MR. BEGAI. NOT IN TERMS OF MOTOR SKILLS OR PERCEPTUAL RESPONSE, ANYWAY. AND HE'S NOT MAKING A WIDER RANGE OF SOUNDS, IS HE?
WELL... I GUESS NOT. MAYBE WHEN I BRUSH HIS TEETH SOMETIMES...

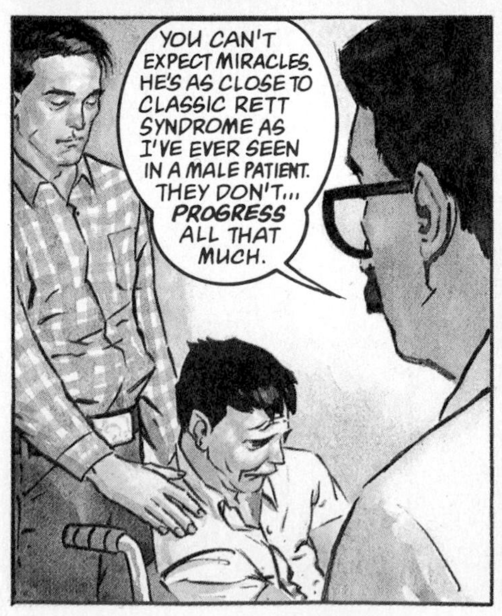
YOU CAN'T EXPECT MIRACLES. HE'S AS CLOSE TO CLASSIC RETT SYNDROME AS I'VE EVER SEEN IN A MALE PATIENT. THEY DON'T... PROGRESS ALL THAT MUCH.

I WAS THINKIN'... I DUNNO... THAT HE WAS LOOKIN' AT ME MORE. LIKE HE WANTED TO TALK TO ME, ALMOST. YOU THINK THAT COULD EVER...?

NO. PUT THAT OUT OF YOUR MIND.

YOU SAID THE FITS ARE ACTUALLY WORSE NOW. DOES THAT MEAN LONGER OR MORE INTENSE?
WELL, BOTH.
I CAN UP THE DOSAGE ON THE LAMOTRIGINE BUT TRY USING THE RECTAL VALIUM TOO, AS A PREVENTATIVE...

"HE'S YOUR BROTHER. YOU'D WANT TO BE THERE FOR YOUR BROTHER, WOULDN'T YOU RACHEL?"
"YEAH, DAD, FINE. IT'S JUST A SCHOOL DAY. I'LL JUST MISS IT. NO PROBLEM. MY TIME IS YOURS."
"...OBVIOUSLY."

HEY, DAD--THERE'S SOME WEIRD WOMAN HANGING 'ROUND YOUR CAR.
I TOLD YOU NOT TO PARK THERE.

SHE'S ACTING REAL CRAZY. SHE'S WAVING THIS FLOWER AROUND LIKE SHE'S DIRECTING TRAFFIC. AND I THINK SHE'S CRYING.

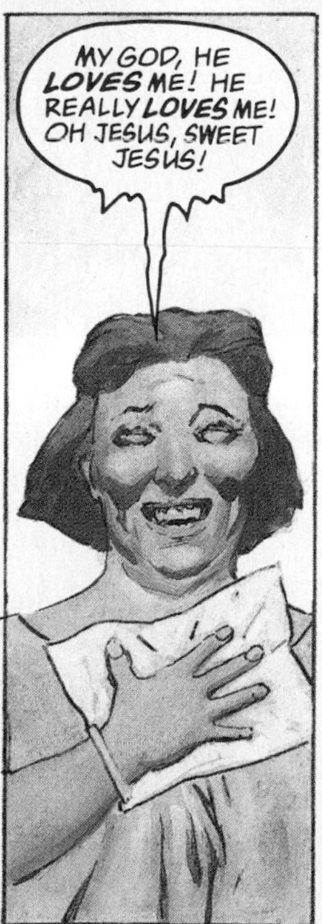
MY GOD, HE **LOVES** ME! HE REALLY **LOVES** ME! OH JESUS, SWEET JESUS!

LOOK! I FOUND THIS!
THAT'S NICE. TAKE CARE. TAKE CARE, NOW.

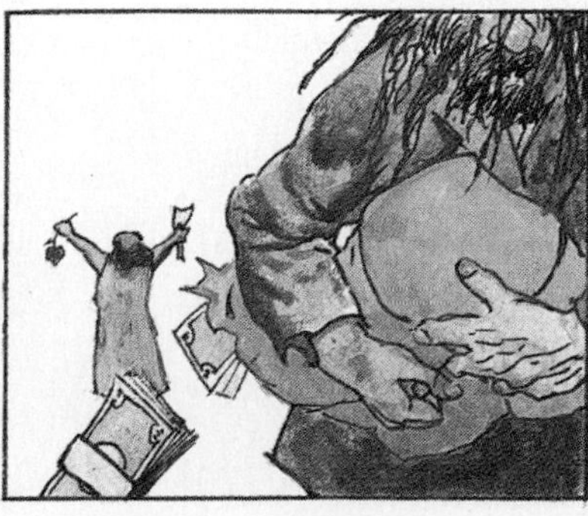

LOCAL MAN JERRY RUFINO SPRAYED HIS BOSS WITH SHAVING FOAM WHEN HE WON THE STATE LOTTERY YESTERDAY, BUT TWELVE HOURS LATER HE WAS ASKING FOR HIS OLD JOB BACK...
I DUNNO ABOUT USIN' MORE OF THAT LAMOTRIGINE STUFF. IT ALWAYS LEAVES 'IM DOPEY. WHAT D'YOU RECKON, RACH?

...BECAUSE A STAGGERING EIGHT HUNDRED PEOPLE PICKED THE WINNING NUMBERS, EACH COLLECTING LESS THAN THREE THOUSAND DOLLARS! DON'T GIVE UP YOUR DAY JOB, JER.
WELL IF IT'S A CHOICE BETWEEN DOPEY AND FRENZY, I KNOW WHICH DWARF I'D GO FOR.

WHAT'S THAT, FLOWER?
NOTHING, DAD.

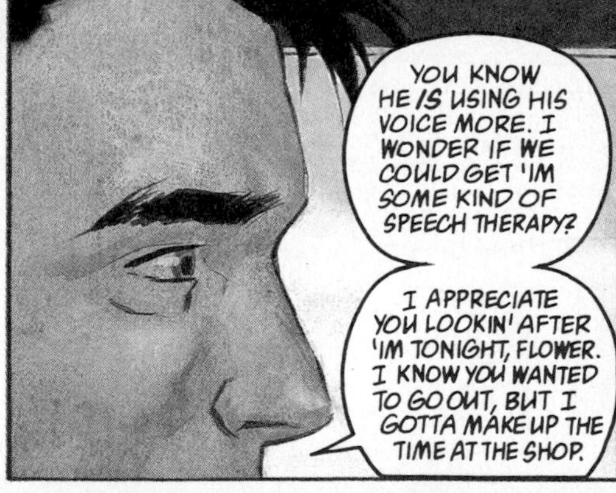
YOU KNOW HE IS USING HIS VOICE MORE. I WONDER IF WE COULD GET 'IM SOME KIND OF SPEECH THERAPY?
I APPRECIATE YOU LOOKIN' AFTER 'IM TONIGHT, FLOWER. I KNOW YOU WANTED TO GO OUT, BUT I GOTTA MAKE UP THE TIME AT THE SHOP.

NO PROBLEM. ALL PART OF THE SERVICE.
TCH. COME ON, PAUL, MOST CHICKS WON'T EVEN LOOK AT A GUY WITH DROOL ON HIS CHIN.

"THEN AGAIN, MOM LOOKED AT DAD.
"SO I GUESS THERE'S HOPE FOR ALL OF US."

LOS ANGELES, CALIFORNIA.
I have said that I wish to see the proprietor.

YES SIR. MAY I REFRESH YOUR NUTS?
You may leave my nuts exactly as they are. Tell your employer that I will speak with him.

NO I CAN'T. THERE'S THIS FREAKY GUY SITTING OUT ON TABLE SEVEN, ALL BY HIMSELF. HE'S BEEN ASKING AFTER YOU.
YOU CAN CLOSE UP UNTIL TONIGHT, BEATRICE.

YES. I IMAGINE HE HAS.
AS HOC OPUS HIC

LOCK THE DOOR ANYWAY.
MAZIKEEN, BRING US TWO GLASSES FROM MY SPECIAL BOTTLE-- THE ONE ON THE LEFT.

"WHOSE FEET MAY NOT TOUCH THE GROUND, NOR ANY FOULNESS STAIN THEIR GARMENTS, FOR THEY ARE OF THE SEVENTH SPHERE WHICH IS ABOVE CORRUPTION."

The devil can cite scripture for his purpose. Good day to you, Lucifer Morningstar.

HARDLY SCRIPTURE. JOHN TRITHEMIUS, ON ANGELS. HE WAS TALKING ABOUT THE THRONES, AND GETTING IT WRONG AS USUAL.
YOU'RE THE ONES WHO LIKE TO GET DIRTY, AREN'T YOU, AMENADIEL?

There is no room for doubt or scruple in the service of the name. If you'd realized that, you might still be of the host.

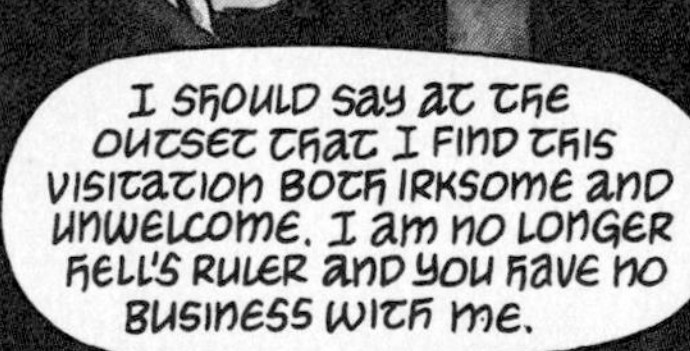

I SHOULD SAY AT THE OUTSET THAT I FIND THIS VISITATION BOTH IRKSOME AND UNWELCOME. I AM NO LONGER HELL'S RULER AND YOU HAVE NO BUSINESS WITH ME.

And how are you *finding* your retirement, Prince of the East?

RESTFUL.

I would have thought you'd be bored. It's difficult to let go of power when you've been used to exercising it.
To settle down and grow roses up the door.
AND YET HERE I AM.

AND THE OLD FIRM IS IN NEW HANDS. AND THE WORLD GOES ON.

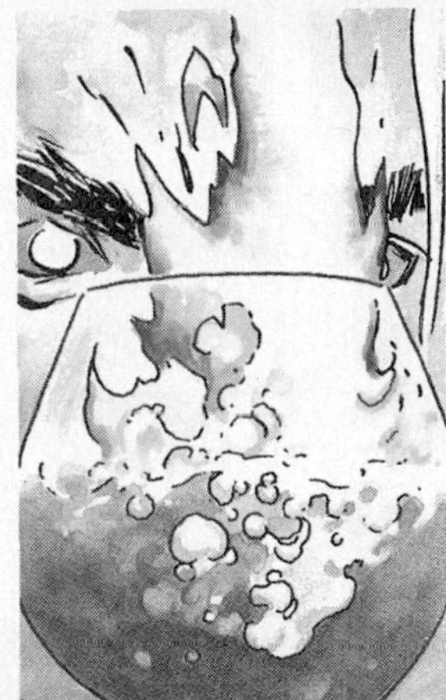

THAT'S AN EIGHTY-YEAR-OLD JANNEAU ARMAGNAC. IF I'D KNOWN YOU WERE GOING TO WASTE IT ON MELODRAMA I'D HAVE GIVEN YOU THE '78.
The world is on fire, Lucifer Morningstar. I wanted to make that point forcefully.
Otherwise we could squander the whole evening in stale repartee.

I'VE NO DESIRE TO TRESPASS ON YOUR EVENING AT ALL, AMENADIEL. I'M SURE THERE ARE MANY PLACES WHERE YOUR COMPANY WOULD BE ALMOST WELCOME.
NO NEED, MAZIKEEN. LEAVE IT.

I am to place a proposition before you. Against my will. Against my judgment. Knowing you to be the king of liars and traitors.
Say **no** right now and you will spare me consider-able effort.

There is a power at work on Earth which is granting human wishes.
SO? THERE ARE *MANY* SUCH. THERE HAVE ALWAYS BEEN AGENCIES THAT TRAFFIC IN THAT WAY.

Ah, but this is different. For one thing, it is new. For another, it is **growing** by increments. We have collated examples.

SHOULDN'T THIS BE ON MICROFILM?

The instances so far are trivial--treasures found in old mattresses, unexpected sexual encounters of surprising sweet-ness, the sudden death of rich relatives. But you know the nature of human desire.
They'll rip each other apart like rats in a sack.

Why me?
Because heaven wishes neither to intervene directly in this nor to stand by and let it happen.
You represent a third option. I am told that you will name your price.

That I *may* name my price or that I *will* name it?
Will.
You'd think part of omniscience would be knowing when to stop.
But still...

Living here among them-- watching them live and die and build and break--you can't help but think about how *impermanent* everything is in this universe. Nothing really workman-like. Nothing made to last.
A letter of passage.
Your pardon?
Say that my price is a letter of passage.

Ah, but he'll already *know* that, won't he?

I do not grasp your meaning.
IT'S NOT NECESSARY THAT YOU SHOULD.
THERE IS ANOTHER SIDE TO THE SKY, THAT'S ALL. I'M SURE THEY'LL TELL YOU ABOUT IT SOME DAY. SOME BIG, HAIRY ARCHANGEL WILL SIT YOU ON HIS LAP AND GIVE YOU THE TALK.

Your mockery demeans you. You have accepted the commission.
Do you require anything else of me before I leave?

YES. I'D LIKE AN APOLOGY.
An ap...?
FOR THE DAMAGE YOU CAUSED TO THE TABLE.

Then... in accordance with my instructions, which were to give you anything you asked for...
I apologize, Lucifer Morningstar, for the damage to your table.

GOODBYE, AMENADIEL.

MAZIKEEN, TELL THE STAFF THEY CAN LEAVE. WE WILL NOT BE OPENING THIS EVENING.
YEHSZ, NGY RROAHD.
LIGHT SOME CANDLES. KEEP THEM LIT FROM NOW ON. AND BRING ME A KNIFE AND A DOVE -- ACTUALLY A PIGEON WILL DO.

OH WHERE ARE YOU GOING... SAID THE FALSE KNIGHT ON THE ROAD...

NGY RROAHD, HRRALL I NGRING HEOU A BOWL TO CASZSZ GHE VHLOOD?
THANK YOU, MAZIKEEN. NO, THE BIRD'S NOT FOR SACRIFICE. WHO WOULD I SACRIFICE IT TO?

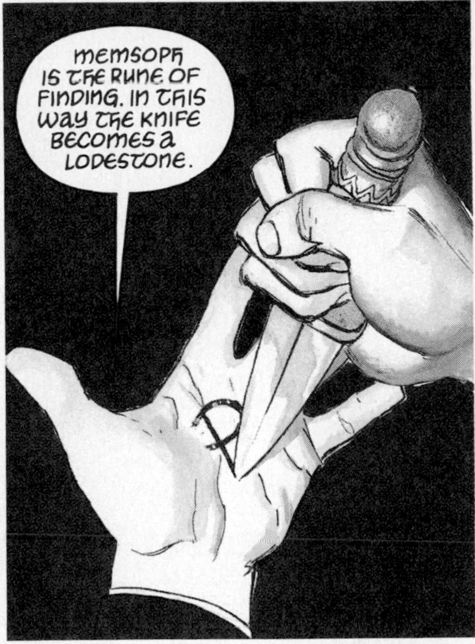
MEMSOPH IS THE RUNE OF FINDING. IN THIS WAY THE KNIFE BECOMES A LODESTONE.

I MAY NOT KNOW WHERE I'M GOING, BUT I SEE NO REASON TO TRAVEL BLIND.

NOW YOU. DON'T BE SO FRIGHTENED. I'M NOT HUNGRY.

I'LL JUST TROUBLE YOU FOR A LOAN OF THESE. I MAY NEED TO FLY BEFORE THIS BUSINESS IS DONE WITH, AND I FORFEITED MY OWN WINGS SOME TIME SINCE.

MAZIKEEN.
YEHSZ, NGY RROAHD.
MY COAT, PLEASE. AND BRING ME MY OTHER BOTTLE. THE ONE ON THE RIGHT.

I'M GOING OUT.

DID YOU EVER EXPECT TO SEE YOUR SON AGAIN?

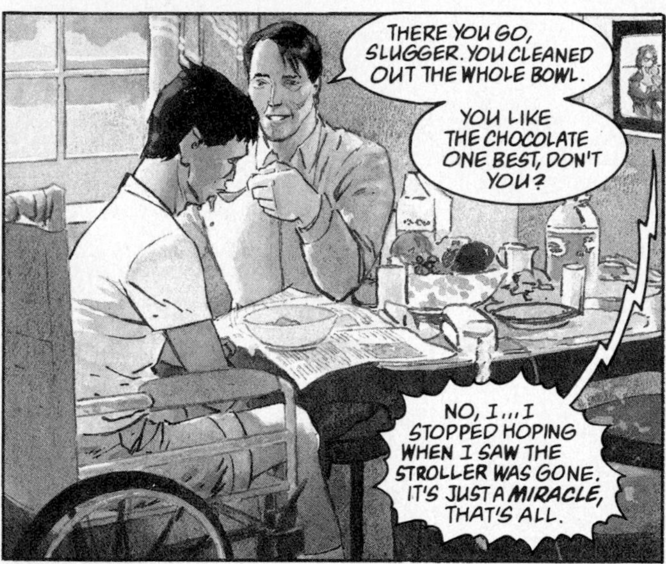
THERE YOU GO, SLUGGER. YOU CLEANED OUT THE WHOLE BOWL.
YOU LIKE THE CHOCOLATE ONE BEST, DON'T YOU?
NO, I...I STOPPED HOPING WHEN I SAW THE STROLLER WAS GONE. IT'S JUST A MIRACLE, THAT'S ALL.

I'M GONNA LEAVE YOU AT THE WINDOW HERE. YOU CAN WATCH THOSE KIDS PLAYING.
YOU HEAR 'EM SHOUTING? NOISY LITTLE SHITHEADS.

IT'S FUNNY. YOU LOOK SO MUCH LIKE HER, BUT SHE NEVER STOPPED TALKING. THAT'S PROBABLY WHY I FEEL LIKE I KNOW WHAT YOUR VOICE WOULD SOUND LIKE.

ANYWAY, I'M GONNA BE BACK AROUND ELEVEN. YOU'LL BE ASLEEP THEN, SO I'LL SEE YOU IN THE AM.

I'M OUTTA HERE. TALK TO 'IM A BIT, WILL YOU, FLOWER?
OKAY, DAD.
AND MOVE 'IM IN THE CHAIR ONCE IN A WHILE TO STOP 'IM GETTING SORE. SEE YOU LATER.

OKAY, LINDA. YOU'RE CLEAR TO COMMENCE APPROACH.
I'M HEARING YOU, RED LEADER. YOU WANT PRETZELS?
NAH, JUST CORN CHIPS.

I'M MOVING YOU INTO YOUR ROOM, PAUL. IT'LL BE NICE AND QUIET THERE.

LOOK, YOU'VE GOT TEDDY AND RABBIT AND SOPHIE.
OKAY?

GUY IN ROWLEYS DIDN'T EVEN LOOK AT MY I.D.
JUST AS WELL. YOU DON'T LOOK ANYTHING LIKE ARLENE DIAZ.
THAT'S WHAT LETS ME SLEEP AT NIGHT. HERE, RACHEL...

...GET HAPPY.

FAR ENOUGH, PRINCE OF HELL.

FAR ENOUGH AND A LITTLE MORE.

AH, THE HOSPITALITY OF THE LILIM! I WONDER WHAT IT DIED OF. HELLO, MAHU. HOW IS YOUR MASTER THESE DAYS?
I ACKNOWLEDGE NO MASTER.

THEN HOW IS BRIADACH THE BLIND, LORD OF THE LILIM IN EXILE? IS HE HEALTHY? I MEAN, WITHIN THE USUAL PARAMETERS?
HIS LUNGS *BURN*. HIS EVERY HEARTBEAT TEARS HIS SIDE LIKE A *FLENSING KNIFE*.
AH. WELL WITHIN THE USUAL PARAMETERS, THEN.

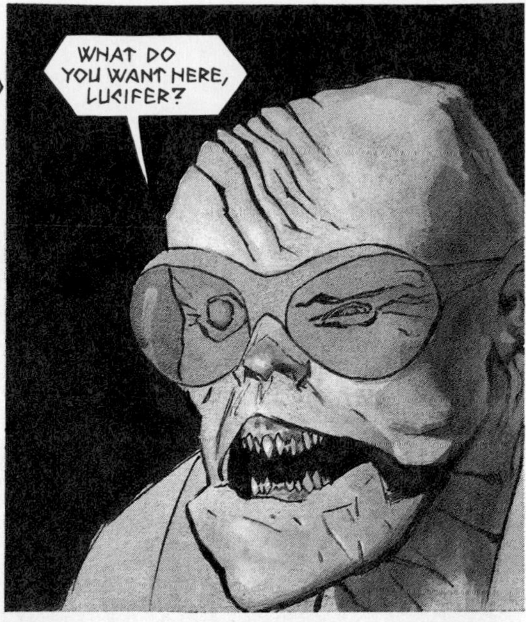
WHAT DO YOU WANT HERE, LUCIFER?

INFORMATION. I HAVE AN OCCASIONAL ARRANGEMENT WITH YOUR MASTER WHICH HE MAY HAVE MENTIONED TO YOU.
AN ARRANGEMENT?
AN ARRANGEMENT, YES.

THEN GO UP, AND BE DAMNED TO YOU. WHEN THE LILIM CLAIM THEIR RIGHT, YOU'LL LAST NO LONGER THAN THE ANGELS. YOU'LL JUST BURN WITH A DIFFERENT COLORED FLAME.
OH, NOTHING WILL BE BURNING BY THEN. EVEN SOLAR FUSION ONLY LASTS SO LONG.

WHO'S THERE, MANU? I HEAR VOICES.
IS IT THE CHALDAEAN BITCH, COME GRUBBING FOR NEWS OF THE DEAD CITIES? OR FALLEN SAMAEL, WITH HIS HURT PRIDE AND HIS SAVAGE TONGUE? WHO'S THERE, I SAY!

NOBODY'S CALLED ME SAMAEL FOR SUCH A LONG TIME. IT'S LIKE SOMEONE USING YOUR MAIDEN NAME.
LORD LUCIFER!
BRIADACH. STILL SICK, I SEE.

SICK? THAT'S A SHALLOW WORD TO MEASURE THE FATHOMS OF MY SUFFERING. MY LORD, IF YOU HAVE ANY OF THAT HEALING WATER ABOUT YOU I'LL TAKE IT NOW AND PAY YOU IN SOME LITTLE SPACE.

BUT IT DULLS YOUR EYES.

DULLS MY EYES! YOU KNOW EXACTLY WHAT I SEE. YOU KNOW EXACTLY HOW MUCH BLINDNESS HEAVEN HAS ALLOWED TO ME!
"THE SEED AND THE ROT." THERE'S NO NEED TO REMIND ME OF YOUR CURSE. DO YOU THINK THIS IS A SOCIAL CALL?
IF YOU WANT THE LETHE WATER, DEMON, YOU'LL HAVE TO WORK FOR IT. THE SAME RULES AS ALWAYS.

ASK ME THEN, BUT IN HELL'S NAME BE BRIEF! A BIRTH AND A DEATH. I'LL GIVE YOU TWO MOMENTS FOR TWO SIPS OF OBLIVION.
ONE MOMENT.

IT WILL BE BOTH, YOU SEE.

A BIRTH AND A DEATH.

THE BIRTH AND DEATH OF WHAT? TELL ME WHAT YOU WANT--AND LET ME HEAR YOU POUR, FOR INSPIRATION'S SAKE.

THE BIRTH AND DEATH OF A DESIRE. A DESIRE SATISFIED IN THE MOMENT IT'S CONCEIVED. A WISH...

...A WISH BEING GRANTED. YES, YES, I'M NOT SIMPLE. THEY'RE RARE ENOUGH SINCE MAB CLOSED HER BORDERS, BUT TODAY THEY SEEM TO BE AS COMMON AS RAIN.

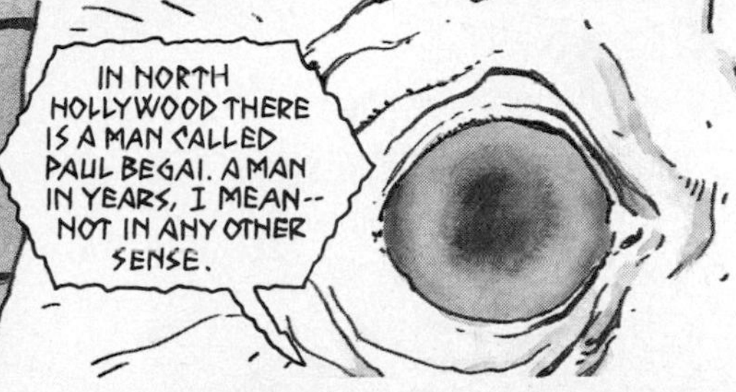
IN NORTH HOLLYWOOD THERE IS A MAN CALLED PAUL BEGAI. A MAN IN YEARS, I MEAN--NOT IN ANY OTHER SENSE.

WHY HIM?

BECAUSE THE POWER LINGERS AROUND HIM. IT WINDS OVER AND THROUGH HIM.
WHAT IS IT, LUCIFER? THIS THING THAT OPENS AND OPENS AND SEEMS TO HAVE NO DEATH? HAVE YOU SEEN IT? HAVE YOU TRIED TO TALK TO IT?

NO. NOT YET. DRINK SPARINGLY, BRIADACH. I DON'T HAVE A STEADY LINE OF SUPPLY THESE DAYS.

SO KEVIN'S STILL SITTING THERE WITH HIS DICK OUT, BUT SUZIE'S CLIMBED OUT OF THE BATHROOM WINDOW. SHE'S HALFWAY DOWN THE STREET. AND THE LAST THING SHE HEARD HIM SAY WAS, "SUUUUZIE! I'VE GOT THE CONDOM ON!"
HAHAHAHAHA!

HEY, SUZIE SAID NO WAY ARE YOU A NAVAJO, COS NAVAJOS ARE BRIGHT RED LIKE TOMATOES. I TOLD HER TO SUCK IT.
UMM, HALF NAVAJO. DAD'S THE REAL THING. HE WAS BORN ON A RESERVATION. AND MY GRANDAD'S SOME KIND OF WITCH DOCTOR. SHAMAN. THING.

MMMMMUUUUH!

NNNNNNAAAAH!

KRAASH!
HEY, WHAT WAS THAT? IS THERE SOMEONE ELSE HERE?
SHIT. JUST MY BROTHER. GIVE ME A SECOND, GUYS.

YOU OKAY, PAUL?
AW, NO!

YOU LITTLE RATBAG, YOU THREW UP ALL DOWN THE BED. AND THE LAMP! DAD IS GONNA KILL ME!
AND IT HAD TO FUCKING SHATTER IN A MILLION GOD-DAMN PIECES. IT COULDN'T JUST BREAK IN TWO, COULD IT?
RAAAAA
AAAAA EL
OW! HEY!
AWWWW, FOR GOD'S SAKE!
YOU DIRTY LITTLE BASTARD! WHY DON'T YOU JUST **CHOKE!**
PAUL? HEY, PAUL! ARE YOU OKAY?
PAUL?

OH MY GOD! PAUL, PLEASE! DON'T DO THIS TO ME! BREATHE! PLEASE BREATHE!

EXCUSE ME. I'D LIKE TO EXAMINE HIM.
WH...? WHO ARE YOU? WHAT ARE YOU DOING?

CURIOUS. THIS WAS A MORE COMPLEX TRANS-ACTION THAN I THOUGHT.
AN EXCHANGE-- A TWO-WAY FLOW. POWER WAS EXPENDED HERE, BUT POWER WAS GENERATED TOO.

A VELLEITY. SOME MORON HAS CREATED A VELLEITY.
LISTEN, ARE YOU SOME KIND OF DOCTOR? ARE YOU GONNA... ARE YOU GONNA RESUSCITATE HIM?
BUT HE SAID THAT THE POWER LINGERED HERE...

COULD HE TALK?
WHAT?
YOUR BROTHER. COULD HE TALK?

NO. HE JUST... HE JUST MADE NOISES, YOU KNOW.

THEN PERHAPS IT'S DRAWN TO SILENCE. PERHAPS IT HOVERED OVER HIM LONG ENOUGH TO SENSE YOUR DESIRE.
MY WHAT?
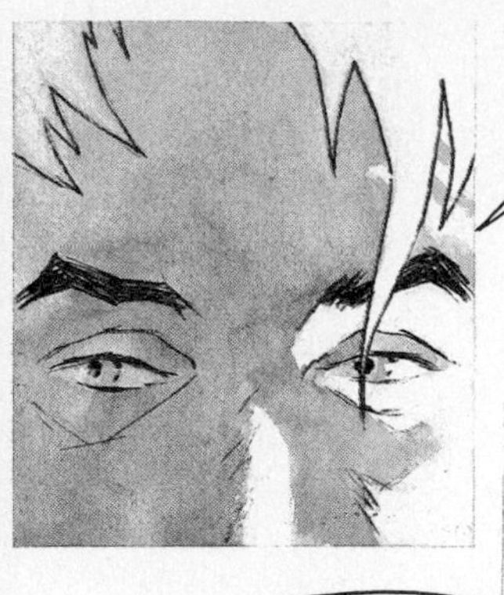

YOUR DESIRE. WHEN YOU WISHED HIM DEAD.

WHEN I WHAT? ARE YOU CRAZY? I DIDN'T WANT THIS TO HAPPEN!
OF COURSE YOU DID.

YOU...YOU COLD BASTARD! HE'S MY BROTHER! GO TO HELL! GO STRAIGHT TO FUCKING HELL!

YES.
I'D BEEN HOPING TO AVOID THAT. BUT YOU'RE RIGHT. THERE'S NO GETTING AROUND IT, IS THERE?

HEY! HEY, WHERE ARE YOU? WHERE DID YOU GO?

OH GODDDDDD!

HOME AGAIN, HOME AGAIN.
JIGGETTY JIG.

S. Hampton

THE CUP IS EMPTY. HARD TO REMEMBER THE COMFORT IT HELD. ALL GONE NOW. ALL DRIED UP.
BRIADACH SETS HIS TEETH IN THE HOT DUSK. THE BLINDFOLD IS NO HELP TO-NIGHT. HE IS ASSAILED BY IMAGES. SEEDS. BEGINNINGS. GAPING MOUTHS THAT ISSUE FORTH THE END-LESS SPEW OF FUTURE TIME.
I WISH I MAY, I WISH I MIGHT... A SWEET POISON IS SPREADING OUT ACROSS THE EARTH.
DANNY FOLGER IS A CROUPIER, BUT NOT AFTER TONIGHT. NO MATTER HOW FAST HE SLAMS THE BRAKE, THE WHEEL IS FASTER. THE LAW OF PROBABILITY JUST TURNED AND BIT HIM IN THE HAND.
BRENDA LIMOTO FINDS HER WEDDING RING, WHICH SHE GAVE UP FOR LOST SIX YEARS AGO, INSIDE THE HOLE IN THE WALL THAT SHE FINALLY DECIDED TO PLASTER.
HYDRANTS BURST IN EVERY DOWN-TOWN AREA. STREET PUNKS DANCE IN THE SPRAY LIKE A SCENE FROM SOME CORNY MOVIE.
COST
I WISH I MAY...
AND LUCIFER, HEAVEN'S FALLEN AGENT...
...WALKING THE ROCKY PATHS OF THE NINTH CIRCLE, SURROUNDED BY HORRORS AS WIDE AND VARIOUS AS THE HUMAN MIND CAN HOLD...
...EVEN LUCIFER IS COMING HOME.

IT'S HIM. IT'S LORD LUCIFER.
BOLLOCKS. THAT TREACHEROUS BASTARD WOULDN'T DARE SHOW HIS FACE AROUND HERE.
AAH! AAH!

UMM... JUST HOLD YOURSELF IN FOR A MINUTE OR TWO, WOULD YOU? NORMAL SERVICE WILL BE, WHAT IS IT, RESUMED. SHORTLY.
GAH...

Insupportable. Simply insupportable.

LITTLE PIG, LITTLE PIG, LET ME IN.

This is no longer your domain, Lucifer Morningstar. You have no right of entry here. No right even to walk on this ground without our leave.
HMM. IN MY DAY WE TOOK IN ANYONE WHO HAPPENED BY. THAT'S PART OF THE POINT, ISN'T IT?

You will not face me down and you will not sway me. Our work of redemption is at a delicate stage, and your presence here drags everything back into question.
REMIEL, YOU ONCE BEGGED ME TO RETURN...
I HAVEN'T FINISHED YET!
OH WELL.
You come here with all your old arrogance—like a visiting head of state, when the truth is you've evaded your responsibilities. You resigned.
You resigned, Lucifer.

YOUR GRASP OF CURRENT AFFAIRS IS AS KEEN AS EVER.
Spare me your sarcasm. I have nothing more to say to you.
REMIEL...

HOW MANY DEMONS STAND BEHIND US? I RECKON AT LEAST A THIRD OF THE INFERNAL HOST.
IF YOU DON'T LET ME COME INSIDE I'LL HUMILIATE YOU SO BADLY THAT YOUR PRESTIGE HERE-- WHICH I IMAGINE IS ALSO AT A DELICATE STAGE--WILL CATCH COLD AND DIE.

GOOD LAD. ALWAYS KNOW YOUR LIMITATIONS, EH?

AND WHY AM I SEEING THIS, BRIADACH WONDERS.
RACHEL BEGAI, FIFTEEN MINUTES AFTER HER BROTHER'S DEATH.
WHAT SEED OPENS HERE?
AHUH. AHUH. AHUH.

THAT'S OKAY, RACHEL. LET IT OUT.
SHE IS LETTING IT OUT, LINDA. SHE'S BEEN CRYING FOR A QUARTER OF AN HOUR.

I'M ONLY TRYING TO HELP, XIMENA.
I THINK I GOT THE VOMIT OUT OF THE SHEET. SHOULD I HANG IT ON A RADIATOR?

WHAT ARE YOU EVEN BOTHERING WITH THE FUCKING SHEET FOR? YOU'RE NOT SUPPOSED TO TOUCH ANYTHING!
THE COPS WILL PROBABLY HAUL YOU IN FOR TAMPERING WITH THE EVIDENCE.
I DIDN'T... I ONLY...

I DON'T THINK WE CALLED THE COPS YET, DID WE?
DID YOU GUYS CALL THE COPS?

WE CAN'T. MY DAD'S GONNA KILL ME FOR THIS.
PAUL'S DEAD, AND I WAS HAVING A... A PARTY. AHUH. AHUH.

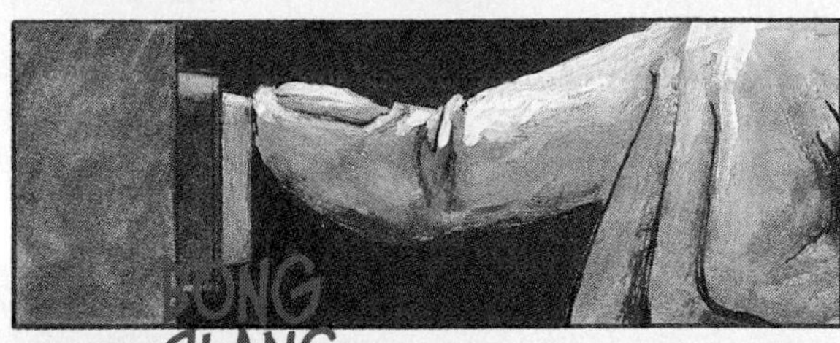
DONG
CLANG

OH NO.
WELL I GUESS SOMEONE CALLED 'EM.

IT'S MY DAD! IT'S MY DAD! DON'T LET HIM IN!
IT'S NOT YOUR DAD, IT'S A SHORT BALD GUY, ANYWAY, HE'S GOING AWAY.
OH NO. HE'S JUST STEPPING BACK TO--

AH YES.
MAHU'S LITTLE POWER PLAY.
UHH!
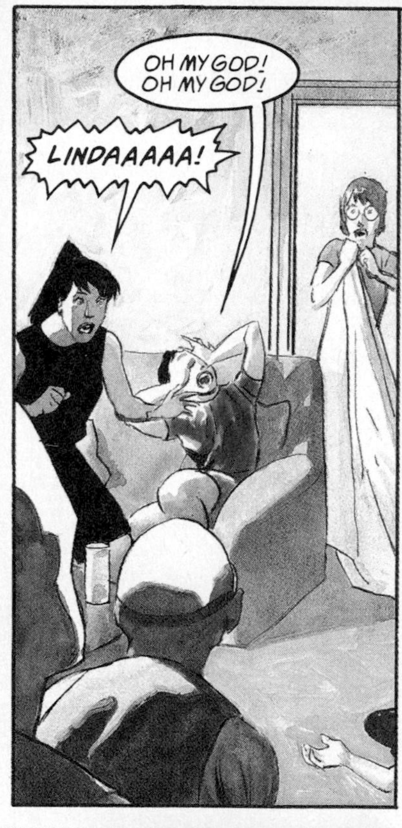
OH MY GOD! OH MY GOD!
LINDAAAAA!

THAT ONE. TAKE HER.
SO MUCH ANGER. SO LITTLE SENSE OF DIRECTION.

"ANNIHILATING ALL THAT'S MADE, TO A GREEN THOUGHT IN A GREEN SHADE." DO I INTRUDE, DUMA?

I CARRIED THIS BURDEN FOR LONG ENOUGH TO KNOW HOW IRKSOME IT CAN BE. NOR WOULD I TRESPASS HERE NOW EXCEPT THAT I AM IN THE SERVICE OF...

...THE SERVICE OF HEAVEN. THAT WAS HARDER TO SAY THAN I'D ANTICIPATED.

BEFORE YOU TOOK UP YOUR PLACE HERE YOU WERE A TUTELARY SPIRIT. YOU HAD CARE OF SILENCE. IT'S IN THAT CAPACITY THAT I COME TO YOU NOW.

I WAS NEVER A GUARDIAN, OF COURSE, BUT I ALWAYS FELT THAT YOU GOT THE SHITTY END OF THE STICK.
ADAM'S CHILDREN ALLOW SO LITTLE ROOM IN THEIR LIVES FOR SILENCE--AND YET DESPITE ITS RARITY THEY SEEM INCAPABLE OF VALUING IT.

BUT THERE WERE AGES OF SILENCE. DO YOU REMEMBER, DUMA? BEFORE THEY CRAWLED OUT OF THE SEA--WHEN YOU COULD STILL HEAR YOURSELF THINK?
MY OWN TASTES TEND MORE TO THE BAROQUE, BUT I DID APPRECIATE THAT...

AND EVEN WHEN THE HOMINIDS ARRIVED THEY COULDN'T SPEAK, OF COURSE. SO THEY WERE STILL YOUR CHARGES.
YOUR GOLDEN AGE, WASN'T IT? MINE TOO. WHEN THE GAS CLOUDS WERE COALESCING INTO SUNS AND I WAS GOD'S LAMPLIGHTER.

I DID DROP IN ON THE EARTH, ONCE IN A WHILE. I REMEMBER THE SILENCE--LIKE AN OCEAN WITH NO TIDES.
AND THE LITTLE GODS. THEY FLOATED IN THE AIR LIKE FLIES. THAT BRINGS ME TO MY POINT, ACTUALLY.

"THE POOR, NAKED HALF-MEN, SCARED OF THEIR OWN SHADOWS... THEY MADE THE BEST GODS THEY COULD, BUT THEY HAD NO LANGUAGE TO GIVE SHAPE TO THEIR IMAGININGS. SO THE FIRST GODS WERE THIN GRAY SHADOWS, WITHOUT FORM AND WITHOUT SPEECH, DREDGED INTO BEING BY THE DUMB LONGINGS OF THEIR WORSHIPPERS.

"FOR THREE HUNDRED THOUSAND YEARS THESE SHADOW THINGS WERE THE ONLY PANTHEON THERE WAS. WE CALLED THEM THE VOICELESS GODS. THEN WE IGNORED THEM.
"WHEN THE OTHERS CAME ALONG, THE GODS WITH THE FIRM HANDSHAKES, IT WAS EASY TO FORGET ABOUT THE LITTLE SILENT ONES."

BUT IT WOULDN'T TAKE MUCH TO KEEP THEM GOING. JUST THE OCCASIONAL HEARTFELT PRAYER TO NOBODY IN PARTICULAR, THE "OH THANK GODS" OF PEOPLE WHO DON'T REALLY KNOW WHICH GOD THEY MEAN.
THEY'RE STILL THERE, AREN'T THEY, DUMA?

AND NOW THERE'S A POWER LOOSE ON THE EARTH THAT MANIFESTS ITSELF IN SILENCE-- THAT SEEMS DRAWN TO SILENCE.
A VELLEITY. I RECOGNIZED IT BECAUSE I MADE ONE MYSELF ONCE, WHEN I HAD LESS PATIENCE AND LESS FORESIGHT.

BUT THIS ONE BELONGS TO THEM. THE VOICELESS ONES. PERHAPS THE GENERAL WASH OF BELIEF AS THE NEW MILLENNIUM APPROACHES GAVE THEM THE INITIAL SURGE OF POWER TO MAKE THE WEAVING.
IT'S A DANGEROUS MAGIC, DUMA. IT GRANTS WISHES AND ACCUMULATES POWER FROM THE WISHER'S FEELINGS OF GRATITUDE OR GUILT. IT GETS BIGGER ALL THE TIME.

THE SPELL MUST BE UNWOVEN BEFORE IT DEVOURS THE WORLD. PLEASE. TELL ME WHERE I HAVE TO GO TO FIND THEM.
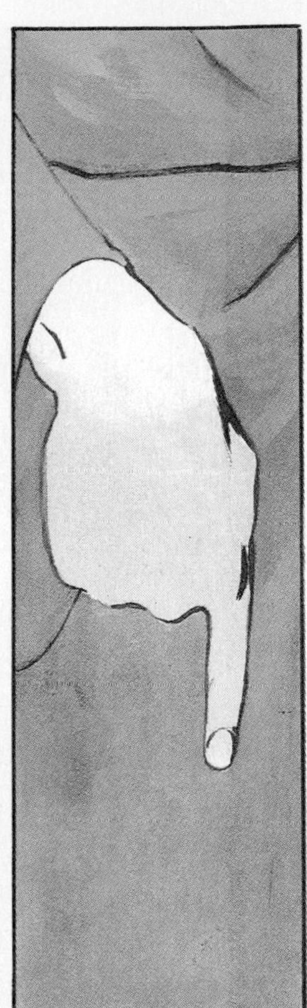
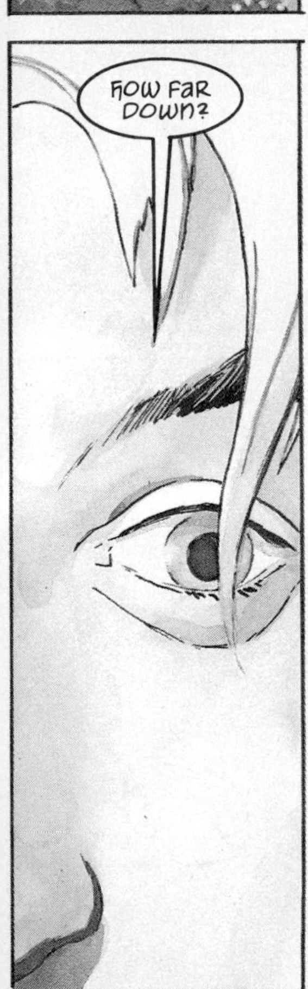
HOW FAR DOWN?
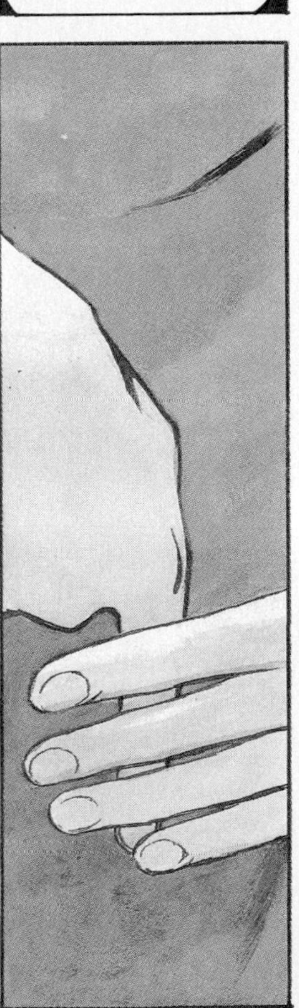

I SEE.
THANK YOU, DUMA.
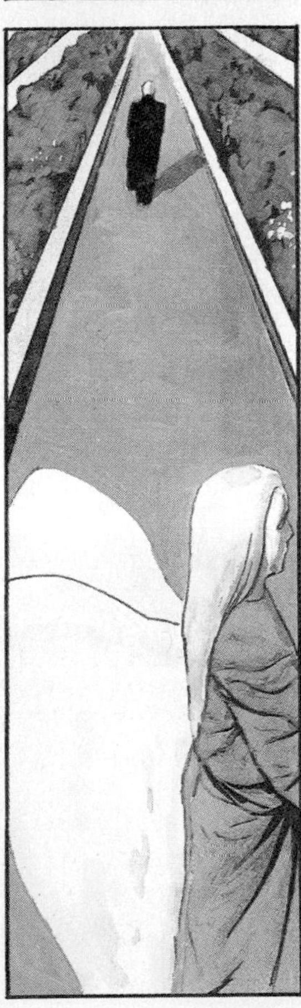

"DO YOU HAVE ANY ENEMIES, MR. BEGAI? ANYONE WITH A GRUDGE AGAINST YOU?
"DO YOU OWE MONEY TO ANYONE?"
POLICE

NO, I CAN'T THINK OF ANYONE WHO'D... WHO COULD...
JESUS CHRIST. I DON'T BELIEVE THIS IS HAPPENING.

WELL, CAN YOU AT LEAST TELL ME YOUR DAUGHTER'S BLOOD TYPE?

YEAH. SHE WAS B NEGATIVE, LIKE HER MOTHER. WHY DO YOU...?
THEN THE BLOOD IN THE FOOTPRINTS BELONGS TO THE FRIEND, LINDA MALPASS. THAT'S GOOD NEWS, I GUESS.

BUT YOU'D BETTER FACE IT, MR. BEGAI. THEY KNEW WHAT THEY WANTED, AND WHAT THEY WANTED WAS YOUR DAUGHTER.
NOW ONE OF THE WITNESSES IS DEAD, AND THE OTHER TWO ARE UNDER SEDATION.

IF YOU WANT RACHEL BACK IN ONE PIECE, THEN FOR GOD'S SAKE THINK. IS THERE ANYTHING YOU CAN TELL ME THAT WOULD NARROW DOWN THE SEARCH AT LEAST A LITTLE?

NO.

PHONE

HELLO. I WISH TO SPEAK TO YOUR MR. FARRELL, PLEASE. I BELIEVE HE IS IN CHARGE OF TRANSPORTATION.
YES, WE'VE HAD DEALINGS BEFORE. TELL HIM IT'S SAM.

PHARAMOND? YES, IT'S ME. JUST FINE, THANKS. WELL, ACTUALLY, I NEED YOU TO ARRANGE ME A PASSAGE TO... AH.
I'LL HAVE TO CALL YOU BACK.

PHONE
I'M DISAPPOINTED IN YOU, LUCIFER MORNINGSTAR.
I'D TAKE IT AS A FAVOR IF YOU'D GET TO THE POINT. THIS IS AN AWKWARD TIME.

THE GREAT REVOLUTIONARY TURNED INTO HEAVEN'S HANDMAID. I RESPECTED YOU. I DIDN'T LIKE YOU, BUT I RESPECTED YOU. BUT NOW... PFAH!
TELL ME, COLLABORATOR. THIS GREAT WEAVING --THIS VELLEITY. WHAT WILL IT DO FOR US?

WHY, IT WILL MAKE YOUR DREAMS COME TRUE, MAHU. UGLY AS THAT SOUNDS.

MY DREAMS ARE IRRELEVANT. I CLAIM THIS MAGIC FOR THE ARMIES OF THE LILIM IN EXILE. GIVE IT TO ME AND YOU CAN HAVE THE GIRL BACK UNHARMED.

HMM? WHAT GIRL WOULD THAT BE?

THE HALF-CASTE. RACHEL BEGAI. I FOLLOWED YOU THERE, LUCIFER. I KNOW EVERYWHERE YOU WENT AND EVERYTHING YOU DID.

THEN HOW COULD YOU MISS THE POINT SO SPECTACULARLY? THE GIRL'S OF NO IMPORTANCE. OH, SOME SLIGHT SPARK OF POWER, PERHAPS, BUT IN HERSELF... NOTHING.
LUX

STILL, THERE ARE SYNCHRONICITIES OPERATING HERE.
PERHAPS... YES.

THEN YOU AGREE TO MY TERMS?

OF COURSE NOT.
TSSSS

AH! AH! AH!
NUUUUH! MY EYES! MAHU, MY EYES!
BUT I WILL TAKE THE GIRL.
AYE! IN BLOODY GOBBETS YOU'LL TAKE HER, RECREANT! THESE PARLOR TRICKS HAVE DECIDED HER FATE AND YOURS!
NO TRICKS, MAHU--PURE SYMPATHETIC MAGIC. A BITCH TO USE, MOST OF THE TIME, BUT NOW...
PUSH THE WORLD IN ANY DIRECTION YOU LIKE AND IT MOVES. EVEN YOU MUST HAVE NOTICED.

DON'T STRUGGLE, MAHU. YOU'LL MAKE ME LOSE MY GRIP.
YOU THINK A FALL WILL KILL ME? GO AHEAD. I CURSE YOU, LUCIFER! I SPIT ON YOU!
I'M NOT GOING TO DROP YOU.
I'M GOING TO GET A BIT MORE HEIGHT AND A BIT MORE SPEED, AND THEN I'M GOING TO THROW YOU STRAIGHT UP.
YOU'LL ORBIT THE EARTH AS A LITTLE FROZEN MOON. REENTRY WILL KILL YOU, BUT NOT FOR A VERY LONG TIME.
WHERE IS SHE?
THERE'S A CAR. BEHIND THE BUS STATION. SHE'S IN THE TRUNK.
MAY FOULNESS AND DECAY ATTEND YOU, YOU WHORESON BASTARD!
LUCIFER I'LL KILL YOUUUUUUU
THEY GENERALLY DO. BUT AS YOU SAID, TODAY I'M ONE OF THE GOOD GUYS.

"and now there's a power loose on the earth that manifests itself in silence..."

"It's a dangerous magic..."

Mazikeen, I shall require your assistance.

I C'N WALK. PUT ME DOWN.
I HOPE THAT SHOW OF BRAVADO ISN'T MEANT TO BE ENDEARING. MAZIKEEN, SOMETHING RESTORATIVE -- AND QUICKLY, PLEASE.

HMMM. YES. SOME POWER THERE, PERHAPS, IF WE HAD TIME TO SIT AND TEASE IT OUT. NEVER MIND.
MAZIKEEN?

OH. I SEE.

VERY WELL. I PRESUME THAT POSSESSING HER IS A MEANS OF SPEAKING TO ME.
I'M LISTENING. BRIEFLY.

A MESSAGE WRITTEN IN BLOOD. EVERYONE INVOLVED IN THIS DRAMA SEEMS COMPELLED TO OVERACT.

I'M THE PAID AGENT OF THE TRIUNE GODHEAD, THE KING OF HEAVEN. I WILL NOT RELENT.
UNLESS YOU WANT TO MAKE ME A SUBSTANTIALLY HIGHER OFFER.
WELL, I SHOULD HAVE SEEN THAT ONE COMING.
HEY! HEY, WHERE DID THE BAR GO? WHAT IS ALL THIS? I WANNA GO HOME! YOU HEAR ME, MISTER?
HMMM?
TALK TO ME, FOR CHRIST'S SAKE! AM I RESCUED, OR KIDNAPPED AGAIN, OR WHAT? WHAT IS THIS PLACE?

THE REFLECTION OF A REFLECTION.
MORE SPECIFICALLY, THE REFLECTION OF MAZIKEEN'S EYE ONTO THE SURFACE OF THE BAR MIRROR. A REALITY TRAP.
THAT DOESN'T MAKE ANY...
BE **QUIET,** CHILD, AND LET ME THINK.
THIS IS SERIOUS. WE'RE TWO LEVELS ABSTRACTED FROM REALITY, SO THE RUNE OF FINDING IS UNLIKELY TO WORK.
I COULD TEAR US A WAY OUT, GIVEN TIME. GIVEN TIME IN **GEOLOGICAL** AMOUNTS.
THAT'S IT! IT'S THE BAR! CAN WE JUST BREAK THROUGH HERE SOMEHOW?
NO. IF IT WERE THAT EASY I'D HAVE DONE IT ALREADY.
BUT THIS IS MAZIKEEN'S BLOOD. WE'LL JUST HAVE TO HOPE IT KNOWS ITS WAY HOME.
BLOOD? THIS IS BLOOD?
WHY DIDN'T YOU **TELL** ME THAT BEFORE I TOUCHED IT?

COME.
YOU KEEP YOUR HANDS TO YOURSELF, PAL!
I'M COMING, BUT I'LL TELL YOU THIS MUCH--SOON AS I'M OUT OF HERE, I'M ON THE PHONE AND THE COPS'LL BE ALL OVER YOUR PEDOPHILE KID-NAP RING *ASS!*

STAY IN THE CENTER OF THE CORRIDOR.
DON'T TOUCH ANYTHING. AND IF ANYTHING SPEAKS TO YOU, DON'T ANSWER.

UMM... MAYBE THAT WAS OUT OF ORDER. I APOLOGIZE. FOR THE PEDOPHILE BIT, ANYWAY.
IT'S NOT IMPORTANT.
I MEAN, I KNOW YOU *SAVED* ME FROM THOSE GUYS. I'M JUST FREAKED OUT, IS ALL.

SO HEY. ARE THESE THINGS *DANGEROUS?*
EVERYTHING THAT LIVES BETWEEN THE WORLDS IS DANGEROUS.
OH. RIGHT.

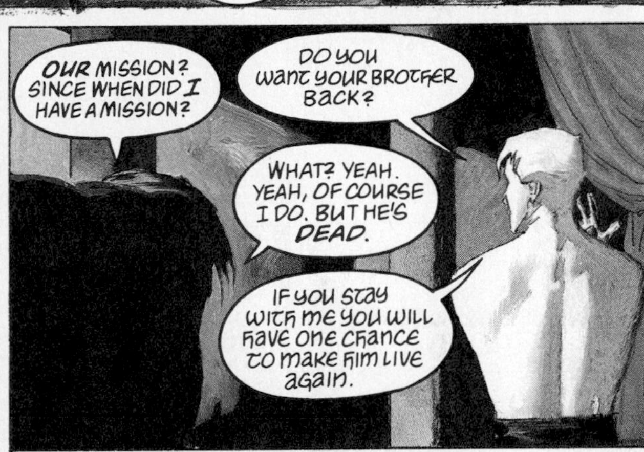

I KNOW. IT DOESN'T MATTER. THIS POWER IS NOT A TOOL TO BE USED.

THE WORLD... MAHU, THE WORLD IS BEGINNING TO *MELT*. ALREADY THE DEAD RETURN, AND THE MAPS RE-DRAW THEMSELVES TO ACCOMMODATE THE LANDS THAT NEVER WERE.

THE LANDS THAT...?

YES, YES, YOU KNOW. ALL THE GREATER ISRAELS AND PALESTINES. THE IRELANDS UNITED AND DIVIDED. THE SWEATSTAIN PRINCIPALITIES OF EASTERN EUROPE WHOSE NAMES WERE MERCIFULLY ERASED FROM HISTORY.

OR PERHAPS YOU *DON'T* KNOW. YOU'VE LET A LOT OF THE LAST QUARTER OF A MILLION YEARS GO RIGHT OVER YOUR HEAD, HAVEN'T YOU?

I BEG YOUR PARDON, LORD MORNINGSTAR, MISS BEGAI... I DON'T NORMALLY TAKE BREAKFAST IN THE OFFICE, BUT TONIGHT I HAVE NOT BEEN HOME.

A NUMBER OF MY ENTERPRISES HAVE BEEN... HOW SHALL I PUT IT... DISRUPTED TONIGHT, IN SMALL BUT ANNOYING WAYS. IT WAS NECESSARY FOR ME TO OVERSEE MANY THINGS PERSONALLY.
MAY I POUR SOME MORE TEA FOR EITHER OF YOU?
NO THANK YOU, PHARAMOND.

PLEASE. I PREFER IN THIS PLACE TO BE CALLED FARRELL.
AND YOU, LORD LUCIFER? WHAT NAME DO YOU GO BY THESE DAYS?
SPLOOF!

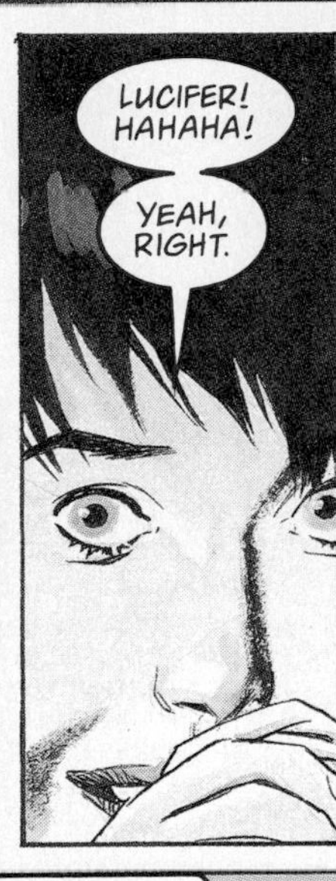
LUCIFER! HAHAHA!
YEAH, RIGHT.

I HONESTLY DON'T CARE. NOT "LORD," THOUGH. IT'S ANACHRONIS-TIC.

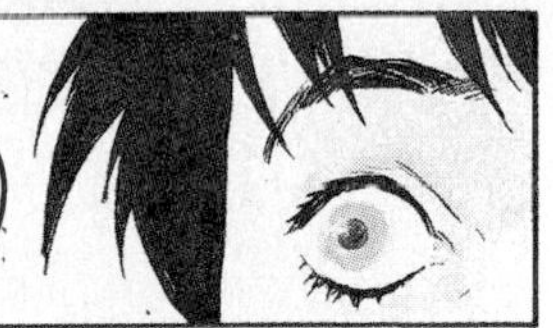
YES, I HAD HEARD THAT YOU RESIGNED YOUR OFFICE. I WAS SORRY, ON THE WHOLE.
CHANGES IN ANCIENT ORDERS DEPRESS ME MORE AS I GROW MORE ANCIENT MYSELF.

YOU... YOU'RE REALLY HIM? JESUS.
AAAAH, SORRY. I MEAN... WHAT'S THE DEAL WITH PAUL? YOU TOOK HIS SOUL, AND NOW I'VE GOTTA PLAY SOME KIND OF GAME WITH YOU TO GET HIM BACK?
NO, THAT'S NOT THE DEAL.

PHARAMOND, WE NEED PASSAGE AND A GUIDE TO FIRST WORLD. HOW SOON CAN THAT BE ARRANGED?
FUCK.

HAH. YOU ASK HOW SOON. EVEN IN NORMAL TIMES, I FIND THIS HARD TO ANSWER. YOU UNDERSTAND, MY FRIEND...
...SUCH JOURNEYS ARE ALWAYS AT LEAST PARTLY SHAMANISTIC. IT'S HARD, THEREFORE, TO GUARANTEE SUCCESS. OR EVEN SURVIVAL.
I DIDN'T ASK FOR ANY GUARANTEES.

TRUE. BUT THEN THE MATTER OF **PAYMENT** BECOMES PROBLEMATIC. THE SITUATION IS NOT PROPITIOUS, AND THE ARRANGEMENTS INVOLVED ARE...

TWO HUNDRED AND FORTY COPPER AES, COLLECTED IN THE USUAL WAY. YOU MAY COUNT THEM, ALTHOUGH TO DO SO WILL LIMIT THEIR USEFULNESS.
THERE IS TRUST BETWEEN US, MORNINGSTAR. I DON'T **NEED** TO COUNT THEM.

RACHEL, YOU ARE NAVAJO, YES?
WELL, PART NAVAJO. MY DAD IS...

HER FATHER IS BORN TO THE FEATHER CLAN AND BORN FOR THE MANY HOGANS CLAN. HER MOTHER IS NOT OF THE DINEH. WHY DO YOU ASK?

YOU CAN GO TO TSOODZIL.

HOW'D YOU KNOW ALL THAT STUFF ABOUT US?
MY DAD'S CLAN AND ALL. EVEN I DIDN'T KNOW THAT.
THE WORLD IS A BOOK. SOME WORDS STAND OUT FROM THE PAGE.

COMPLIMENTS OF MR. FARRELL, SIR. WHERE TO?
THANK YOU. LAX, PLEASE.

THAT'S NOT AN ANSWER. AND WHAT'S WITH THE CAR? CAN'T YOU JUST DO THE DOOR-OUT-OF-BLOOD THING AGAIN?
THIS IS A PILGRIMAGE. THERE ARE PROTOCOLS.

PLEASE PHONE AHEAD AND BOOK US ON A FLIGHT TO ALBUQUERQUE.
I BELIEVE MR. FARRELL HAS ALREADY TAKEN CARE OF THAT, SIR.

AND WHY EXACTLY ARE WE GOING TO ALBUQUERQUE?
I KNOW NEW MEXICO'S A HELLHOLE BUT I DON'T BELIEVE MY BROTHER WENT THERE WHEN HE DIED.

YOU REALLY HAVE NO KNOWLEDGE OF YOUR OWN HERITAGE AT ALL, DO YOU?
NEVER MIND. WE'RE ON HEAVEN'S BUSINESS, GIRL. THE ONE JOB THAT CAN'T BE LEFT TO THE REGULAR STAFF.

WE'RE GOING TO KILL SOME GODS.

s. hampton

"I'M REALLY SORRY," THE RECEPTIONIST SAID. "UNLESS THERE'S SOME KIND OF EMERGENCY..."
"YEAH, THERE IS," RACHEL WANTED TO SAY. "WE'RE GOING TO SAVE THE WORLD. ME AND LUCIFER HERE. THERE ARE THESE GODS WHO ARE FUCKING WITH PEOPLE'S HEART'S DESIRE AND WE'RE GONNA KILL THEM."
BUT "NO," HE SAID. "IT'S JUST A VISIT. IT CAN WAIT."

WHAT DID YOU SAY THAT FOR? I THOUGHT...
IF ALL REGULAR FLIGHTS ARE SUSPENDED, I CAN ONLY GET US ONTO A PLANE BY LIES OR COERCION. AS I'VE ALREADY SAID, THIS IS A SHAMANISTIC JOURNEY.
LIES AND COERCION WOULD HURT OUR CHANCES OF SUCCESS.

"SO WE'LL DO IT THE HARD WAY," HE SAID, AND PHARAMOND SUPPLIED A TRUCK.

A MIDNIGHT SKATER RUNNING BOOTLEG LIQUOR AND PORNOGRAPHY DOWN TO THE RESERVATIONS.
SOME PILGRIMAGE, RACHEL THOUGHT. SOME SHAMAN.

I DON'T HAVE TO DO THIS, YOU KNOW? I'M NO FUCKIN' TOURIST BUS. I GOT MY OWN WAYS OF WORKIN'. FUCKIN' FARRELL.
I OWE 'IM MONEY, NOT FUCKIN' BLOOD, OKAY? I GOT MY RIGHTS.

ARE YOU GONNA TELL ME WHERE WE'RE GOING?
I'VE ALREADY TOLD YOU. TSOODZIL, THE TURQUOISE MOUNTAIN, KNOWN IN THE MUNDANE WORLD AS MOUNT TAYLOR. YOUR PEOPLE'S MOST SACRED PLACE.

DON'T KEEP SAYING MY PEOPLE. ONLY MY DAD IS NAVAJO. IF I HAVE ANY PEOPLE THEY'RE IN L.A.
SO APART FROM BEING SACRED, WHAT ELSE HAS THIS PLACE GOT GOING FOR IT?
IT'S WHERE THE WORLD BEGAN.

THE WORLD BEGAN IN ALBUQUERQUE?
THIS COULD KICKSTART A WHOLE NEW RELIGION.
I NEED A FUCKING SMOKE. YOU PEOPLE TALK TOO MUCH. EXCUSE ME.

OKAY. I'M SORRY. BAD JOKE.
SO TELL ME ABOUT TSOODZIL.

IT'S NOT ABOUT TSOODZIL, GIRL. IT'S ABOUT YOU.
ME?
HUMANITY.

ALL THE RACES OF MAN TELL THE STORY OF THEIR OWN ORIGINS, BUT THEY ALL DISAGREE ON THE DETAILS.
DO THE DETAILS MATTER?
THE DETAILS ARE ALL THAT MATTERS.

THE BIBLE TELLS THAT STORY IN TERMS OF TIME--ONE THING AFTER ANOTHER. FIRST THERE WAS DARKNESS, THEN THERE WAS LIGHT.
YOUR PEOPLE REMEMBER IT DIFFER-ENTLY.

THEY SEE THE DARKNESS AS A TUNNEL THAT THEY CRAWLED THROUGH TO REACH THE LIGHT. A VERTICAL TUNNEL. THE LIGHT WAS IN ANOTHER PLACE, FAR ABOVE. THIS MEANS NOTHING TO YOU, DOES IT?
UMM...NOT A LOT. IS IT A BIRTH METAPHOR?
NO. IT'S THE THING FOR WHICH BIRTH IS A METAPHOR.

IN ANY CASE, THE DINEH TELL THE STORY AS A JOURNEY. A HARD AND TERRIBLE JOURNEY. THE PLACE THEY STARTED FROM WAS FIRST WORLD.
WHERE THE DARKNESS WAS. WHERE IT STILL IS.

"UNDERSTAND ME. WHATEVER LIVED THERE THEN LIVES THERE STILL, THOUGH YOUR KIND ABANDONED THIS PLACE HALF A MILLION YEARS AGO. THERE ARE FORESTS OF BLACK OAKS, A HUNDRED FEET TALL, STANDING INVISIBLE IN THE DARK. THERE ARE CREATURES ...PREDATORS... THAT HAVE NOT EATEN IN GEOLOGICAL AGES."

"YOU HAVE FORGOTTEN THE VOICELESS, BUT THEY HAVE NOT FORGOTTEN YOU. THEY WANT YOU TO COME HOME. WANT THE FEEL OF YOUR FEAR AND YOUR WORSHIP. BUT WHILE THE DARKNESS IS A HOME FOR THEM, FOR YOU IT WAS ONLY A WOMB."

CAN WE... STOP... FOR... A REST?
WE'RE NEARLY THERE. YOU CAN REST AT THE TOP.

HUFF
FUNNY. IT DIDN'T LOOK SO STEEP FROM DOWN THERE.
IT WASN'T. THAT WAS MOUNT TAYLOR. THIS IS TSOODZIL.

YOU SAID MOUNT TAYLOR IS TSOODZIL. TWO NAMES FOR THE SAME THING.
THEN IMAGINE WE'RE CLIMBING THE NAME RATHER THAN THE MOUNTAIN, IF THAT MAKES IT ANY EASIER.
TRUTH IS A LOCAL PHENOMENON, LIKE A MICRO-CLIMATE.

WELL YOU KNOW, I FUCKING HATE BEING PATRONIZED AND I FUCKING HATE BEING USED, SO I'M JUST GONNA SIT HERE TILL I GET AN ANSWER I UNDERSTAND.

ALL RIGHT. YOU FELL ASLEEP. BUT BECAUSE OF YOUR FEELINGS OF GUILT OVER PAUL'S DEATH, IT'S A SHALLOW, RESTLESS SLEEP. YOU'RE DREAMING ME. YOU'RE DREAMING ALL OF THIS.
YEAH, THAT'S JUST ABOUT POSSIBLE. I THINK I WOULD'VE PUT IN A BOB'S BIG BOY HALFWAY UP, THOUGH.

PHARAMOND SAID WE COULD COME UP HERE BECAUSE I'M NAVAJO. IS THAT THE ONLY REASON YOU BROUGHT ME? BECAUSE YOU COULDN'T GET IN BY YOURSELF?

NO. NOT THE ONLY REASON. ARE YOU RESTED NOW?

IT SOUNDS PLAUSIBLE ENOUGH, IN THIS PLACE AND AT THIS TIME. SHE PLAYS WITH THE IDEA. A DREAM-RACHEL CARRYING OUT A DREAM-QUEST. A FIGURE OUT OF FANTASY TO GUARD AND SAVE HER...
DREAMS HAVE THEIR OWN LOGIC, OF COURSE, AND THEIR OWN AGENDAS.

WHOA.

WE'RE NOT GOING DOWN THERE...
ARE WE?
NOT YET. WE HAVE TO SPEAK TO BLUE FLINT GIRL FIRST. THIS IS WHERE SHE LIVES.

IS THAT BLUE FLINT GIRL'S GRANDMA OR WHAT?
IT'S JUST HER NAME--ONE OF HER NAMES. SHE'S OLDER THAN YOUR ENTIRE RACE.
COME ON. I'D LIKE TO GET THIS PART OVER WITH.

AH, YOU'RE HERE AT LAST. YOU MUST BE TIRED. SIT, AND EAT WITH ME.

ACTUALLY, MOTHER OF WHIRLWINDS, OUR BUSINESS IS FAIRLY PRESSING. WE'D LIKE TO GO STRAIGHT--
BE QUIET, ATSE'HASHKE. I WAS SPEAKING TO MY GRAND-DAUGHTER.

WHO? ME?
COME DOWN HERE, CHILD. SIT WITH ME ON THE GROUND. I WANT TO TALK TO YOU.

UMM. HI. HOW'S IT GOING?
NOT WELL. NOT WELL AT ALL. YOUR SPIRIT CRIES OUT LIKE AN ANIMAL IN A TRAP. IT HURTS ME TO SEE YOU IN SUCH PAIN.

YEAH, EVERYTHING'S PRETTY FUCKED UP RIGHT NOW. I DID SOMETHING TERRIBLE AND I'M ... I'M TRYING TO MAKE IT OKAY AGAIN. LUCIFER'S HELPING ME.

I'VE COOKED CORN PANCAKES IN BEAR'S GREASE. EAT. THEY'LL GIVE YOU STRENGTH.
ATSE'HASHKE, I HAVEN'T MADE ENOUGH PANCAKES FOR YOU. GO FILL THE JUG WITH WATER AND I'LL MAKE SOME MORE.
YOU JUST LOVE TO TWIST THE KNIFE, DON'T YOU?

THEY'RE GOOD?
THEY'RE...THE WORST THING I'VE EVER TASTED IN MY WHOLE LIFE.
BUT STILL THEY'RE GOOD. EAT THEM ALL.

GRANDDAUGHTER, HE IS NOT HELPING YOU. BE SURE OF THAT. ATSE'-HASHKE HAS HIS OWN REASONS FOR EVERY-THING HE DOES.
BUT HE SAID IF I CAME WITH HIM I'D GET MY BROTHER BACK.

THAT IS NOT WHAT HE SAID. THE CRYING OF YOUR OWN SPIRIT MADE YOU DEAF TO HIS WORDS.
AND NOW HE HAS WALKED IN YOUR FOOTPRINTS TO THIS HOLY PLACE.

I WALKED IN HIS FOOTPRINTS, OKAY? HE GOT ME HERE, AND HE'S GIVING ME A CHANCE TO DO WHAT I NEED TO DO.
NO--WHAT HE NEEDS TO DO. BUT NO MATTER. YOU'LL REMEMBER THE WAY HERE ANOTHER TIME, AND YOU'LL BE WELCOME--IF YOU COME ALONE.

LOOK, I'M STAYING WITH HIM. HE PULLED ME OUT OF A LOT OF SHIT ALREADY.
CHRIST, MY STOMACH! THOSE WERE JUST CORN PANCAKES, RIGHT?
YES. BUT THE GREASE OF A BEAR GIVES STRENGTH TO THE HEART AND MIND. YOU WILL NEED THAT.

ONE JUG OF WATER. IF YOU'RE REALLY GOING TO MAKE ME EAT THOSE THINGS, GO LIGHT ON THE BEAR'S GREASE. VERY LIGHT.
TCH. THIS IS NO TIME TO SIT AND FILL YOUR STOMACH, ATSE'HASHKE. I THOUGHT YOU WERE IN A HURRY.
HERE, GRANDDAUGHTER. I HAVE A GIFT FOR YOU.

WHAT IS IT?
A JISH.
WHAT'S A JISH?
A MEDICINE POUCH. IT WILL TAKE YOU WHERE YOU HAVE TO GO, AND IT WILL BRING YOU BACK.

MOTHER OF WHIRLWINDS, I WAS PROMISED A GUIDE.
SO? AND NOW YOU HAVE ONE.

THIS GIRL? HOW CAN SHE GUIDE ME WHEN SHE DOESN'T KNOW THE WAY HERSELF? THIS IS ABSURD.
BUT THESE ARE STRANGE TIMES, ATSE'HASHKE--THE WISEST ARE LOST. AND YOUR LITTLE TRICK WITH THE KNIFE WILL ONLY TELL YOU WHEN YOU'VE ARRIVED. OPEN THE POUCH, CHILD.
I CAN'T UNTIE THE... OH YEAH. OKAY.

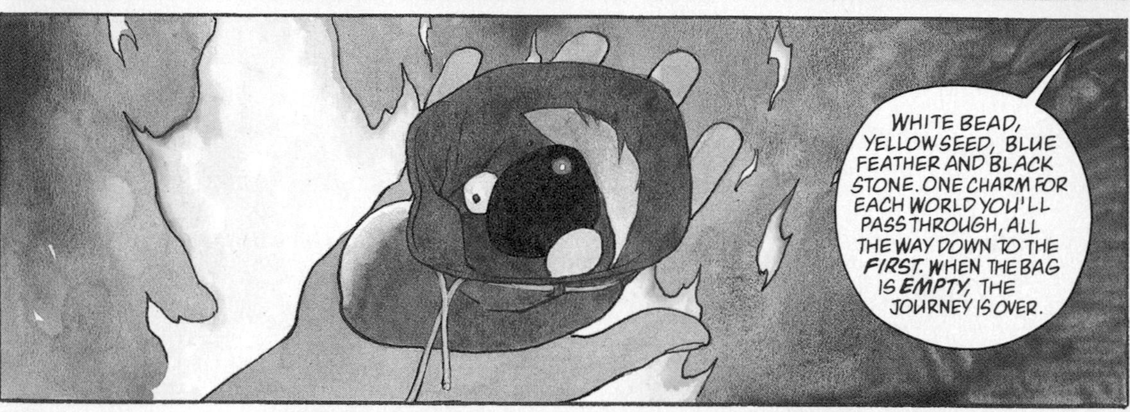
WHITE BEAD, YELLOW SEED, BLUE FEATHER AND BLACK STONE. ONE CHARM FOR EACH WORLD YOU'LL PASS THROUGH, ALL THE WAY DOWN TO THE FIRST. WHEN THE BAG IS EMPTY, THE JOURNEY IS OVER.

THANKS. THANK YOU. BUT... I MEAN... IS THIS GONNA WORK? AM I GONNA SEE PAUL AGAIN?
SOMETIMES THE TRUTH IS FALSER THAN ANY LIE. I CAN'T ANSWER THOSE QUES-TIONS. WHEN THIS IS OVER, GO TO YOUR GRANDFATHER. ASK HIM TO SING A BLESSING WAY FOR YOU.

MY GRAND-FATHER? YOU KNOW HIM?
OH YES. I HAVE HAD TO DEAL WITH HOSTEEN SAM THREE TIMES. BUT YOU MUST GO NOW. WE'LL TALK AGAIN.

SA'AH NAAGHÁII BIK'EH HÓZHÓ, RACHEL.
AND WHILE YOU OPEN THE WAY FOR HIM, KEEP YOUR EYES AT YOUR BACK.
WORDS TO LIVE BY, RACHEL. I HOPE YOU'RE WRITING THEM DOWN.

THOSE LOOK LIKE FISH SKELETONS.

THEY **ARE** FISH SKELETONS.

THERE WAS A FLOOD HERE IN THE DAWN AGE THAT KILLED MANY OF YOUR PEOPLE.

PLEASE. KEEP YOUR EYES ON THE PATH.

RACHEL...
YOU STOLE MY BARBIE DREAM 'VETTE. YOU KNOW YOU DID.

EWWW!
RACHEL, YOU SHOULDN'T HAVE LAUGHED AT MY BRACE.
RACHEL, THIS IS YOUR MOTHER. WHY DO YOU NEVER WRITE TO ME, DARLING?
DON'T LEAVE ME, RACHEL.
WHY DID YOU KILL ME, RACHEL?

WHAT THE HELL IS THIS?
FOURTH WORLD. THE SALT WASTE LEFT BY THE FLOOD, WHERE NO SEED GROWS.
AS FOR THE FISH... THEY'RE SPEAKING TO YOU, NOT ME, SO I CAN'T COMMENT.

SO THEY'RE THE VOICES OF MY SUBCONSCIOUS GUILT OR SOMETHING, RIGHT?
PERHAPS. I'M NOT BIG ON PSYCHO-ANALYSIS.
IN WHICH CASE THEY CAN GO SCREW THEMSELVES. ENOUGH IS ENOUGH!

IF THIS IS A SPIRIT JOURNEY, EVERY-THING'S GONNA TURN OUT TO BE SOME HOKEY SYMBOL.
LIKE THIS IS A BARREN LAND WHERE SEEDS DON'T GROW...
...AND I JUST HAPPEN TO HAVE A SEED RIGHT HERE IN THE POUCH.

OKAY. THERE WE GO.
LET'S MAKE THE DESERT BLOOM, WHY DON'T WE?

PLISH!

CHRIST ON A BIKE!
WELL DONE. YOU'VE FOUND OUT WHERE THE FLOOD WATERS WENT.

AND I THINK YOU'VE SUCCEEDED IN ATTRACTING THEIR ATTENTION.

GREAT.
FUCKING PERFECT.
WHAT DO WE DO NOW?
WE WAIT. THIS WON'T TAKE LONG.
LUCIFER, I CAN'T SWIM. I'M GONNA DROWN!
NOT IF THE WATER IS ONLY SYMBOLIC.
OH FOR CHRIST'S SAKE! DON'T JUST STAND THERE TAKING CHEAP SHOTS, DO SOMETHING!

TRY BREATHING. YOU'LL BE AMAZED HOW MUCH MORE COMFORTABLE YOU'LL FIND IT.

IT'S BACK UP IN THE SKY, WHERE IT WAS. YOU SAVED US. YOU HIT THE REWIND BUTTON.
NO. IT ALLOWED US TO PASS THROUGH IT. WE'RE IN THIRD WORLD NOW, BENEATH THE FLOOD.

THERE'S A LOT OF STUFF THAT'S GOING OVER MY HEAD HERE.
YOU ASTONISH ME.
I MEAN, THIS PLACE IS SMACK IN THE MIDDLE OF THE DESERT. OUT IN THE REAL WORLD, I MEAN.

THE REAL WORLD?
YOU KNOW WHAT I MEAN. SO WHERE DID ALL THE WATER COME FROM? HOW COME THERE WAS A FLOOD?

THE USUAL REASONS-- THE EVIL OF THE PEOPLE MADE THE ELEMENTS MOVE FROM THEIR PROPER ORDER. BE CAREFUL HERE. THIRD WORLD IS STILL FULL OF THE RESIDUE OF THAT EVIL.

MAYBE IT'S TIME FOR SOME MORE MEDICINE MAN STUFF.
I'VE JUST GOT THE FEATHER AND THE STONE LEFT NOW. WHICH ONE D'YOU RECKON COMES NEXT? I'M THINKING MAYBE THE FEATHER...

BRING IT HERE, RACHEL. I'LL SHOW YOU WHAT TO DO.
HUH?

IT'S EASY. GIVE ME THE JISH AND I'LL SHOW YOU. I'LL TEACH YOU HOW TO BE A SKINWALKER AND CHANGE YOUR SHAPE.
PAUL! OH MY GOD! WHAT ARE YOU DOING HERE?

THIS IS CRAZY. YOU'RE TALKING. YOU'RE TALKING LIKE THERE WAS NEVER ANYTHING WRONG WITH YOU.
THERE'S STRONG MAGIC HERE. GIVE ME THE JISH.
YOU KNOW I NEVER WANTED TO HURT YOU, PAUL. IT WAS AN ACCIDENT. IT JUST...

NOW, WHORE, LET ME SHOW YOU WHAT HURT IS. LET ME TEACH YOU ALL THE WAYS OF IT.
UUUUH!

GET OFF ME! YOU'RE NOT PAUL! LET ME GO!
I AM THE GREAT STONE. IF YOU STRUGGLE IT WILL BE BETTER FOR ME, WORSE FOR YOU.

LUCIFER! LU...
KKKKHHHHH!

...?
BUT THE HOLY PEOPLE HAVE GONE. THERE'S NO POWER HERE GREAT ENOUGH TO...

NO! I WAS BORN FROM A WOMAN'S WOMB! I AM FLESH NOW, WARM FLESH! I WON'T...

I TOLD YOU TO BE CAREFUL.
YEAH. YEAH, YOU DID.
OH.
OH FUCK.
COME HERE. THERE'S SOME-THING I NEED TO SHOW YOU.

THIS GULF IS SECOND WORLD, AND AT THE BOTTOM IS FIRST WORLD.
WE CAN'T GO ANY FURTHER--UNLESS YOU CAN FIND US A WAY DOWN.
FINE. LET'S TRY THE MAGIC FEATHER. IT WORKED FOR DUMBO.

OKAY. WE CAME. WE SAW. WE ALMOST GOT RAPED BY A ROCK. NOW CAN WE...

WHOOOAAA!

IS THIS THE PLACE?
FIRST WORLD?
CAN YOU DOUBT IT? THIS **DARKNESS** IS PROOF ENOUGH, EVEN WITHOUT THE KNIFE.
THEN WHERE ARE ***THEY?*** THE VOICELESS GODS.
LET YOUR EYES ADJUST TO THE DARK. THEN LOOK UP.

SHIT. WHAT ***IS*** THAT THING?
THE VELLEITY, THEY WOVE IT OUT OF THEIR OWN **BODIES**. THEY'RE NOT TOOL-USERS.
BUT LET'S SEE HOW STRONG THEIR WEAVING IS.

SSSSSSSSSSSS

SSSHRAKKK!

OH, WE HAVE ARRIVED, HAVEN'T WE? VOICES. A PLACE OF POWER. A CAR IN THE GARAGE. HOW DISMAYINGLY BOURGEOIS YOUR ASPIRATIONS ARE.
THE MAGIC YOU'VE MADE TURNS FAITH INTO POISON. THE EARTH WILL DROWN IN IT--AND SO WILL YOU, YOU ECTOPLASMIC FOSSILS.

WE WILL NOT GIVE UP THIS STRENGTH. THIS CLARITY. THIS SWEETNESS. WE HAD FORGOTTEN WHAT IT WAS LIKE...TO BE WORSHIPPED.
IF YOU ARE THE BRINGER OF LIGHT, LET US SEE WHAT THE DARK CAN DO.

LUCIFER, WHAT'S THAT NOISE?
AND JESUS! THE SMELL. WHAT'S HAPPENING?
I TOLD YOU THERE WERE THINGS THAT LIVED HERE.

THEY'RE COMING.

THE NOISE ATTRACTS THEM--THAT AND THE SMELL OF LIVING THINGS. THEY'RE COMING TO EAT US.
JESUS.
JESUS CHRIST.
THIS CAN'T BE REAL.

THAT IS FOR US TO SAY, BECAUSE YOUR REALITY BELONGS TO US NOW. YOU MAY PRAY TO US IF YOU WANT TO. WE WOULD LIKE THAT.

WHAT DO YOU SAY, RACHEL? A QUICK PRAYER BEFORE BED-TIME? YOU CAN'T SAY THEY'RE NOT DELIVER-ING THE GOODS.
YOU WANT SOMEONE MURDERED, BANG. ALL YOU HAVE TO DO IS ASK.
I'M NOT A MURDERER!
OF COURSE YOU ARE.
NO.
APOLOGIES CHANGE NOTHING. GUILT CHANGES NOTHING. YOU ARE WHAT THEY MADE YOU.
BASTARDS! SLIMY, TWISTING LITTLE BASTARDS! I'D RATHER DIE THAN PRAY TO YOU! I HATE YOU! YOU KILLED MY BROTHER!
FUCK YOU! FUCK YOU! FUCK YOU!
GOOD. NOW MAKE A WISH.
JUST... FUCKING... DIE!!!

THAT'S THAT, I THINK. TIME TO GO HOME.
I... I DON'T GET IT. WHERE DID THEY GO? WHAT HAPPENED?
YOU HAPPENED.

THE VELLEITY WAS DESIGNED TO SATISFY DESIRE. IT'S A COMMODITY I'M SHORT ON, BUT YOURS DID WELL ENOUGH.
WHEN YOU WISHED IT GONE, IT HAD NO CHOICE BUT TO DESTROY ITSELF. BY THE WAY, YOU'LL BE NEEDING THIS.

WAIT. WAIT A MINUTE. THAT WAS THE THING THAT WAS GRANTING WISHES, RIGHT?
AND NOW IT'S GONE. SO HOW DO I GET PAUL BACK?
YOU DON'T. IT'S TOO LATE NOW.

BUT YOU... YOU SAID...
I SAID I'D GIVE YOU AN OPPORTUNITY.
NOT STEP-BY-STEP INSTRUCTIONS.

YOU TRICKED ME! YOU LIED TO ME!
PERHAPS. BUT IF YOU REALLY WANTED HIM BACK, IT WOULD HAVE HAPPENED.
I SUSPECT THAT WHAT YOU ACTUALLY WANTED WAS AN EXCUSE TO FORGIVE YOURSELF.

I'VE STILL GOT THE JISH, LUCIFER. I'M NOT TAKING YOU BACK WITH ME. I'M GOING TO LEAVE YOU HERE TO ROT, YOU BASTARD!
YES, I THOUGHT WE MIGHT GET TO THAT.
I SAID YOU NEEDED IT, NOT ME. NOW THAT THE WEATHER'S CLEARED, I THINK I'LL JUST WALK.

IN ANY CASE, YOU SHOULD BE GRATEFUL THAT YOU'RE LEAVING HERE IN ONE PIECE. I SAVED YOUR LIFE AND YOUR MAIDENHEAD AND I CONSIDER US WELL QUIT.
CONSUMMATUM EST.

I'LL FIND YOU SOMEDAY. I WILL, I MEAN IT. WHEN I'M STRONG ENOUGH TO TAKE YOU ON.
THAT'S A PITY. YOU'D MANAGED TO KEEP YOUR HEAD UP ABOVE THE MELO-DRAMA UNTIL NOW.
GOODBYE, RACHEL.

"The general opinion is that you did well, Lucifer Morningstar.
"It's not an opinion that I share."

This is what you asked for, I believe.
Thank you, Amenadiel. Grudging praise is the most flattering of all.
And the girl?

You took advantage of her innocence and her grief. You have damaged her. You may even have destroyed her.
I don't think I'd have the stomach for them right now.

There's a whole shelfload of Christian commentaries about how good suffering is for the soul. Have you read them? They're great fun.

You hired me, Amenadiel. You gave me free rein and total absolution.
I carried out my...
Yes, of course you did. Now off you go and wash your hands --
-- I suggest steel wool.

THEY CHOSE THE RIGHT TARGET, DIDN'T THEY? NOTHING IS SO PLENTIFUL AS DESIRE, OR SO CONCENTRATEDLY TOXIC.
THANK YOU, MAZIKEEN. LET IT BREATHE A LITTLE WHILE, THEN BRING IT OVER TO THE PIANO FOR ME.
PERHAPS I'LL PLAY A FEW TORCH SONGS. GOD KNOWS, THE BASTARDS DESERVE IT.
THIS IS A LITTLE BILLIE HOLIDAY NUMBER THAT SAYS EVERYTHING THERE IS TO SAY ABOUT HAVING IT AND THEN LOSING IT. "STORMY WEATHER." THANK YOU.
AND HE COUNTS THEM OFF IN HIS MIND AS HE PLAYS, DESIRE'S SLAVES. MAHU OF THE LILIM, SHIPWRECKED ON THE VAST INLAND SEA OF HIS OWN RAGE.
FRANK BEGAI, WAITING FOR THE PHONE TO TELL HIM WHETHER OR NOT HE CAN LIVE AGAIN.
AND RACHEL, HEADING ON WEST FROM GRANTS INTO THE RESERVATION LAND, LOOKING FOR A BLESSING THAT SHE WON'T ACCEPT WHEN IT COMES.
BECAUSE ALL THE WATERS OF THE OCEAN WON'T FILL A BUCKET WITH A HOLE IN IT.
AND THAT'S THEIR FALL, AND THAT'S THEIR FELLOWSHIP. DESIRE. THE HOLE IN THE BUCKET: THE GULF OF YEARNING INTO WHICH THE SOUL EMPTIES ITSELF.
HE DROPS A NOTE.
THE DISCORD IS HIS TRIBUTE TO THEM.
END.

FEGREDO
'99

Divine Susano, son of Izanami, Speaker in Thunder...
Welcome, my Lord. Welcome to Hell.

YOUR KINDNESS IS MORE THAN MY WORTH, REMIEL OF THE SERAPHIM. THINGS HAVE CHANGED SINCE MY LAST VISIT.
YOUR OWN WORK ENTIRELY? OR DO YOU CONSULT WITH LORD LUCIFER FROM TIME TO TIME?

Never.

AH! FORGIVE MY IMPERTINENCE AND INCOMPREHENSION. I HAD HEARD THAT THE STAR OF MORNING HAD MADE HIS PEACE WITH HEAVEN.

No, no! There was a specific and discreet arrangement. He... did the Host a favor and was duly paid for it.
As for Lucifer's advice...

...DUMA and I have done very well without it.

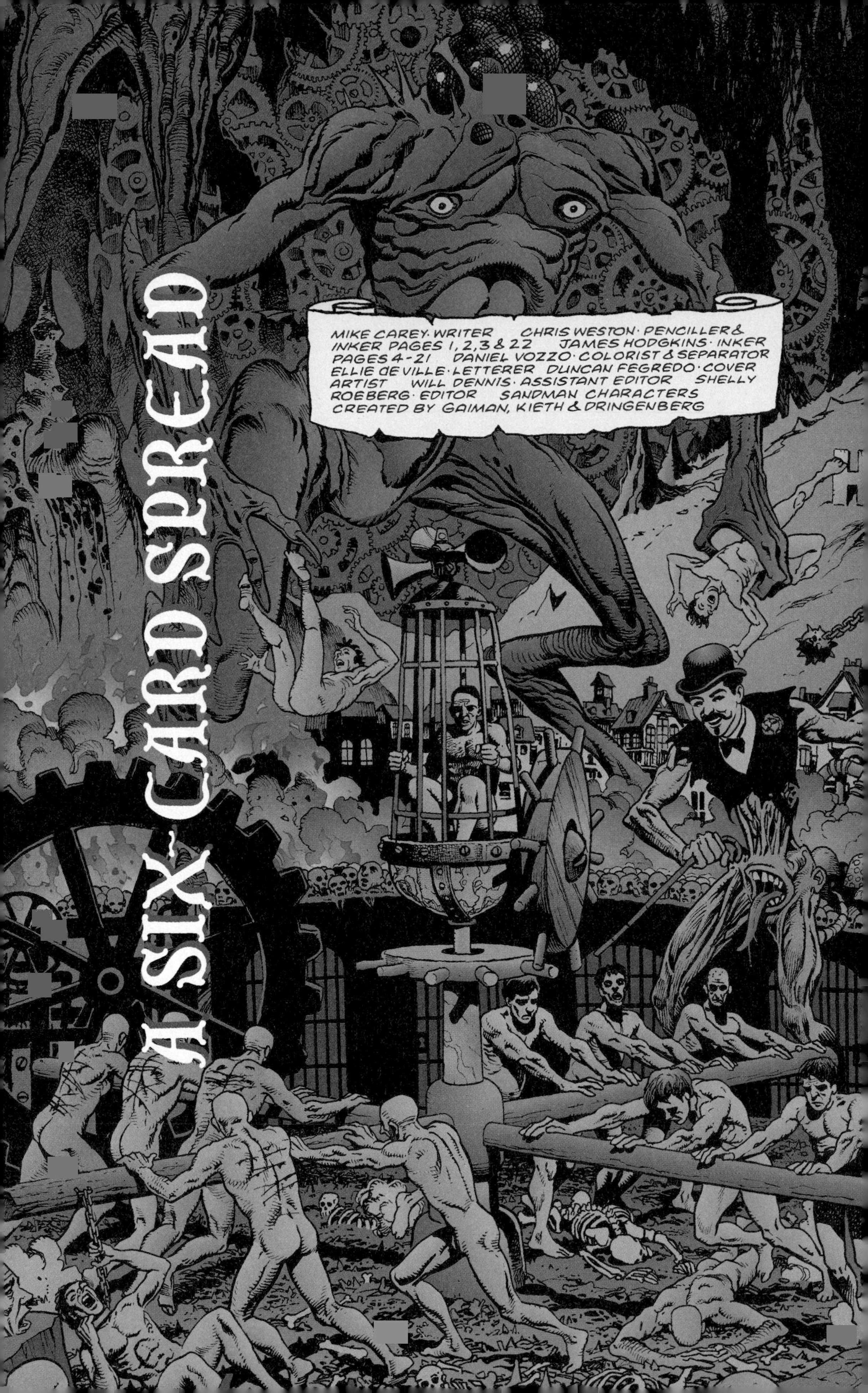
A SIX-CARD SPREAD
MIKE CAREY·WRITER CHRIS WESTON·PENCILLER & INKER PAGES 1, 2, 3 & 22 JAMES HODGKINS·INKER PAGES 4-21 DANIEL VOZZO·COLORIST & SEPARATOR ELLIE DEVILLE·LETTERER DUNCAN FEGREDO·COVER ARTIST WILL DENNIS·ASSISTANT EDITOR SHELLY ROEBERG·EDITOR SANDMAN CHARACTERS CREATED BY GAIMAN, KIETH & DRINGENBERG

LYWOOD
C. Weston
IT IS IMPRESSIVE. MY MOTHER'S REALM IS NOT SO VAST, NOR SO OPEN.
Lucifer designed it so. Freedom is his obsession.
IN THIS LIGHT, I FEEL THAT MY MOTHER'S OFFER IS WORTHY OF YOUR NOBLE COGNIZANCE. SHE VOUCHSAFES ONE HUNDRED MILLION SOULS...
In exchange for Lucifer's wings. What makes you think I have them?
IT IS KNOWN THAT DREAM OF THE ENDLESS SEVERED THE WINGS AT LORD LUCIFER'S REQUEST.
IT IS KNOWN THAT THEY REMAINED HERE.
And why does the Mistress of the windowless rooms wish to acquire them?
MY IGNORANCE SHAMES ME BEYOND BEARING. I AM HER ENVOY ONLY.
I would do nothing to compromise Lucifer. But the great work of redemption is more important than my feelings.
Were he here, I am sure that he would... understand.

HE IS NO LONGER THE LORD OF HELL. HE IS NO LONGER THE AGENT OF HEAVEN. EVEN HIS NAME LUCIFER, THE LIGHTBRINGER, DESCRIBES A FUNCTION FROM WHICH HE HAS RESIGNED.
HE HAS ESCAPED FROM PROVIDENCE. HE HAS BREAKFASTED ON OMELETTE AND SLICED PASTOURMA. AND NOW HE FOLDS THE LETTER--
NOTHING WILL COME OF NOTHING.
--WHICH IS SO SEARINGLY BLANK IT SEEMS TO LEAVE A HOLE IN THE AIR WHERE IT WAS.

HEOU SZHKOKE, NGY RROAHD?
ONLY TO MYSELF, MAZIKEEN.
I'M ONE MOVE AWAY FROM ENDGAME. I WAS JUST REVIEWING MY OPTIONS.

NGY RROAHD... IGH I CAN AKHHH, RHY HHKAVV RE HKONGH HHERE?
WHY? BECAUSE IN ANY DEALINGS WITH HEAVEN I'M INCLINED TO DISSECT THE GIFT HORSE AND HAVE A GOOD LOOK AT ITS GUTS.
I DON'T TRUST THE OLD BASTARD AS FAR AS I CAN THROW HIM.

TO RID HIMSELF OF A MINOR NUISANCE, HE GAVE ME AN OBJECT OF INCONCEIVABLE POWER.
THE LETTER SEEMS GENUINE. BUT IF IT WERE ME, I'D HAVE MADE SURE IT COULD NEVER BE USED.

SO I THOUGHT I'D COME TO HAMBURG, PULL MELEOS OUT FROM UNDER HIS ROCK...
...AND ASK HIM, VERY POLITELY, FOR A SIX-CARD SPREAD.

MUSIC
DER TASCHENTURM
MR. WEISS, WHAT SHOULD I DO WITH THE STUFF THAT CAME FROM ZWEMMERS?
DO YOU WANT ME TO...?
I'M SORRY, KARL. THE ZWEMMER BOOKS. YES. COULD YOU CHECK THEM AGAINST THE INVOICE?
THEN PUT THEM STRAIGHT ON THE SHELVES.
YES, MR. WEISS.

HE'S DISTRACTED. HE HAS BEEN FOR MOST OF THE DAY.
DISTURBED. THROWN OUT. NOT BY THE CRACKED SPINE OF THIS ORLANDO FURIOSO. A CRACKED SPINE CAN BE MENDED WITH PASTE AND STAIN.
IF ONLY ALL HIS PROBLEMS WERE SO TRACTABLE.

THE WOLF AND THE MAN IN MODERN HISTORY ARE DEVOURING EACH OTHER: TAKING TURNS TO BITE INTO FUR AND FLESH, TO SHIFT, GRIP AND TEAR, TO CHEW AND SWALLOW.
HE'S COMING, MELEOS.

THE BLIND WOMAN HOLDS A WHIP, WHOSE NINE HOOKED TAILS ARE STUCK TOGETHER WITH CONGEALING BLOOD. SHE IS SO TIRED FROM HER EXERTIONS THAT SHE HAS LOWERED HER SCALES.
HE IS HUNTING FOR TRUTH. HE WANTS TO CRACK IT BETWEEN HIS TEETH, AND SUCK ITS JUICE AND SPIT OUT ITS GRISTLE.

THE BASANOS REVEALS ITSELF ONLY TO THOSE IT WISHES TO ADDRESS, SO MELEOS SPEAKS IN A MURMUR, HIS LIPS BARELY MOVING.
VERY WELL. SO HE'S COMING. SHOULD I RUN AND HIDE?
DO YOU THINK I'M AFRAID OF LUCIFER?

WHY NOT? YOU'RE AFRAID OF US. SO AFRAID YOU KEEP US BOUND IN A BOX OF OAK AND IRON.
I'M NOT AFRAID OF YOU.
THEN LET US OUT TO PLAY. AND FLY. AND FUCK. AND FEED.
ALL THE THINGS YOU NEVER GET AROUND TO YOURSELF ANYMORE.

HI, KARL. WHERE'S MR. WEISS? I BROUGHT BACK THE BOOK HE LENT ME.
HE'S IN THE BACK. TALKING TO HIMSELF. AGAIN.

SO HOW'S LIFE? YOU'RE GETTING SOME NEW STOCK IN, YEAH?
NO, I'M MOVING OLD STOCK AROUND SO IT STAYS FRESH.
HEH. RIGHT.

YOUR LITTLE PROTEGÉ, MELEOS PHILOSOPHIA, EH? THE PURE LOVE OF WISDOM.
CYNICISM IS EASY.

THANKS FOR THE LOAN, MR. WEISS. I REALLY ENJOYED THIS.
YOU'RE WELCOME, JAYESH. I HAVE MARCUSE'S CRITIQUE OF FREUD IF YOU'RE INTERESTED.
WELL... I DON'T KNOW. IT'S TOUGH STUFF. I'M NOT SURE I'M UP TO IT.

"A MAN GAINS HIS FIRST MEASURE OF WISDOM WHEN HE ADMITS HIS IGNORANCE."
BUT YOU TOOK THAT STEP A LONG TIME AGO, JAYESH. IT'S TIME TO HAVE SOME FAITH IN YOURSELF.

YEAH, WELL, YOU KNOW HOW IT IS.
I GET DISTRACTED TOO EASILY.

IT'S ALL ACADEMIC, ANYWAY. THERE'S NO WAY MY DAD IS GOING TO LET ME GO TO UNIVERSITY.
YOU'LL NEED TO REASSURE HIM, NOT... CONFRONT HIM.
HE HAS HIS OWN AMBITIONS FOR YOU. THAT'S ONLY HUMAN NATURE.

THIS IS HUMAN NATURE, MELEOS. TO SACRIFICE THE OTHER ON THE ALTAR OF SELF.
TAKE A LOOK AT MARCUSE ANYWAY, AND WE'LL TALK TOMORROW. I'M AFRAID I HAVE TO CLOSE UP NOW.
I'M EXPECTING VISITORS.
OH. OKAY. THANKS.
'BYE, KARL. SEE YOU LATER.
YEAH. I'M SURE OF IT.

THIS WILL KEEP UNTIL TOMORROW. TAKE THE POST AND THEN GO ON HOME.
VERY WELL, MR. WEISS.

NOW THAT'S SO MUCH MORE COSY, DON'T YOU THINK?
ES TUT MIR LEID, WIR SIND GESCHLOSSEN: SIE MÜSSEN DIE GELBEN SEITEN LESSEN.

RUPINDER DEV
GEMISCHTWAREN HANDLUN
Phanta-Pop
TIGHT
1.40 DM
3.50 DM
OH NO.

I'M SORRY, DAD. I THOUGHT IT WOULD BE OKAY. I ONLY WENT...
YES, YES. I KNOW WHAT YOU ONLY WENT. YOU LEFT THE KEY IN THE TILL. WE'RE LUCKY IT WAS ONLY CRISPS THEY TOOK.
BUT YOU HAVE YOUR BOOKS SO THAT IS ALL VERY WELL INDEED.

I THOUGHT I'D SEE IF ANYONE CAME IN.
NEVER MIND. I KNOW THE TILL IS A SACRED TRUST. IF YOU'LL HOLD THE FORT HERE I'LL GO OUT BACK AND FLOG MYSELF.

Toffy
DON'T BE SO CLEVER, YAAH. THIS IS A FAMILY BUSINESS, JAYESH. IF YOU WANT TO BE FAMILY, YOU HAVE TO BE BUSINESS, TOO.
YEAH. WELL. OKAY. WHAT NEEDS DOING, THEN?

EVERYTHING NEEDS DOING.
THE COLD CABINET. THE PRICING. THE RUBBISH.
AND OUR SO LADYLIKE, SO CLEAN AND SO RESPECTABLE LODGER HAS ASKED FOR A BLOODY WAKE-UP CALL AT TWO IN THE AFTERNOON!

OH GREAT. I'LL DO THAT.
UMM. I MEAN I'LL DO THAT FIRST.
CAFE
KUCKE

TCHAH. BLOODY ANARCHIST BOOKS SHOULD BE PILED UP AND BURNED, YOU KNOW.
EROS AND CIVILIZATION

VAN DYKE
TOOT
SWEETS
JET
AEROSOL
JET

JILL? ARE YOU AWAKE? IT'S TEN PAST TWO.
KNKK
I'VE BROUGHT YOU SOME COFFEE. I'LL JUST LEAVE IT HERE, SHOULD I?

HI, JAY. NAH, BRING IT IN. I'M UP ALREADY.
I DON'T SUPPOSE YOU BROUGHT A COUPLE OF YOUR MUM'S SAMOSAS TOO, BY ANY CHANCE?
HUGO
MERVEILLE
AND
JILL PRESTO
THE NEEDLE'S EYE
ZIRKUSWED
HAMBURG
YEAH, AND A BIT OF BRINJAL PICKLE IF YOU WANT.
COOL.

GOD, THIS STUFF IS LIKE ANGELS STABBING YOUR TONGUE TO DEATH. I HAD TO SKIP SUPPER AGAIN.
HUGO HAD ME PRACTICING.
I LIKE THE EYELINER.
THANKS.
YOU WEAR A PADDED BRA? WHY WOULD YOU NEED TO DO THAT?
WHY ELSE? BECAUSE LOTS OF GUYS HAVE A TIT FIXATION.
MOSTLY THEY DON'T EVEN LOOK YOU IN THE EYE UNTIL THEY'VE CHECKED OUT HOW YOU'RE BUILT.

BUT YOU ... I MEAN YOU'VE GOT A PERFECT FIGURE.
THANKS, JAY. I'M TOUCHED. I MEAN, YOU'RE AS BENT AS ...
...BUT I GUESS IT'S THE THOUGHT THAT COUNTS.

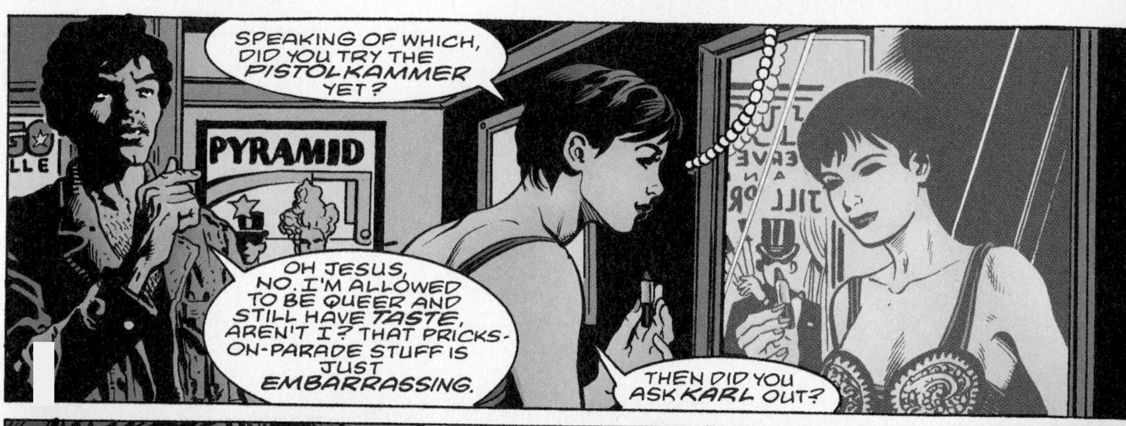
SPEAKING OF WHICH, DID YOU TRY THE PISTOLKAMMER YET?
OH JESUS, NO. I'M ALLOWED TO BE QUEER AND STILL HAVE TASTE, AREN'T I? THAT PRICKS-ON-PARADE STUFF IS JUST EMBARRASSING.
THEN DID YOU ASK KARL OUT?
PYRAMID

I ALMOST DID, BUT I CHICKENED OUT. I MEAN, WHAT IF HE SAYS NO?
HE JUST WORKS TWO DOORS AWAY. AND I'M IN AND OUT OF THE SHOP ALL THE TIME. IT COULD GET PRETTY UNCOMFORTABLE.
HUGO MERVEILLE AND JILL PRESTO

ISN'T WALKING AROUND WITH A PERMANENT HARD-ON PRETTY UNCOMFORTABLE TOO?
I MEAN, I DON'T HAVE A DICK SO THIS ISN'T A VALID COMPARISON, BUT WHEN I'M HORNY I TEND TO...

I DON'T KNOW WHY I EVER CONFIDED IN YOU. YOU'RE A FOUL-MOUTHED TART WITH SMALL TITS.
GUILTY AS CHARGED. COME ON, JAY--PUT UP OR SHUT UP. YOU'VE BEEN MOONING AFTER HIM FOR THREE MONTHS NOW.
I MEAN, LET'S FACE IT...

"...ANYONE WHO CAN'T GET LAID IN ST PAULI ISN'T TRYING."
HEY. HEY, MISTER. YOU WANT SOMETHING A BIT FRESHER?
GUCK MAL!
CLUB ORGASM
COMET
SEX SHOW
TOPLESS
VIDEO
SEXY

NO. THANK YOU. YOU HAVE NOTHING THAT I WANT.
YOU DON'T KNOW TILL YOU'VE TRIED. COME ON, MISTER. WHEN DID YOU LAST GET YOUR PIPE CLEANED?
golden Wildlife
CLU
TEL
GIRLS
SEX
PEEP
IN THE Pink
BOTTOM DRAWER
LESBIAN TEENS

GO HOME NOW, SIGRID MAHLER, AND YOU MAY BE IN TIME FOR YOUR FATHER'S FUNERAL.
WH... WHAT?

Oh. Oh god.
Papa.
Oh god forgive me.
BOYS

ANG HHKISZ ISZ RHRERE RHRE RRIGSZ? HHKE ISZ ANG ANKHYELH.
HE'S A HISTORIAN. HE LIVES AMONG HUMANS IN ORDER TO CHRONICLE THEM.
ALTHOUGH PERHAPS IT'S ALSO A DECLARATION OF NEUTRALITY.
HOT HOT HOT
KINO
VIDEO
PEEP

THIS WILL BE EASIER IF WE'RE NOT INTERRUPTED, MAZIKEEN. IF ANY BIBLIOPHILES SHOULD PASS THIS WAY, PERSUADE THEM TO KEEP ON GOING.
YESZ, NGY RROAHD.

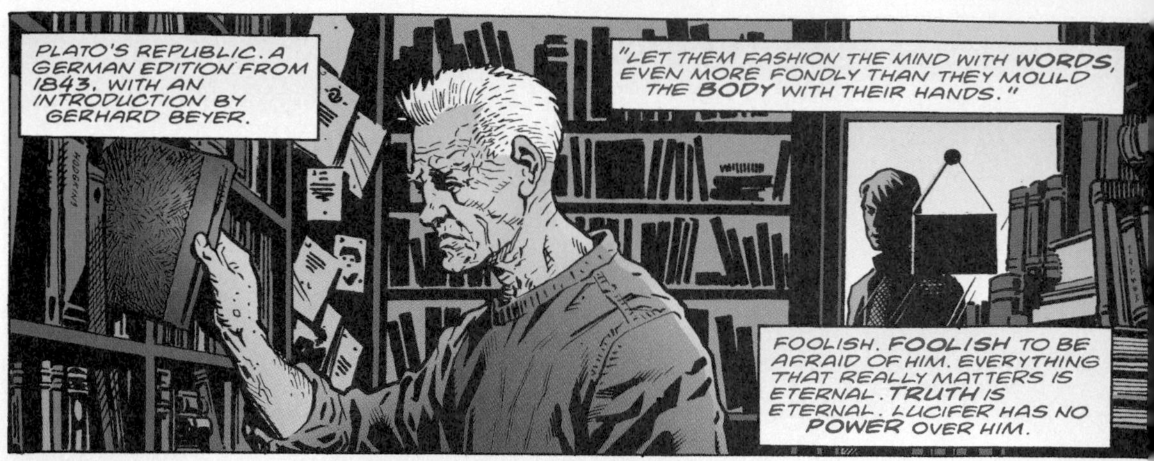
PLATO'S REPUBLIC. A GERMAN EDITION FROM 1843, WITH AN INTRODUCTION BY GERHARD BEYER.
"LET THEM FASHION THE MIND WITH WORDS, EVEN MORE FONDLY THAN THEY MOULD THE BODY WITH THEIR HANDS."
FOOLISH. FOOLISH TO BE AFRAID OF HIM. EVERYTHING THAT REALLY MATTERS IS ETERNAL. TRUTH IS ETERNAL. LUCIFER HAS NO POWER OVER HIM.

OH, MELEOS, YOU HAVE NO IDEA AT ALL HOW DEEP A SILENCE IS ABOUT TO FALL ON YOU.
BE QUIET.
NOTHING IS ETERNAL, MELEOS. EVEN THE SILVER CITY WILL END. SO HOW SHOULD THE SOUL OF MAN ENDURE?

I SAID BE QUIET! YOU'RE NOT EVEN HERE! YOU'RE BURIED!
BURIED SO DEEP THAT NO ONE WILL EVER FIND YOU!
TING-TING

GOOD AFTERNOON, LUCIFER. WAS IT SOMETHING SPECIFIC YOU WERE LOOKING FOR, OR WOULD YOU LIKE TO BROWSE?
HELLO, MELEOS. NO, THANK YOU.
I'M NOT LOOKING FOR A BOOK.
POLITIK
HESSE

TO TELL YOU THE TRUTH, I'M MORE IN THE MOOD FOR A GAME OF CARDS.

OUCH!

OW. SHIT. SORRY.

HEY. SIE SIND SCHAUSPIELERIN, YEAH? A *PERFORMER*?

COOL MASK. WHERE ARE YOU PLAYING?

I NEED TO CARRY OUT A DIVINATION.

WHICH MEANS THAT I NEED THE DECK YOU'VE CREATED.

THE BASANOS? HAH. YOU'LL FORGIVE ME IF I DON'T BELIEVE YOU.
WHAT WOULD YOU ASK IT? YOU'VE NEVER KNOWN THE FEELING OF DOUBT. YOU'VE NEVER NEEDED A BLESSING OR AN ABSOLUTION FOR ANY-THING YOU DID.
EVEN WHEN YOU PLUNGED US ALL INTO WAR.

I MAKE MY OWN CHOICES. AS YOU'VE DONE. AS EVERYONE DOES.
I'M LOOKING FOR INFORMATION, NOT A BLESSING.

DO YOU SEE THIS?
IT'S A LETTER OF PASSAGE, AND IT BEARS GOD'S IMPRIMATUR.
YES. THE CARDS HAVE TOLD ME ALL ABOUT YOUR PLAN.

LUCIFER.
I CAN'T. I CAN'T LET YOU CONSULT THEM.
I DON'T KNOW WHAT THE DECK'S CAPABLE OF. I DON'T TRUST IT ANYMORE.

LOOK AROUND YOU, MELEOS. YOUR WHOLE LIFE IS FLAMMABLE.
SAYING NO TO ME IS AN OPTION YOU JUST DON'T HAVE.

YES. I... I SEE.
BUT I CAN'T JUST FETCH IT. IT NEEDS TO BE WOKEN. PREPARED.

YOU HAVE UNTIL TONIGHT. I'LL COME AT SUNSET. UNDERSTAND ME, MELEOS. I WILL HAVE THIS DIVINATION.
IF THE CARDS ARE UNAVAILABLE I'LL JUST HAVE TO USE YOUR ENTRAILS.

YOUR MIND WANDERS WHEN YOU'RE ON LOOKOUT.
YOU SPEAK GERMAN, MAN?
YOU SPEAK DEUTSCHER FUCKING LANGUAGE?
YOU ASK US TO STOP IN GERMAN AND WE'LL LEAVE YOU ALONE.
uhhhh!

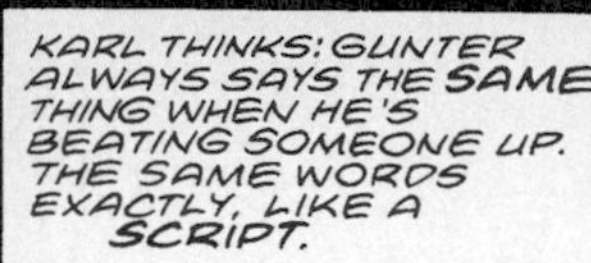
KARL THINKS: GUNTER ALWAYS SAYS THE SAME THING WHEN HE'S BEATING SOMEONE UP. THE SAME WORDS EXACTLY, LIKE A SCRIPT.
THEN THE TALKING GIVES WAY TO REPETITIVE IMPACT SOUNDS AND HE THINKS ARBEIT MACHT FREI. BUT NOT FOR THE GASTARBEITEN, WHO STEAL OUR JOBS.

MIND YOUR FOOT, ERICH, FOR CHRIST'S SAKE!

WORK IS FOR GERMANS. FREEDOM IS FOR THOSE WHO DESERVE IT.
KEINE JUDE
NAZI
IT'S HALTEN. HALTEN SIE BITTE. YOU THINK YOU'LL REMEMBER THAT NEXT TIME?
LET'S PISS ON HIM.
DON'T BE STUPID, MAN. HE'S GOING TO DIE. WE SHOULD GET OUT OF HERE.

JET

RAUS

FUCK, NO NEED TO RUN, KARL. IT LOOKS BLOODY SUSPICIOUS. WE'RE JUST WALKING, OKAY?
YEAH, WHAT ARE YOU PANICKING FOR? IT'S NOT LIKE YOU EVEN DID ANYTHING.
WHAT DO YOU MEAN? I WENT LOOKOUT.

YES, KARL. YOU WENT LOOKOUT. AGAIN. WITHOUT BEING ASKED TO.
I THOUGHT YOU WANTED TO BE FULLY INVOLVED IN THE POLITICAL DIALECTIC.
OF COURSE I DO.

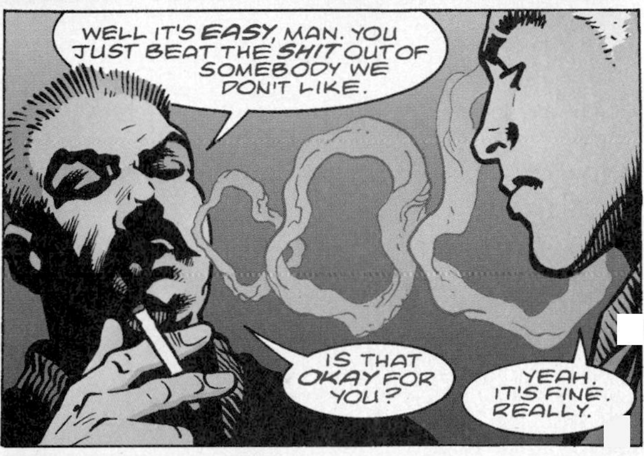
WELL IT'S EASY, MAN. YOU JUST BEAT THE SHIT OUT OF SOMEBODY WE DON'T LIKE.
IS THAT OKAY FOR YOU?
YEAH. IT'S FINE. REALLY.

SO WHO DON'T WE LIKE, KARL?
WELL. YOU KNOW...
YEAH, I DO. TELL ME.

JEWS. TURKS. PAKIS. LEFTIES.
QUEERS.

YEAH, YOU GOT TO LOOK OUT FOR THOSE QUEERS, KARL. A GOOD-LOOKING BOY LIKE YOU. BUY YOURSELF A CAN OF PAINT AND DO SOME HOMEWORK, OKAY?
YOU'RE IN OR YOU'RE OUT. WE DON'T NEED A FAN CLUB.

"WE DON'T NEED A FAN CLUB..."
NO, THEY NEED A SACRIFICE. AN OFFERING. THE PRICE OF ADMISSION.
AND HE WANTS TO PAY IT. WANTS TO PROVE THAT HE BELONGS. THEN HE CAN STEP THROUGH THE DOOR...

...THE ONE MARKED ADULTS ONLY.
NEEDLE'S EYE
PRIVAT KABERATT
BAR

HELLO, JILL. HUGO WAS LOOKING FOR YOU. HE WAS SEEMING PRETTY PISSED OUT.
THAT'S PISSED OFF, LOTTE. NEVER MIND HUGO, WHAT ABOUT MR. METTERLINCK? IS HE IN YET?

I DON'T THINK SO. WHY?
I ASKED HIM ABOUT A SOLO SPOT. YOU KNOW, SINGING.
I THINK HE'S GONNA GO FOR IT. THEN HUGO CAN KISS MY RING.

HOW WOULD IT BE IF HUGO JUST WRINGS YOUR NECK?
UMM...YEAH, MAYBE. BUT MY IDEA HAS MORE IMMEDIATE VISUAL APPEAL.

I ASK YOU TO COME AN HOUR EARLY, PETERSON. FOR PRACTICE. BECAUSE EVERY MISTAKE YOU DO LOOKS BAD FOR ME.
I DON'T WANT TO BE WORKING BLOODY HAMBURGER CABARET UNTIL I RETIRE, YOU KNOW?

IT'S PRESTO. JILL PRESTO.
I DON'T GO BY PETERSON ANYMORE, HUGO.

YOU CAN CALL YOURSELF THE VIRGIN BLOODY MARY IF YOU WANT TO. BUT YOU MAKE ME LOOK BAD, I FUCKING PAY YOU OFF. YOU UNDER-STAND ME?
RIGHT. WHERE DO WE START?
DOVE IN A FRY-ING PAN. THEN FLYING KNIVES.

AND SWING FROM THE HIP, AND BEND AT THE KNEE, AND OFF WITH THE LID.
AND ONE TWO THREE FLY. SATISFIED?
NO. SMOOTHER. ONE SMOOTH MOVEMENT. CHRIST.

HEY, HUGO. WHEN I DO MY SOLO ACT... YOU THINK I'D LOOK COOL IN, LIKE, A MASK OVER JUST ONE HALF OF MY FACE?
SOMETHING IS AMISS.
HE THINKS FLEETINGLY OF HIS WINGS. NOSTALGIA OR PREMONITION?

NEW VARIABLES ARE BEING ADDED TO A SITUATION ALREADY COMPLICATED.
HE HAS TO ACT BEFORE ACTION BECOMES IMPOSSIBLE.
THIS IS UNDIGNIFIED...
...BUT IN THE ABSENCE OF ANYTHING BETTER YOU'LL HAVE TO DO.

THERE IS A DOOR AT THE BACK OF MELEOS'S SHOP THAT REQUIRES MORE THAN A KEY TO OPEN IT. MOST OF THE TIME IT ISN'T EVEN VISIBLE.

PRIVAT

HE NEVER STANDS HERE WITHOUT FEELING THE WEIGHT OF AGES PRESSING AGAINST THE DOOR FROM THE OTHER SIDE.

THERE IS A CELLAR ROOM IN THE PLANS, IF ANYONE EVER WANTED TO LOOK. TWELVE FEET BY FIFTEEN, WITH A SMALL UTILITIES CUPBOARD.

HE COULD FLY DOWN, OF COURSE. THE STAIRWELL IS WIDE ENOUGH FOR HIS WINGS, IF HE CHOSE TO MANIFEST THEM.

BUT THE TRUTH IS, HE'S IN NO HURRY TO REACH THE BOTTOM.

NOT TO HIM. NOT TO YOU.

YOU'RE NOTHING BUT A PACK OF CARDS.

BUT AS HE TURNS TO FACE THEM HE KNOWS IT'S TOO LATE. ALL THEIR GOADING. ALL THEIR MANEUVERING, HAS BEEN TO BRING HIM TO THIS POINT.

THERE IS A HOT METAL SMELL. THERE IS A SOUND THAT DRAGS ITSELF LIKE A DULL BLADE ACROSS HIS EARS.

WHEN THE BATTLE IS OVER, THEY DANCE. IT'S GOOD TO BE FREE. TO RIDE THE STILL AIR WITH THE GRACE OF RAZORS.
THEY'VE GOT A LOT OF LOST TIME TO MAKE UP.
OH, MELEOS. HOW FAR DID YOU THINK YOU'D GET ON GUILT AND GOOD INTENTIONS?
YOU'VE LET YOUR RABID LITTLE CHILDREN OFF THE LEASH.
"AND ALL BLOODY HELL IS OUT FOR NOON."
THE SUN

HAMBURG. THE DAWN OF A NEW MILLENNIUM.
A SIX CARD SPREAD
THE SUN
THE LOVERS
RAGE
THE TOWER
DEATH
TEMPERAN
THE HANGED MAN
THE EMPERO
THE WHEEL
MIKE CAREY · WRITER
CHRIS WESTON · PENCILLER
JAMES HODGKINS · INKER
DANIEL VOZZO · COLOR & SEPS
ELLIE DEVILLE · LETTERER
DUNCAN FEGREDO · COVER ART
WILL DENNIS · ASST. EDITOR
SHELLY ROEBERG · EDITOR
BASED ON THE CHARACTER CREATED BY GAIMAN, KIETH & DRINGENBERG

"ARE THEY NOT WONDERFUL, THESE HUMANS, WITH THEIR MAYFLY LIVES AND MAD DREAMS ?
"I WILL CHRONICLE THEM. I WILL BE THE KEEPER OF THEIR MEMORY."
MELEOS'S OWN WORDS. BUT NOW HE IS CRIPPLED FROM HIS FIGHT AGAINST THE CARDS, AND THE CHRONICLE HE HAS MADE IS AN UNDERGROUND TOWER MORE THAN A MILE HIGH.

THE SCAR ON HIS FACE BURNS LIKE A BRAND.
AND IT WILL NOT CLOSE, EVEN THOUGH HE HAS FOCUSED THE FULL FORCE OF HIS WILL UPON IT.
IT IS THE MARK OF HIS SIN.

THE MIND AND THE SOUL TRACE THE LINE THAT THE HAND WILL FOLLOW. BUT THE MOVEMENTS THAT THE HAND DOES NOT MAKE MATTER JUST AS MUCH.
THE DRAWING MUST SUBSUME ALL UNDRAWN LINES AND ALL POTENTIAL FIGURES INTO A PERFECT STASIS.

WE'RE FIGHTING FOR FREEDOM, MELEOS. FREEDOM TO DEFINE OURSELVES. FREEDOM FROM THE TYRANNY OF PREDESTINATION.
AS AN ARTIST, ISN'T THAT YOUR FIGHT TOO?
I DO NOT FIGHT. BUT IT MAY BE THAT I CAN HELP YOU IN ANOTHER WAY, LUCIFER.

I VISITED DESTINY OF THE ANEUTELOI RECENTLY.
HE WAS NOT... CORDIAL. BUT HE ALLOWED ME TO EXAMINE HIS BOOK.

YOU'RE INCREDIBLE. YOU'RE AFRAID TO FIGHT WITH US, BUT YOU'D BEARD THE ENDLESS IN PURSUIT OF YOUR ART.
ONE DAY THIS OBSESSION WILL DESTROY YOU.
YOU MISUNDERSTAND ME. MY PASSION IS FOR THE SUBJECTS WHICH I EXPLORE-- FOR LIVING MINDS.
DESTINY'S BOOK IS THE ULTIMATE CHRONICLE OF WHAT WE HAVE THOUGHT AND SAID AND DONE. AND THESE CARDS I MAKE WILL HAVE THE SAME WORKMANSHIP.
THE SAME AFFINITIES.

THINK ABOUT IT, MORNINGSTAR. YOU MIGHT READ YOUR ENEMY'S MIND BY CONSULTING THIS DECK.
THE LIGHT
INGER
OR YOUR OWN, FOR THAT MATTER.
BUT THAT WAS IN ANOTHER COUNTRY. ALL HIS ARROGANCE IS LONG SINCE GONE.
MELEOS HAS NO WINGS. HE HAS NO STRENGTH TO SUMMON THEM.
AND IT IS NOT TOWARD HEAVEN THAT HE RISES NOW.

CAN YOU GET...UH... WORDS WITH THAT?
YEAH, SURE. THE STANDARD DESIGN HAS FC ST. PAULI FOREVER, BUT YOU CAN HAVE WHATEVER YOU LIKE.
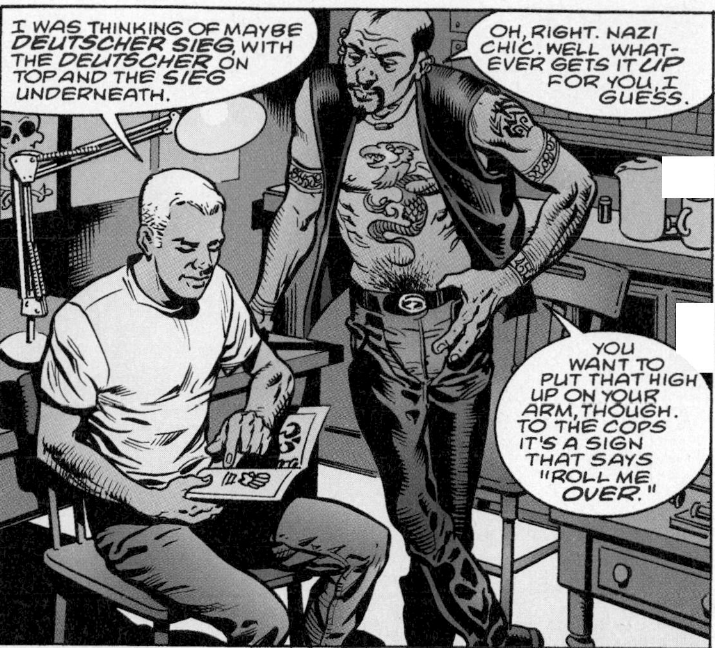
I WAS THINKING OF MAYBE DEUTSCHER SIEG, WITH THE DEUTSCHER ON TOP AND THE SIEG UNDERNEATH.
OH, RIGHT. NAZI CHIC. WELL WHAT-EVER GETS IT UP FOR YOU, I GUESS.
YOU WANT TO PUT THAT HIGH UP ON YOUR ARM, THOUGH. TO THE COPS IT'S A SIGN THAT SAYS "ROLL ME OVER."

DON'T I GET A LOCAL ANAESTHETIC?
SORRY. FOR TWO HUNDRED MARKS YOU DON'T EVEN GET A PIN THAT SAYS "I WAS BRAVE AT THE TATTOO PARLOR TODAY."
IS HERE OKAY FOR YOU?

AAH!
AAH!
SCHEISSE!
SWEAR BOX. YOU'D BETTER SAVE THE CHOICEST ONES FOR LATER. IT GETS WORSE WHEN THE NERVES WAKE UP PROPERLY.

OKAY, MAN! ENOUGH! ENOUGH!
SORRY ABOUT THAT. YOU MUST HAVE A LOW PAIN THRESHOLD.
SIEG

I'LL FINISH IT ANOTHER TIME, OKAY?
THERE'S ALWAYS MARKER, I SUPPOSE.

SHIT, THAT'S NOT EVEN...
WHAT THE FUCK DOES THAT LOOK LIKE, MAN?
SHIT SHIT SHIT SHIT SHIT.

NOW, THAT-- THAT'S A REAL TATTOO.
THE EMPEROR

BUT FOR SOMETHING THAT BIG, YOU'D BE LOOKING AT TWO THOUSAND MARKS.
AND YOU'D BE LUCKY IF YOUR WHOLE FUCKING ARM DIDN'T DROP OFF.

BUT WHY WEAR IT WHEN YOU CAN BE IT?

YOU'VE GOT THE SEEDS OF GREATNESS. GUNTER KNOWS. THAT'S WHY HE'S SO HARD ON YOU. HE'S TESTING YOU.
THAT'S WHAT THIS IS ALL ABOUT, SON.
DEUTSCH
SIEG
YOU'VE GOT TO PAY THE PRICE OF ADMISSION. YOU SAID SO YOURSELF.
BE DECISIVE. BE STERN AND SWIFT.

SEXY
BEEP
"BE MAGNIFICENT."
THE EMPEROR

ELSA KRETCHNER SELLS FUR COATS TO RICH BITCHES IN A SHOP THAT WOULDN'T EVEN OPEN ITS DOORS FOR HER IF SHE DIDN'T WORK THERE.
HERR KRETCHNER FELL INTO THE HARBOR THREE YEARS AGO ON A SATURDAY NIGHT. ELSA'S CHANCES OF OWNING A FUR, NEVER VERY GOOD, DIED WITH HIM.
THE CARDS SPEAK TO ELSA OF SIMPLE JUSTICE.

WHILE TO HUGO POULENC-- KNOWN TO THE MASSES AS THE AMAZING HUGO MERVEILLE-- THE SIREN SONG IS ABOUT THE SHOW THAT HE WILL PERFORM TONIGHT. IT WILL BE THE GREATEST PERFORMANCE OF HIS LIFE.
HE'S READY. HIS CRAFT IS PERFECT. HE WILL JOIN THE CANON AND SIT WITH HARRY AND DAVID IN GLORY FOREVER.

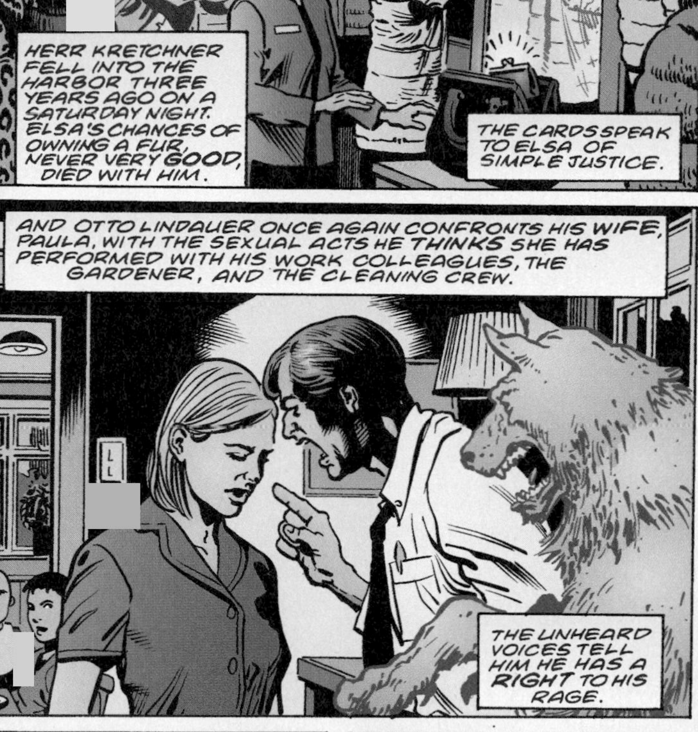
AND OTTO LINDAUER ONCE AGAIN CONFRONTS HIS WIFE, PAULA, WITH THE SEXUAL ACTS HE THINKS SHE HAS PERFORMED WITH HIS WORK COLLEAGUES, THE GARDENER, AND THE CLEANING CREW.
THE UNHEARD VOICES TELL HIM HE HAS A RIGHT TO HIS RAGE.

NIEDERHAFEN. ST. PAULI. AUSSENALSTER. THE CHORUS EBBS AND FLOWS WITH THE WIND ALONG THE URBAN CANYONS AND THE ARTERIAL ROADS.
PROMISING. MOCKING. URGING.
PLAYING THE GAME OF THE BASANOS WITH HUMANKIND.

BUT IN THE PARK CALLED THE PLANTEN UN BLOMEN LUCIFER WALKS, WATCHING THE PLAY OF LIGHT ON WATER, THINKING ABOUT FLUX AND PERMANENCE.
AND AROUND HIM, AT LEAST, THERE IS A SANCTIFIED SILENCE.

MAZIKEEN. I'M SORRY TO INTERRUPT SUCH A SPECIAL MOMENT, BUT I NEED YOU.
YEHKHHH, RROAHD.

THERE ARE PLACES IN ANY TOWN WHERE SHARPENING A KNIFE WILL PASS WITHOUT COMMENT.
GENERALLY SPEAKING, PUBLIC PARKS ARE A POOR BET EXCEPT MAYBE IN NEW YORK CITY.
I HHELT I NUKHT VHE REAGHY, RROAHD. IHHH RE NUKHT HHIGHT HHHE CARGHHS...

WE NEED TO FIND THEM BEFORE WE CAN FIGHT THEM. AND WE NEED TO APPROACH THEM ON THEIR BLIND SIDE, OR THEY'LL GET SKITTISH AND RUN.
I NEED YOU TO BLEED ON THESE LEAVES, AS I HAVE DONE.

I WATCHED MELEOS DESIGN THEM. THE BASANOS IS AN EXQUISITE PIECE OF WORK, BUT NO MAKING IS PERFECT.
IF WE CAST OUR BLOOD ON THE WINDS THEY'LL SEE SHADOWS OF US EVERY-WHERE.
THE VERY SHARPNESS OF THEIR SIGHT IS A WEAKNESS WE CAN EXPLOIT.

THERE. NOW I HAVE ONE SMALL MATTER TO ATTEND TO BEFORE WE CAN BEGIN.
NEREOKHH?
MELEOS. OF COURSE.

WE HAVE PERHAPS TWO HOURS. I'LL GIVE HIM THE FIRST TEN MINUTES.
AND THEN WE'LL HUNT.

AUSGANG
THE NEEDLE'S EYE.
ANY SIGN OF MR. METTERLINCK, LOTTE?
HE CAME IN, JILL. I DON'T KNOW WHERE HE IS NOW, THOUGH. DID YOU TRY THE BAR?
YEAH. TWICE.

HER INTERIOR SOUNDTRACK IS THE SAME AS IT'S EVER BEEN FOR ALL THE YEARS OF SLAMMED DOORS AND SCUT WORK.
IF IT'S A LITTLE FAINTER NOW, THAT'S ONLY BECAUSE SHE'S TIRED.

HEY, HUGO, DID YOU SEE METZ YET TONIGHT?
DID I...?DID I WHAT?

NO, PETERSON, I DIDN'T SEE HIM. WHAT ARE YOU WANTING TO DO, ANYWAY, TO COME IN WITHOUT KNOCKING?
GIVE ME SOME FUCKING PRIVACY, WOULD YOU MIND? AND CLOSE THE DOOR!

FUCK YOUR MOTHER, HUGO.
IF YOU DIDN'T ALREADY.
SLAM

JILL WILL BE HIS HAND-MAIDEN, THE VOICES WHISPER.
AND, AT LONG LAST SHE'LL LEARN TO SHOW THE PROPER RESPECT.

HA! CAUGHT YOU.
OOPS. SORRY, SOLA.
UH... THAT'S OKAY, JILL.

I'LL SEE YOU LATER, MAYBE. I HAVE TO PRACTICE MY NUMBER.

GIVEN THAT SHE'S A STRIPPER SHE WAS GETTING PLENTY OF PRACTICE RIGHT HERE, WASN'T SHE?
IS THIS SOMETHING THAT CAN WAIT, JILL? YOU'VE PICKED A LOUSY TIME.
I JUST WANTED TO ASK ABOUT MY SOLO SPOT--

I CAN'T THINK ABOUT IT JUST YET. I'VE GOT A DEPOSITION TO MAKE TO PETRA'S LAWYER TOMORROW.
AND NOW SHE SAYS SHE'S GOING TO SUE FOR CUSTODY OF MAX.

OH. YEAH. LOTTE TOLD ME THAT.
I'M SORRY, METZ, THAT'S REALLY...

HOLD ON THERE, BALD EAGLE. LOTTE TOLD ME PETRA SERVED YOU THOSE PAPERS THREE WEEKS AGO. SO WHY ARE YOU BRINGING THEM UP NOW?
WELL IT'S ON MY MIND A LOT. I KEEP--
BULLSHIT.

YOU USED YOUR PRIVATE LIFE TO CHANGE THE SUBJECT ON ME, METZ. FOR ABOUT THE FIFTH TIME.
NOW GIVE ME A STRAIGHT ANSWER.

OKAY, JILL. THE STRAIGHT ANSWER.
YOU'RE NOT UP TO IT. YOU SING OKAY, BUT YOUR MOVES ARE AWKWARD AND YOU DON'T PROJECT YOUR PERSONALITY ALL THAT WELL.

MY MOVES? SONOFABITCH! WHAT ABOUT YOUR MOVES? YOU ONLY GAVE SOLA HER BIG CAGE ROUTINE BECAUSE SHE WENT DOWN ON YOU!
ON SECOND THOUGHT, YOU PROJECT JUST FINE-- YOU COME ACROSS AS LOUD AND COARSE.
COARSE? YOU WANNA SEE COARSE?

GIMME MY COAT, LOTTE. I NEED A DRINK.
JUST WAIT UNTIL I FINISH THIS PARAGRAPH--

HIS WIFE DIES OF LEUKEMIA AND HE MARRIES THE NURSE, OKAY?
YOU'RE ON AT TEN THIRTY, YOU KNOW. I COULD GET YOU A DRINK FROM THE BAR.

THEN THE NURSE DIVORCES HIM AND HE SPENDS THE REST OF HIS BEER-BELLIED LIFE FUCKING EIGHTEEN-YEAR-OLD STRIPPERS.
IT'S BASED ON A TRUE STORY. RIGHT METZ?
LOTTE--

--GO INTO THE OFFICE AND TYPE UP A TERMINATION LETTER.

"AND LEAVE SOME SPACES FOR ADJECTIVES."
NEEDLE'S EYE
BAR
BAR

OKAY, DAD, I'M BACK.
JAYESH, THANK GOD YOU'RE HERE. THERE IS A SKIN-HEAD IN THE MIDDLE AISLE. A SKIN-HEAD!
I ASKED IF I COULD HELP HIM AND HE GAVE ME FOUL LANGUAGE! CALL THE POLICE, YAAH.

SHIT! THE POLICE WON'T DO ANYTHING. THEY NEVER DO.
LEAVE HIM TO ME.

LISTEN, FRIEND, MY DAD'S ALREADY CALLED THE POLICE, SO IF YOU DON'T MIND...
FUCK.

KARL...
DEVA. DO YOU HAVE ANY ANTISEPTIC OINTMENT? I... I CUT MY ARM AND IT'S SWOLLEN UP.
SURE. SURE WE DO.

YEAH, HERE WE GO. ELOTOX -- DISINFECTS MINOR WOUNDS AND RELIEVES ITCHING. DO YOU HAVE AN ITCH?
NO. I TOLD YOU. A SWELLING, NOT AN ITCH.

AND OH FUCK, JAYESH THINKS, THE HAIRS IN HIS EAR, THE SLIDING OF THAT MUSCLE IN HIS ARM.
THANKS.

AND HE THINKS HE'LL NEVER...
KARL...
...IF HE DOESN'T DO IT NOW.
I WAS WONDERING...UMM... IF YOU...

WHAT?
WELL, YOU KNOW...
TAB
TAB
DUZ
DUZ
...IF YOU'D LIKE TO COME OUT FOR A DRINK LATER.

HAH. THAT'S FUNNY, YOU KNOW? AFTER A DAY LIKE THIS.
YEAH, SURE A DRINK. WHY NOT?
REALLY?
YES, REALLY. THEN MAYBE YOU'LL GIVE ME SOME FUCKING PEACE.

LISTEN, JAYESH. I'VE GOT FRIENDS THAT'LL LITERALLY FUCKING KILL ME IF THEY SEE US TOGETHER.
MEET ME AT THE BACK DOOR OF THE SHOP AT TEN. NOT ON THE STREET.
ELOTOX
RIGHT. OKAY.

TCHAH. HE IS A ROUGH ELEMENT. AND A RACIST. HE HAS A FOUL TONGUE.
KARTEN-P
YEAH...
STERN

...AND HAIRY EARS.
10.05

"I WILL CHRONICLE THEM," HE HAD SAID.
I'M SORRY. I'M SO SORRY...
NOW ONE OF THE TOOLS HE MADE HAS SPILLED RED INK ACROSS THE PAGES OF THE CHRONICLE. AND HE IS LEFT STARING HELPLESSLY AT HIS STAINED HANDS.

GOOD EVENING, MELEOS. I WAS BEGINNING TO WONDER IF YOU'D MAKE IT. THOSE LAST TWENTY FLIGHTS NEARLY FINISHED YOU.
...PLEASE...

TWO COPIES OF JEROME'S BIBLE MIGHT BE SEEN AS EXCESSIVE, EVEN IF ONE DOES HAVE A PSALM MISSING.
DID THE BASANOS DO THAT TO YOUR FACE?

WE FOUGHT. THEY... THEY BROKE MY CONCENTRATION, AND THEN STRUCK ME DOWN. AND NOW I CAN'T HEAL THE WOUND.
LUCIFER, THEY'RE FREE. THEY'VE ESCAPED FROM ME.
I KNOW. THAT'S WHY I'M HERE.

YOU THOUGHT YOU COULD TRAP THEM AGAIN IN THE SAME BOX.
DON'T YOU KNOW THE PROVERB ABOUT WORMS AND CANS?

CRRRK

WHAT SHOULD I DO WITH YOU, MELEOS? I NEED SOMETHING QUICK BUT UNFORGETTABLE.
I WASN'T TRYING TO SET THEM FREE! I WANTED TO KILL THEM! YOU MUST KNOW THAT!
YOU DISOBEYED ME. THAT'S THE ISSUE AS I SEE IT.

I WOULD HAVE DONE A SIMPLE SIX-CARD SPREAD, AND THEN I WOULD HAVE GONE.
IT WOULD HAVE BEEN PAINLESS. COMPARATIVELY.
AND WHAT IF THEY'D OVERPOWERED YOU? THEY MIGHT HAVE--
ESCAPED? YOU'RE A FOOL, MELEOS.

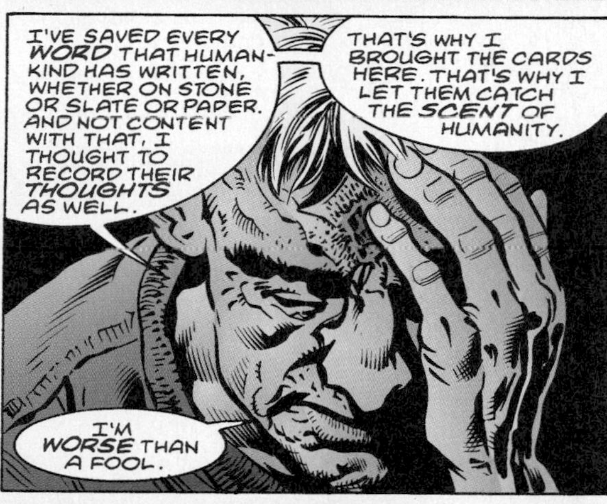
I'VE SAVED EVERY WORD THAT HUMANKIND HAS WRITTEN, WHETHER ON STONE OR SLATE OR PAPER. AND NOT CONTENT WITH THAT, I THOUGHT TO RECORD THEIR THOUGHTS AS WELL.
THAT'S WHY I BROUGHT THE CARDS HERE. THAT'S WHY I LET THEM CATCH THE SCENT OF HUMANITY.
I'M WORSE THAN A FOOL.

I SUPPOSE IT'S BECAUSE WE DON'T BREED THAT WE PUT SO MUCH OF OURSELVES INTO OUR TOOLS.
FROM ONE POINT OF VIEW YOU'VE ALREADY PUNISHED YOURSELF ENOUGH.
SO DON'T SEE THIS AS A PUNISHMENT.

SEE IT AS AN HONEST CRITIQUE OF YOUR... PROJECT.

WHAT HAVE YOU DONE? LUCIFER, PLEASE! TELL ME!
YOU HAVE A FINE MIND, MELEOS.
PROCEED BY OBSERVATION AND INFERENCE.

AND THE CHILD WALKS AMONG THE YOUNG, TIRED WHORES ON THE REEPERBAHN, LOOKING INTO EVERY FACE. SHE IS SEARCHING, AND SO SHE IS FULLY INCARNATE.
SHE IS SEARCHING, AND SO SHE HAS NO TIME TO PLAY. BUT TO PLAY IS TO FEEL YOURSELF ALIVE; TO WEAVE THE INVISIBLE THREADS OF FATE INTO FANTASTIC PATTERNS THAT NO ONE ELSE CAN SEE.
FOR HER KIND IT IS SEX AND FOOD AND REST--THE ONLY IMPERATIVE.

HER CARD IS INNOCENCE, BUT THAT IS NOT A SIGN THAT DEFINES HER. IT IS A DRESS SHE WEARS.
WHERE SHE WALKS, THE STREET GIRLS ARE ASSAILED BY MEMORIES. ALL THE STATIONS OF THE NIGHT. ALL THE MOMENTS OF SURRENDER AND DEGRADATION.

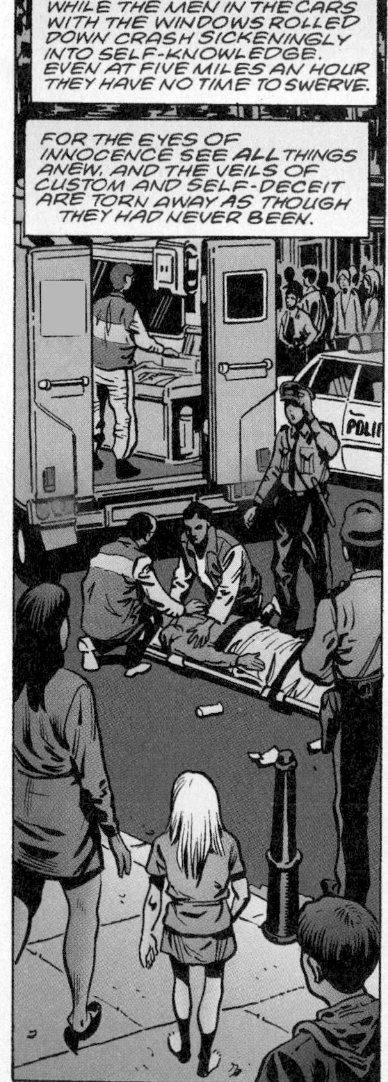
WHILE THE MEN IN THE CARS WITH THE WINDOWS ROLLED DOWN CRASH SICKENINGLY INTO SELF-KNOWLEDGE. EVEN AT FIVE MILES AN HOUR THEY HAVE NO TIME TO SWERVE.
FOR THE EYES OF INNOCENCE SEE ALL THINGS ANEW, AND THE VEILS OF CUSTOM AND SELF-DECEIT ARE TORN AWAY AS THOUGH THEY HAD NEVER BEEN.

SORRY, KID. YOU CAN'T COME THROUGH HERE.
GET ME ANOTHER DRESSING!
SHIT, WHY WOULD A MAN POKE HIS OWN EYES OUT?
HE PUT HIS EYES OUT BECAUSE HE DIDN'T WANT TO SEE.

GET THESE PEOPLE MOVING, GERD. WHAT WAS THAT LOVE?
IT WILL BE DIFFERENT FOR YOU. YOU'LL WANT TO PASS THE PAIN ON TO SOMEBODY ELSE.

THERE IS A TRILLING IN THE WIRES--A HIGH, INHUMAN SOUND.
A MILLION CATS ARE MEWLING IN A MILLION HYPOTHETICAL BOXES. A MILLION TRIGGERS ARE PULLED.
DESTINY RIDES ON THE BULLETS.

NINE FORTY FIVE. THERE IS A SCENT IN THE AIR LIKE HOT METAL.
AS IF THE CITY HAS BEEN PLUNGED INTO A FORGE, AND NOW IT'S LYING ON THE ANVIL WAITING TO BE HAMMERED INTO A NEW SHAPE.
JAYESH IS WAITING FOR HIS MAN.
JAYESH. OVER HERE.
HAVE YOU BEEN WAITING LONG?
AGES. BUT DON'T WORRY. YOU'RE WORTH IT.
YOU REMEMBER THOSE FRIENDS I MENTIONED?
THEY WANTED TO MEET YOU, SO I THOUGHT I'D BRING THEM ALONG.
HELLO, BHAJI BOY. KARL TELLS ME YOU'RE A QUEER.
SO HOW'D YOU LIKE TO TAKE ALL FOUR OF US ON? PRETTY EXCITING, EH?
LOOK, THIS WAS MY MISTAKE. I'M SORRY. REALLY. I'M GOING TO LEAVE NOW.
NO, NO, JAYESH. STICK AROUND. THIS IS YOUR PARTY.
PLEASE, KARL--
KARL TOLD YOU TO STAY, BHAJI BOY. DON'T YOU SPEAK GERMAN?
VERSTEHEN SIE NICHT THE FUCKING DEUTSCHER LANGUAGE?

THE MUFFLED SCREAM. THE SCUFFLING FEET. THE SMACK AND THUD OF HUMAN FLESH BEING TESTED TO DESTRUCTION. THE SOUNDS ARE SOFT BUT UNMISTAKABLE.
No. Oh no.
BUT MELEOS DOESN'T HEAR THEM.

SURELY... IT'S ONLY THE ONE BOOK. THE ONE HE TOUCHED. THIS IS SOME SORT OF WARNING.
PLEASE... PLEASE DON'T...
BUT NO. LUCIFER DOES NOT THREATEN BEFORE HE STRIKES.

FROM LEVEL TO LEVEL HE RUNS. SPINOZA, ARISTOTLE, LAO-TZU...
THE FRAGILE LINES LIKE OPENED ARTERIES OF THOUGHT RUN OFF THEIR PAGES AND POOL ON THE FLOOR.

THEY HAVE BEEN STRUCK DOWN BY A HEMORRHAGIC PLAGUE.
MORNINGSTAR--
LUCIFER'S PLAGUE. FOR HE IS OLDER THAN THE ANGEL OF DEATH, AND GREATER.
AND WHEN HE COMES IN JUDGMENT HE SPARES NONE.

TOO CRUEL... EVEN FOR YOU.

MELEOS KNEELS AMONG THE VIOLATED BODIES OF HIS CHILDREN. TO MOURN THEM ALL WILL TAKE A LIFETIME.

AFTER THE FIRST KICK IT BECOMES LARGELY ABSTRACT.
A TERM IN AN ARGUMENT. A PROOF-- LIKE THE PROOF THAT ALL THE ANGLES ADD UP IN A TRIANGLE.
KRASSH
SHOVE HIM UP AGAINST THE WALL AND GET HIS PANTS DOWN. HERE YOU GO, KARL.
WHAT? WHAT DO YOU MEAN?
POETIC JUSTICE.
COME OFF IT, GUNTER. I'M NOT GOING ANYWHERE NEAR HIS FUCKING ASS, MAN.
WHY NOT? HE WAS AFTER YOURS.
YOU'RE NOT IN THE FAN CLUB ANYMORE.
WELL, GET A MOVE ON. THE FUCKER'S DOZING OFF ON US.
HE'S FUCKING HEAVY, TOO.
DU BIST UNSER MENSCH NOW, KARL.
YOU'RE ONE OF US.

IN MOVIES WHEN YOU'RE DOWN, THE BARMAN LISTENS TO ALL YOUR PROBLEMS.
DISPENSES HOMESPUN WISDOM WHILE HE'S CLEANING GLASSES WITH A CHECKERED CLOTH.
BUT THIS ISN'T HER COUNTRY, AND THERE ISN'T ANYONE WHO KNOWS HER FUCKING NAME.

HEY. HEY, GIRL. YOU'VE GOT STAR QUALITY, REMEMBER.
YOU DIDN'T COME ALL THE WAY FROM PITTSBURGH JUST TO ROLL OVER AND BEG WHEN SOME...
...SOME SWEAT-STAINED FLEAPIT WHORE-RUNNER SNAPS HIS FINGERS.

DO YOU WANT ANOTHER DRINK, FRAULEIN?
NAH. WHEN YOU START GIVING PEP TALKS TO YOUR REFLECTION IT'S PROBABLY TIME TO QUIT.
JUST POINT ME TO THE TOILETS.

SERVE HUGO RIGHT IF HE HAD TO WIGGLE HIS OWN ASS AT THE CHEAP SEATS TONIGHT.
BUT I GUESS THE SHOW MUST GO ON.

HELLO. YOU'RE JILL PRESTO, AREN'T YOU? THE CABARET STAR?
HUH?
HEY.
AREN'T YOU A LITTLE YOUNG TO BE IN HERE?

OH, DON'T WORRY. I'M HERE WITH FRIENDS.
WE'RE COMING TO SEE YOUR ACT TONIGHT. WE'RE REALLY LOOKING FORWARD TO IT.

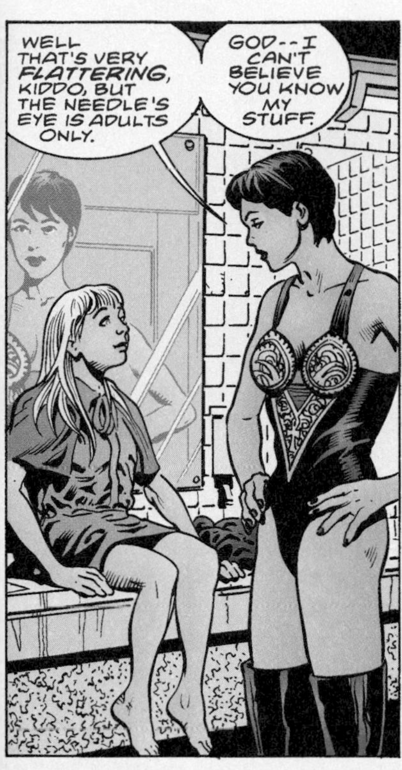
WELL THAT'S VERY FLATTERING, KIDDO, BUT THE NEEDLE'S EYE IS ADULTS ONLY.
GOD--I CAN'T BELIEVE YOU KNOW MY STUFF.

WE KNOW EVERYTHING ABOUT YOU, JILL. YOU SEE, WE'VE SORT OF BEEN AUDITIONING. LOOKING FOR SOMEONE TO WORK WITH.
YEAH? WHAT SORT OF ACT?
VARIETY. LIMITLESS VARIETY. ALL WE NEED IS A HOST. TAKE A LOOK.

YOU MEAN AN M.C.? THAT REALLY DOESN'T SOUND LIKE MY LINE.
UMMM... WHAT AM I MEANT TO BE LOOKING AT?
YOUR FUTURE. YOUR PAST. YOUR DESTINY. CAN'T YOU SEE?

DEATH

CUTE, BUT WEIRD. ARE YOU A LITTLE CULT KID? DO YOUR FOLKS SELL FLOWERS AT MAJOR AIR-PORTS?
LOOK, YOU CAN KEEP THE CARDS. I'M NOT INTERESTED.

YOU'VE ALREADY ACCEPTED THEM, JILL. DON'T BE AFRAID--THE DEATH CARD STANDS FOR CHANGE AND REBIRTH. IT'S A GOOD OMEN.
WHAT DIES IS JUST THE PART OF YOU YOU DON'T NEED ANYMORE.

I FEEL AS THOUGH I'M AWAKENING FROM A LONG SLEEP. TWICE NOW I'VE WALKED OUT ON HIM, AND THEN BOTH TIMES I'VE LET HIM RECAST ME -- FIND ME A NEW ROLE IN THE UNFOLDING DRAMA.
AND EVERY TIME I TRY TO IMPROVISE I FIND MY MOVES WERE RIGHT THERE IN THE SCRIPT ALL ALONG.

BUT HIS OMNISCIENCE ONLY WORKS BECAUSE THERE ARE NO ALTERNATIVES. I SEE THAT NOW.
AND I HAVE CONCEIVED OF A REVOLUTION THAT MAY SURPRISE EVEN HIM.

NGY RROAHD, KHARGHON NE. IFH THIKH NÓTHHH THE TINE TO HHHTRIKE? RRHILE THHEY ARE DIKHHRACTED?
KAISER
BEE
NO. NOT YET.
AUSGANG

WE CAN'T MOVE UNTIL THEY'RE ALL TOGETHER IN ONE PLACE. THEY'VE BEEN WINDOW SHOPPING.
AND NOW I THINK THEY'VE DECIDED TO BUY.

WATCH CLOSELY.
THIS IS ONE YOU PROBABLY HAVEN'T SEEN BEFORE.

HOLY FUCK!
IT'S HOLY, YES. FUCKING APPEARS ELSEWHERE IN THE EQUATION.
COMFORTABLE, JILL? THEN MAKE ROOM FOR ME.
THE MORNING STAR IS CLOSE AT HAND.
IT'S TIME FOR THE HIGH-STAKES GAME.

FEGREDO

THE NEEDLE'S EYE. HOW ABOUT THAT. SHE MADE IT.
STAGE DOOR
RAIDER!
CLUB DESE

JILL PRESTO NEVER MISSED A GIG IN HER LIFE, AND SHE'S NOT ABOUT TO START NOW.
WHOA! WHAT'S THIS? WHO SAID YOU COULD PINCH-HIT FOR ME?
JILL! YOU CAME BACK. I THOUGHT--
--METZ SAID--

GO FUCK YOURSELF, SOLA. IT'S THE ONLY OPTION YOU HAVEN'T TRIED, ISN'T IT?
COME SNIFFING AROUND MY JOB AGAIN, I'LL STRIP YOUR ASSETS.

BUT GRAVITY, DAMEN UND HERREN, IS AN ILLUSION.
IT IS PART OF MAYA, THE GRAND ILLUSION THAT IS THE WORLD.
LET ME SHOW YOU THE TRUTH.

HI. REMEMBER ME?
...

HUGO'S A TROOPER. SKIPS ONE BEAT, THEN ROLLS WITH THE PUNCH AND JUST GETS ON WITH IT.
GIVES HER TIME TO PULL HERSELF TOGETHER. ONLY...

...ONLY HER MIND IS WANDERING.
WELCOME TO Fabulous
EILEEN PENN
VEGAS 1979
"Got the world on a string."

STAGE SCHOOL? WHY THE FUCK WOULD YOU WANT TO GO THERE?
I DON'T KNOW. I JUST...
YOU JUST THOUGHT IMITATION WAS THE SINCEREST FORM OF COP-OUT.

CHRIST, YOU'RE YOUR FATHER'S DAUGHTER, AREN'T YOU?
FOLLOW THE DREAM. EVEN IF IT TAKES YOU UP SOMEONE ELSE'S ASS.

LAS VEGAS. 1979.
THE WORLD.
ON A STRING.

THE CARDS WILL RESIST ME. A SHOW OF FORCE IS GOING TO BE NECESSARY AT SOME POINT.
JUST OUT OF INTEREST, ARE YOU CARRYING A WEAPON? SOMETHING WITH AN EDGE?
ALRAYSZH, RROAHD.
GOOD.

A SIX-CARD SPREAD

MIKE CAREY · WRITER CHRIS WESTON · PENCILLER + INKER PPS. 14, 17-19, 21 JAMES HODGKINS · INKER PPS. 1-13, 15-16, 20, 22 DANIEL VOZZO · COLOR + SEPS ELLIE DE VILLE · LETTERER DUNCAN FEGREDO · COVER ART WILL DENNIS · ASST EDITOR SHELLY ROEBERG · EDITOR
BASED ON THE CHARACTER CREATED BY GAIMAN, KIETH AND DRINGENBERG

I'M AFRAID THE CLUB IS MEMBERS ONLY. WOULD YOU LIKE TO JOIN?
I WOULD LIKE YOU TO REMOVE YOUR HAND.
OR IF YOU HAVE A CONCESSIONARY TICKET, THEN I COULD--

I DON'T HAVE THE TIME FOR THIS.
WHICH FOR YOU IS SOME-THING OF A MIXED BLESSING. EXCUSE ME.

GUUUH!

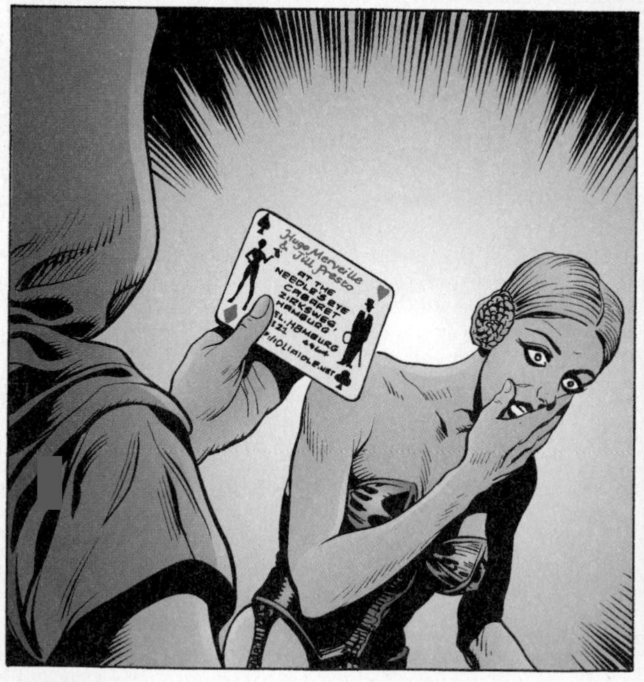
Hugo Merveille
& Jill Presto
AT THE
NEEDLE'S EYE
CABARET
ZIRKSWEG,
HAMBURG

HUUUULCH!

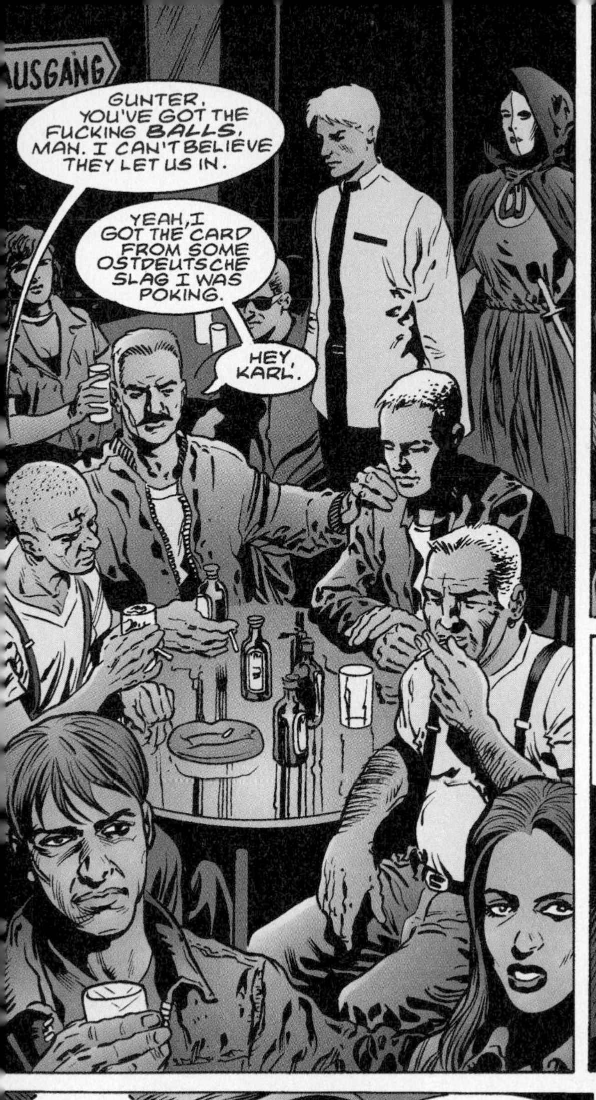
AUSGANG
GUNTER, YOU'VE GOT THE FUCKING BALLS, MAN. I CAN'T BELIEVE THEY LET US IN.
YEAH, I GOT THE CARD FROM SOME OSTDEUTSCHE SLAG I WAS POKING.
HEY, KARL.

YOU WANT ANOTHER BOTTLE?
CHRIST, GUNTER. DON'T.

A HANDFUL OF FEATHERS, DAMEN UND HERREN. SOME COOKING FAT...
NO MORE THAN THAT. BUT SEE WHAT AN EXOTIC DISH WE CAN COOK UP FROM THESE MODEST INGREDIENTS.

ARE YOU MADE OF WOOD?
SORRY, HUGO. I... I FEEL--
GIVE ME SOME COMMITMENT, YOU STUPID BITCH!
GIVE ME ALL YOU'VE GOT!

GO AHEAD, JILL. WHY NOT?
YOU CAN'T HOLD IT IN MUCH LONGER ANYWAY.

FUCK, MAN, THAT WAS PRETTY *IMPRESSIVE*.
YEAH, IT WAS OKAY. WHERE ARE YOU GOING, KARL?
I NEED TO PISS.

EMERGENCY 110. CANN ICH IHNEN HELFEN?

I WANT TO REPORT A...AN ACCIDENT.

WHICH SERVICE, CALLER?

I *TOLD* YOU. THERE'S A MAN IN AN ALLEY OFF THE FRIEDRICHSTRASSE. I THINK HE'S BEEN BEATEN UP.

HE NEEDS AN ***AMBULANCE***.

I SAID THE ALLEY BEHIND FRIE...

OKAY, SO THERE'S MORE THAN ONE. LOOK IN ***ALL*** OF THEM.

LOOK, IT'S YOUR ***JOB*** ISN'T IT? THERE'S A FUCKING MAN LYING ON THE ***GROUND***. HE'S NOT GOING TO BE HARD TO FIND!

JUST FUCKING... DO YOUR JOB, MAN!

FOR CHRIST'S SAKE! WELL, JUST SEND IT TO THE ***BOOKSHOP***-- THE TASCHENTURM.

I'LL ***TAKE*** YOU THERE, YOU INCOMPETENT BASTARDS!

IT'S UNBELIEVABLE. LIKE HITTING A HUNDRED AND TWENTY ON THE STRAIGHT AND THE ENGINE ISN'T EVEN MAKING A SOUND.

LIKE SHE'S HOLDING A REMOTE IN HER HANDS AND IT WORKS THE WORLD.
STOP IT! WHATEVER YOU'RE DOING, STOP IT!
WHAT'S THE MATTER, HUGO?
DON'T YOU LIKE MAGIC?
NOT YET, MAZIKEEN.
LET HER SPEND THE COIN OF THEIR POWER AS PRODIGALLY AS SHE LIKES.
WHEN SHE'S DOWN TO SMALL CHANGE, THEN WE'LL MOVE.

THIS IS WHAT GOD FELT LIKE WHEN HE MADE THE WORLD.
THIS IS WHY HE DID IT. FOR THE POWER. FOR THE HIGH.

SHE CAN SEE THEIR LIVES. THE PAST STRAIGHT LIKE A WIRE, THE FUTURE BRANCHING INTO A MILLION FILAMENTS.
WHAT THEY ARE AND WERE AND COULD BE.

AND INSIDE THEM... IN THEIR MINDS...
SHE CAN SEE THAT TOO.
HUGO. CHOKING ON TEARS OF ANGER AND HUMILIATION. HE'S THINKING "THE BEST PERFORMANCE OF MY LIFE" AGAIN AND AGAIN.

METZ WANTS TO TEAR UP THE LETTER THAT TELLS HER SHE'S UNEMPLOYED.
HE'S THINKING NUMBERS.
ALL THIS BEAUTY AND STRANGE-NESS FLATTENED BETWEEN THE COLUMNS OF A BALANCE SHEET.

AND THERE'S LOTTE. WHY ISN'T SHE READING HER CRUDDY ROMANCE? SHE'S THINKING ABOUT A PAIR OF EYES SHE STARED INTO. IT WAS HALF AN HOUR AGO AND SHE STILL CAN'T LOOK AWAY.

SHE'S SEEING THE WORLD THROUGH A HUNDRED STAINED GLASS WINDOWS.
THERE ARE NO BARRIERS, NO DISGUISES. THERE'S NOTHING
NOTHING SHE CAN'T
SEE.

YOU BASTARDS! YOU ROTTEN, COWARDLY SCUMBAGS!
HOW COULD YOU?
HOW COULD YOU DO THAT?

WELL LET'S SEE HOW YOU LIKE IT!

AND SHE BECOMES A LIGHTNING ROD. THE POTENTIAL FUTURES MOVING THROUGH HER INTO THE PRESENT.
SHE FINDS THEIR PAIN. SHE FINDS THEIR DEATHS. THE CURRENT FLOWS.

THE FIRST ONE'S ERICH. THREE YEARS FROM NOW, THERE'S A STRONG POSSIBILITY THAT HE'LL CRASH HIS CAR ON THE AUTOBAHN, DRIVING WITHOUT A SEATBELT.
THE ONE NAMED ECKERHART COULD MEET A RAZOR GANG IN BERLIN WHEN HE'S CELEBRATING THE NEW YEAR WITH HIS SISTER.
THE WOUNDS OPEN ON HIS BODY LIKE RED FLOWERS. HE CAN'T EVEN SCREAM. THE FIRST SLASH CUTS HIS THROAT.
THIS MOMENT MEETS THAT ONE. WHAT MIGHT BE BECOMES WHAT IS.

AND YOU'RE... WHAT? GUNTER?
THERE'S A STROKE THAT'S WAITING FOR YOU WHEN YOU TURN SIXTY. BUT YOU CAN HAVE IT NOW INSTEAD.
YOU CAN HAVE IT ON ME.
GWWA--
VERSTEHEN SIE NICHT DEUTSCH YOU FASCIST PIECE OF SHIT?
DON'T YOU SPEAK THE LANGUAGE?
ENOUGH.
REVEAL YOURSELVES. I DIDN'T COME HERE TO WATCH A PUPPET SHOW.
RAGE
AND THEY COME AT HIS COMMAND, RISING LIKE FLIES FROM A BLOWN CARCASS.
THE BASTARD CHILDREN OF CHANCE AND DESTINY. THE BEASTS OF REVELATION. THE BASANOS.

WHILE ELSE-WHERE...
THE RIPPLES SPREAD FROM TRICKS ALREADY PLAYED.
RAUS
JAYESH? THERE'S AN AMBULANCE COMING.
THEY'RE GOING TO HELP YOU, MAN.
I'M JUST... I'M JUST GOING TO...
...WAIT FOR THEM. OUT ON THE STREET. SHOW THEM THE WAY.
I'LL...I'LL COME BACK.
AAAH!
MISTER WEISS! I DIDN'T SEE YOU!
RAUS
NO. I'M SURE YOU DIDN'T.
THAT COULD ALMOST BE YOUR MOTTO, COULDN'T IT, KARL?
"I HAD MY EYES CLOSED, SO I DIDN'T SEE YOU."
I DON'T KNOW WHAT YOU...
AKKK!
BUT HOW COULD YOU MISS SO MUCH?
HOW COULD YOU FAIL TO SEE EVEN YOURSELF?

IT WASN'T HIS LOVE FOR YOU THAT MADE YOU HATE HIM.
IT WAS THE FACT THAT YOU WERE AROUSED BY HIM.
ONE MORE PIECE OF BRUTALITY MAKES NO DIFFERENCE, I KNOW.
BUT IT SEEMS SO TYPICAL. IT SEEMS TO SUM UP SO MUCH.
I'VE GIVEN MY LIFE TO YOUR SPECIES. KEPT EVERY WORD YOU WROTE.
I SPENT TEN THOUSAND YEARS BUILDING A CARD HOUSE, AND THE DARK ANGEL KNOCKED IT DOWN WITH ONE SWEEP OF HIS HAND!
IT'S IRRELEVANT NOW. I DON'T HAVE ANY RESPONSIBILITY FOR YOU.
KRAASH
I DON'T NEED TO WARN YOU WHERE YOUR NEED FOR FORGIVENESS WILL BRING YOU.
ATONEMENT IS AT BEST A JOURNEY OF UNCERTAIN LENGTH TO AN UNKNOWN DESTINATION.
BUT SO IS REVENGE, OF COURSE. WE BOTH EMBRACE OUR OWN DESTRUCTION.
GOODBYE, KARL.
DID SOMEBODY HERE CALL AN AMBULANCE?
AMBULANCE

THE CARDS SEEM TO KNOW THAT THEY CAN'T WIN BY DIRECT ATTACK. THESE ARE THE TACTICS OF DIVERSION.
FEINT AND WEAVE, STAB AND RETREAT.
FOR A MOMENT, AT LEAST, THEY SEEM TO WORK.
THAT ONE, MAZIKEEN.
NOW.
NOTHING HUMAN COULD MOVE SO FAST. THE CARDS RISE LIKE STARTLED BIRDS.
ALL BUT ONE.
SOMETHING TEARS INSIDE HER. SOFT MEMBRANES SLICED CLEAN THROUGH. COLD METAL SHEATHES ITSELF IN HER GUT.
SHE TRIES TO SCREAM.
BUT THERE'S NO AIR LEFT.
THE LIGHTBRINGER

LUCIFER. SUNLIGHTER. OATH-BREAKER.

GIVE US OUR BROTHER BACK OR YOU'LL TWIST ON THE AXLE TREE OF HEAVEN LIKE A GAME-COCK ON A GIBBET!
YOU FORGET YOURSELF.

I AM CONSIDERING WHETHER OR NOT TO PARDON YOU. IN THE MEANTIME, I REQUIRE A DIVINATION.
YOU WILL OBLIGE ME.

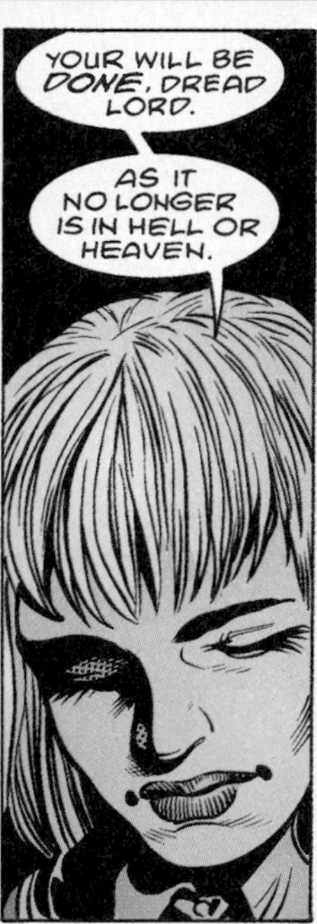
YOUR WILL BE DONE, DREAD LORD.
AS IT NO LONGER IS IN HELL OR HEAVEN.

I STAND AT A CROSS-ROADS. ILLUMINATE THE PATHS.
VERY WELL.

THIS... THIS SHOWS HIM.
THE LORD OF NO REALM. THE APOSTATE. PINNED ON A DILEMMA.
GOD HOLDS THE DOOR FOR YOU LIKE A FAWNING FOOTMAN, BUT WHERE DOES IT LEAD?

The Mounta
LIGHTBRINGER
THIS CROSSES HIM. YOU MUST ASCEND AND YET YOU HAVE NO WINGS.
YOU WILL SEARCH FOR THEM THROUGH WINDOWLESS ROOMS.
Innocence
THIS RAISES HIM. AH, BUT DON'T BE MISLED.
I AM YOUR ENEMY, MORNINGSTAR, NOW AND ALWAYS. THE CHILD THAT LIGHTS THE WAY FOR YOU IS SOMEONE QUITE DIFFERENT.
AND YOU'LL HAVE TO RETURN THE FAVOR.
THIS CASTS HIM DOWN.
YOUR CREATOR HAS GIVEN YOU A POISONED CHALICE. THE LETTER OF PASSAGE WILL OPEN FOR YOU, BUT ONLY ONCE. AND WHEN IT CLOSES BEHIND YOU IT WILL CLOSE FOREVER.
The Fo
IT SEEMS THAT HEAVEN CAN DISPENSE WITH YOUR SERVICES NOW.
e Wheel
THIS IS WHERE HE BEGINS. TREADING THE SAME GROUND AGAIN. FOR THE WHEEL HAS COME FULL CIRCLE, A REVOLUTION.
AND THIS, LUCIFER...
THIS IS WHERE HE ENDS.
NONE TOO SOON, EITHER.
SKIP THE MELODRAMA AND GO STRAIGHT TO THE POINT.
the Tower
GIVE US YOUR PARDON, MORNINGSTAR. AND OUR INJURED BROTHER.
TAKE HIM. AND MAKE SURE THAT YOU PLAY YOUR GAMES FAR AWAY FROM ME.

Bar.
WE HAVE WHAT WE CAME FOR, MAZIKEEN, BUT KEEP THIS HANDY.
YESZH, RROAHD.

UUUUUH!
WELL THAT'S THAT THEN. CONSUMMATUM EST.
TIME FOR YOU TO DECIDE, JILL. YES OR NO?

Y...YES OR NO TO WHAT? I DON'T UNDER-STAND.
TO US.
WE CAN ONLY STAY IF YOU ACCEPT US OF YOUR OWN FREE WILL. IT'S A BARGAIN.
A CONTRACT.

YOU'VE SEEN THE SMALLEST GLIMPSE OF WHAT WE CAN GIVE YOU.
SUCCESS AND FAME WILL COME TO YOU WITHOUT YOUR NEEDING TO TRY. OH, AND YOU'LL LIVE FOREVER, IF THAT'S ANY INCENTIVE.
SAY YES, DAUGHTER OF EVE. LET US LIVE IN YOU.
Death

AND WHAT CAN SHE SAY? THE TASTE IN HER MOUTH IS THE TASTE OF TWELVE WASTED YEARS. CLIMBING. FALLING.
LIKE HER FATHER, DANGLING ON A STRING.
THE SOUND SHE HEARS IS HER MOTHER'S VOICE, TELLING HER SHE'LL NEVER AMOUNT TO JACK SHIT.

AND SHE GETS THIS FEELING, LIKE ALL HER LIFE IS STIGMATA.
OLD WOUNDS THAT STAY MIRACULOUSLY OPEN.

HEY. MISTER DEVA.
EXCUSE ME.
YES?
HAS HE... HAS HE WOKEN UP YET?

THEY CANNOT SAY FOR SURE THAT HE WILL WAKE UP.
THERE IS BLEEDING IN THE BRAIN, YOU SEE.
X-
THEY SAY IT IS A HARD THING TO CURE.

OUR SON WOULD BE DEAD ALREADY IF YOU HAD NOT FOUND HIM.
BLESS YOU FOR THAT. BLESS YOU.
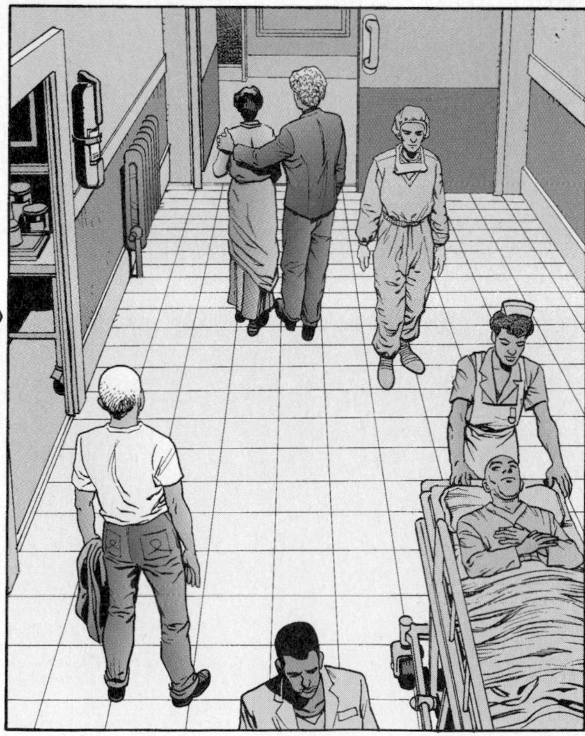

IF HIS BLOOD PRESSURE FALLS ANY FURTHER, PAGE ME. OTHERWISE I'LL SEE HIM ON WARD ROUNDS IN THE MORNING.
YES, DOCTOR.

SO ANYWAY.
HOW WAS YOUR DAY?

TWO OF THEM ARE DEAD, JAY, AND ONE'S QUADRIPLEGIC.
THE ONE OUTSIDE... WELL, TRUST ME WHEN I TELL YOU HE'LL GET HIS SOME OTHER WAY.
I DON'T THINK I COULD KILL HIM IN COLD BLOOD. WELL, MAYBE WITH MY COOKING...

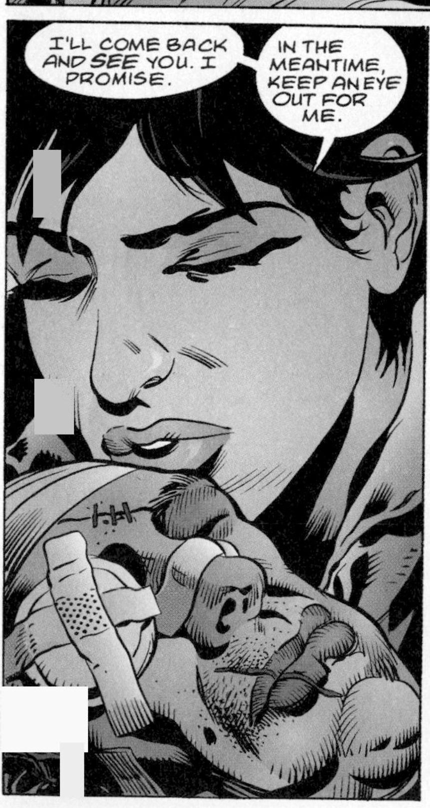
I'LL COME BACK AND SEE YOU. I PROMISE.
IN THE MEANTIME, KEEP AN EYE OUT FOR ME.

"I'LL BE HARD TO MISS."
ALL DONE?
YOU'VE GOT ME COLD, HAVEN'T YOU?

YOU CAN SEE THE INSIDE OF MY HEAD. SO YOU KNEW WHICH WAY I'D JUMP ALL ALONG.
WE KNOW WHICH WAY EVERYONE JUMPS.
THOSE WHO BELIEVE IN FREE WILL MAKE THE BEST PUPPETS OF ALL.

A ONE-WAY TICKET. A DOOR THAT OPENS ONLY FROM THIS SIDE.
I DON'T KNOW IF I'M MORE OFFENDED BY THE DECEIT OR BY THE INSULT TO MY INTELLIGENCE.

I THOUGHT I'D PROVED MY POINT, BUT EVIDENTLY YOU'RE VERY SLOW ON THE UPTAKE.
YOU'VE GOT NO ONE TO BLAME FOR THIS BUT YOURSELF.
MAZIKEEN, GIVE ME THE KNIFE.
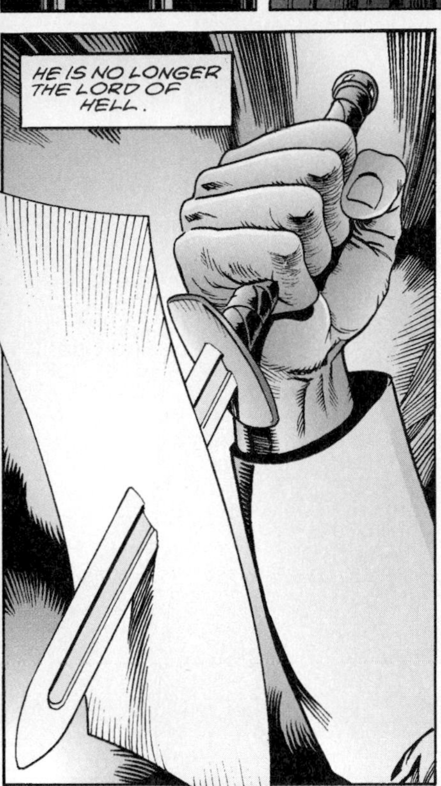
HE IS NO LONGER THE LORD OF HELL.

HE IS NO LONGER THE AGENT OF HEAVEN.

WHAT IS HE NOW? WHAT NAME DENOTES HIS FUNCTION?

YUD. HAY. VAV. HAY.
ONLY ONE OF YOUR NAMES, BUT GOOD ENOUGH. TRY CLOSING IT NOW--
--WITHOUT UNMAKING THE REST OF YOUR CREATION.
HE IS LUCIFER. THE LIGHTBRINGER.
HIS OLDEST NAME. GIVEN BY GOD. BORNE LIKE A BRAND THROUGH THE EONS WHEN HE WALKED IN DARKNESS.
RILL HHHEY COMHHE?
OF COURSE THEY'LL COME. I'M DEPENDING ON IT.
IT WOULD HARDLY BE AN APOCALYPSE WITHOUT ANGELS AND TRUMPETS.

mike carey writer · warren pleece layouts · dean ormston finishes · daniel vozzo colorist & seps · ellie de ville letterer · will dennis assistant editor · shelly roeberg editor

based on the character created by gaiman, kieth & dringenberg

And by this time I REALLY wanted to get it over with.
ELAINE. DON'T TURN ON THE LIGHT. PLEASE.

I LOOK A REAL MESS.

HELLO, MONA. WHAT TOOK YOU SO LONG?
WELL, IT WAS HARD TO THINK, AT FIRST. IT WAS THE NORTH CIRCULAR.
SEVEN OR EIGHT CARS WENT OVER ME BEFORE THEY COULD STOP.

THEN I WENT HOME, BUT NO ONE COULD SEE ME. SO I CAME TO YOU BECAUSE... BECAUSE YOU WERE SORT OF SHINING AND I COULD SEE YOU FROM A LONG WAY AWAY.
I'M SORRY. I'M LEAVING BLOOD ALL ON YOUR BED.

NO YOU'RE NOT. YOU'RE NOT REALLY BLEEDING. AND YOU DON'T HAVE TO LOOK LIKE THAT, EITHER.
I DON'T?

NO, IT'S JUST WHAT YOU...YOU KNOW, WHAT YOU'RE EXPECTING BECAUSE OF HOW YOU DIED. YOU CAN LOOK LIKE BRITTNEY SPEARS IF YOU WANT TO.

WHY'D YOU DO IT, MONA? WHY'D YOU GO AND WALK UNDER A CAR?
THAT'S GREAT! THAT'S REALLY GREAT! I KNEW YOU'D COME ON LIKE MY MUM!
DO YOU THINK I WANTED TO BE DEAD?
WELL DIDN'T YOU? I MEAN, I THOUGHT... YOU KNOW... IT WAS BECAUSE YOUR DAD WAS...

NO I DIDN'T, ELAINE BELLOC!
I WAS BLOODY MURDERED, IF YOU MUST KNOW!

MURDERED?
MONA, DON'T SAY THINGS LIKE THAT!
IT'S TRUE. SOME M...MAN JUST CAME UP BEHIND ME AND THREW ME OFF THE OVERPASS. RIGHT INTO THE TRAFFIC.

OH MY GOD. THEN I... I'VE GOT TO TELL SOMEONE. THIS WAS WHEN YOU WERE COMING OUT OF SCHOOL, RIGHT? DID ANYONE ELSE SEE?
NO. I HAD DETENTION. MR. WADDINGTON GAVE ME A WHOLE HOUR FOR RUNNING IN THE CORRIDORS.
THERE WAS NO ONE AROUND.

I DON'T EVEN KNOW WHY HE DID IT. HE JUST PICKED ME UP AND TH... THREW ME.
OH, I'M SO SCARED, I'M SO SCARED.
PLEASE, ELAINE. PLEASE HELP ME.

And that did it, I guess. At Northcote she was so much TOUGHER than me. She hit Gordon Bosch in the face once because he pushed me.

COME ON, MONA. DON'T... DON'T GET UPSET, OKAY?

She never, NEVER cried.

Then I remembered what Grandma Furness said -- about why some dead people lie DOWN and some don't.

WHAT ARE YOU DOING?

Uhhhhh...
ANYWAY, THEY'RE ON OUR SIDE. IT'S THE GUY WHO KILLED YOU WHO'S GOT TO WORRY.

HELLO, DARLING.
HELLO, LAINIE. WHERE'S THE FIRE?
WHAT ARE YOU GETTING THESE OLD BIDDIES UP SO EARLY FOR?
GRANDMAS, THIS IS MY FRIEND, MONA. SHE... SHE WAS MURDERED.

AND SHE NEEDS A GUIDE TO THE DRY LANDS?
NO. SHE NEEDS REVENGE.

Grandma Furness used to be a WITCH. I knew she'd have some good ideas.
BLACK MAGIC. HEX THE BUGGER TILL 'E BLEEDS OUT OF 'IS EARS.
OH LORD, PEGGY, THAT'S NOT A THING FOR...
YOU CAN DO A SUMMONING. A LESSER DEMON WILL TELL YOU THE KILLER'S NAME.
AND THEN YOU CAN USE THE NAME TO CURSE 'IM.

BUT WE DON'T KNOW HOW TO SUMMON A DEMON, GRANDMA.
NOT EVEN A LESSER ONE.
SPILL BLOOD, MY POPPET, AND THEN DRINK IT. DANCE NAKED. CALL HIS NAME.
IF HE'S MINDED TO COME HE WON'T BE HOLDING OFF FOR SPELLS OR CANDLES.

Great. Where was I going to get fresh BLOOD in Kensal Rise?
I came up with some pretty gross ideas, but in the end I just borrowed some from the kitchen.
Wussy or what?

Then I did a sort of stupid DISCO dance. I kept my underwear on because I didn't want a demon to see me naked.
I shouted three names. Grandma Furness said they were all good.

NOTHING'S HAPPENING, ELAINE.
I DON'T THINK THIS IS GOING TO WORK.

What I did next was pretty stupid. But I felt like such a PRAT standing there in my underwear.
HELLO, SATAN! HELLO, LUCIFER! ARE YOU RECEIVING ME?
ARE YOU MAZED, GIRL? BE SILENT!
IF HE DEIGNED TO ANSWER YOU, HE'D SHRIVEL YOUR SOUL LIKE A SALTED SLUG!
YOU KNOW WE COULD DO NOTHING BUT WATCH!
I'M SORRY.
IT WAS WRONG TO MAKE HER TRY, PEGGY FURNESS.
A CHILD DOING BLACK MAGIC!
AYE, WELL THAT'S THE NUB OF IT, I SUPPOSE.
YOU'RE TOO YOUNG, POPPET.
WHY SHOULD A DEMON HALE HIMSELF FROM THE HOBS OF HELL TO ANSWER A SPOTLESS VIRGIN WHO COULDN'T GIVE HER SOUL AWAY IF SHE TRIED?
THERE'S NO PROFIT IN IT.
That was when Dad called me down for supper.
IT'S OKAY, MONA. THERE'S SOMETHING ELSE WE CAN TRY TOMORROW.
DON'T WORRY. WE'LL GET HIM.
It's a good job I've got the grandmas.
Mum just talks about shares and investments and stuff and Dad's only into his book reviews
They wouldn't know the first THING about finding a murderer.

The next morning we set off for school. When we got to the end of the road I turned LEFT instead of right. To the Roundhey estate. To Mona's school.

But when we got close to the North Circular we could hear the cars. Mona got really scared.
IS THIS WHERE IT HAPPENED?
OVER THERE. BY THE POSTERS.
I'LL STAY HERE, ELAINE. IS IT OKAY IF I STAY HERE?
EELS
KING BALOOKA

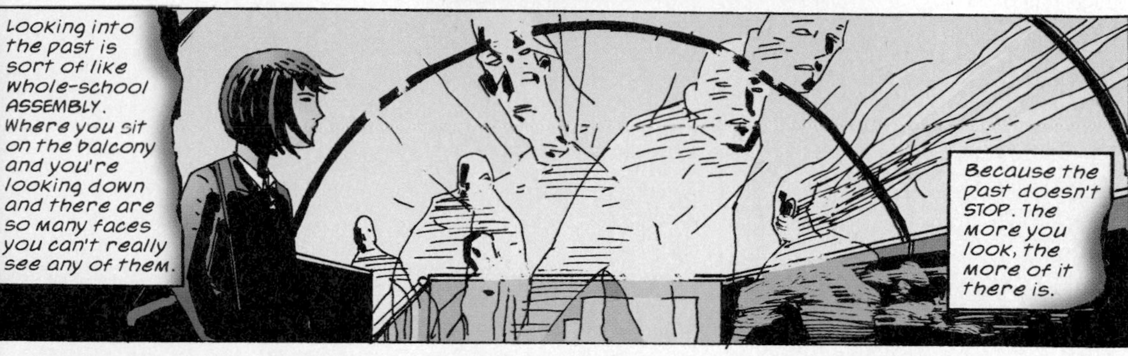
Looking into the past is sort of like whole-school ASSEMBLY. Where you sit on the balcony and you're looking down and there are so many faces you can't really see any of them.
Because the past doesn't STOP. The more you look, the more of it there is.

I thought I could see Mona. And maybe there WAS a man — near her, moving around her, before she fell --
-- But moving too fast, in the dark, and her fear was still fresh, like a big STAIN over everything. I couldn't see his face.

So I kept on looking backwards — further away in time. Keeping my EYES on him as he went back and back, always the same distance behind Mona.
Across the overpass and back down the Sutton Road. To the gates...

He was FOLLOWING her.
ROUNDHEY COMPREHENSIVE
LONDON BOROUGH OF BRENT
All the way from the school.

WHERE DID YOU DO YOUR DETENTION?
B-12. IT'S THAT WAY. ELAINE...
...HOW COME YOU CAN SEE ME WHEN MY MUM AND DAD COULDN'T?

IT'S NOT JUST DEAD PEOPLE. REMEMBER IN YEAR THREE WHEN MRS. SEWELL GOT CANCER?
YOU COULD SEE THAT?
I COULD HEAR IT. B-12, RIGHT?
B12

It was just a ROOM. A school room. Horrible old wood polish smell. Crummy old desks with the chairs fixed in.
At Bishop Laud we have CARPETS. And chairs with legs.
HE WASN'T WITH YOU IN HERE. HE MUST'VE--

EXCUSE ME! YOU, GIRL! WHAT ARE YOU DOING OUT OF CLASS?
OH NO! ELAINE, IT'S MR. WADDINGTON! MY HEADMASTER!

THAT ISN'T A ROUNDHEY UNIFORM. WHO ARE YOU?
I'M SORRY, SIR. I CAME TO... TO TELL MY FRIEND SOMETHING. SHE'S IN...
...IN MONA DOYLE'S CLASS.

IN MONA DOYLE'S CLASS? AND WHO WOULD *THAT* BE?
SAY DIANE HORNBY.
UMM... DIANE HORNBY.

THEN WE'LL JUST GO AND *ASK* DIANE HORNBY IF SHE KNOWS YOU, SHALL WE?
I was in enough trouble already. But I thought, I'll just take ONE look.
See what's on his mind...

COME BACK, GIRL! COME BACK HERE!
ARE YOU *MAD*?

I CAN'T TELL YOU HOW **SORRY** WE ARE. THEY WERE BEST FRIENDS ALL THROUGH PRIMARY SCHOOL...

NO, NO, MR. BELLOC. NO HARM DONE.

IT'S VERY **HARD** FOR CHILDREN TO COPE WITH SUCH A SUDDEN LOSS --HARD FOR ALL OF US.

YOUNG GIRLS GET VERY INVOLVED IN THESE ROMANTIC FRIENDSHIPS. SHARE THEIR... **SECRETS**, AND SO ON.

BUT TIME IS A GREAT HEALER.

I JUST WISH YOU'D **TALKED** TO US, ELAINE.

I'M SORRY, DAD. I WANTED TO SEE... WHERE SHE DIED. **PLEASE** DON'T GET MAD.

I'M NOT MAD. I'M DISAPPOINTED.

I got the Dad treatment, then the Mum treatment, but not the Mona treatment. She didn't come back that night.

She always hated getting into trouble. Maybe she just wanted to forget the whole thing now. Get on with being dead.

But I didn't. Things look DIFFERENT *when you've been inside a murderer.*

And if Mona didn't know how to be an unquiet spirit, I'd just have to do it MYSELF.

I waited until about one -- nothing but snores from Mum and Dad's room. Mr. Waddington lived in Burnt Oak. I fished that out of his SECRETARY'S thoughts.
There was a night bus that would take me to Brent Cross, and then I could walk it.
N3

All the way there I kept seeing that stuff that was in his mind. He was thinking about killing Mona.
But he was thinking about this suitcase, too. In his garage. As though Mona REMINDED him of it.
So I thought, if I get a look inside the case there might be some kind of PROOF that he did it.

Halfway along Burnt Oak Broadway, I felt this kind of prickling. Like someone was BREATHING on my neck.
ELAINE, I'M SORRY I RAN AWAY. I WOULD'VE COME BACK BEFORE, BUT...
...THERE'S THIS GIRL WHO'S FOLLOWING ME AROUND. I'VE BEEN TRYING TO LOSE HER.

BLACK HAIR AND AMAZING EYE SHADOW, RIGHT? YOU CAN'T LOSE HER, MONA.
BUT YOU'RE OKAY IF WE STICK TOGETHER. ANYONE WHO'S WITH ME, SHE SORT OF IGNORES.

YOU SAY "TILL DEATH US DO PART" -- YOU KNOW, LIKE IN A WEDDING. IT MEANS YOU'LL KEEP THE SECRET FOR-EVER.
TILL DEATH US DO PART.

It felt GOOD having Mona there. It made me think about when I was nine and we used to do everything together.
About dancing to THE SPICE GIRLS singing that friendship never ends.
Like THEY know.

Dad used to work for the RAC, and he had a set of keys that he used to open cars when people locked themselves out.
Some of the keys were called SKELETONS, and he told me once they worked on any lock.
CLICK

It didn't take long at all.

MONA?
ARE THESE WHAT I THINK THEY ARE?

WELL, IT DOESN'T MATTER ANYWAY. I'M TAKING SOME OF EVERYTHING.

WE CAN SEND THIS STUFF TO THE POLICE.

I BET HE'LL LOSE HIS JOB, AT LEA...

LOSE MY JOB? LOSE MY JOB?

THAT'S NOTHING COMPARED TO WHAT YOU'RE GOING TO LOSE, GIRL!

It was feeling so scared that woke me up. I was choking on it. I couldn't even THINK except to think afraid, afraid, afraid.
I wanted to run...

And I couldn't move.

I CARE ABOUT MY WORK, YOU KNOW?
I'VE MADE SOME BAD DECISIONS, BUT I REALLY DO CARE. ABOUT THE SCHOOL-- THE KIDS.

IF YOU WEIGH UP THE GOOD AND THE HARM I'VE DONE, ANYONE WOULD SAY I'M A DECENT MAN.
SO... WHO ELSE KNOWS?

I tried to figure that out but I couldn't make my mind work. I was going to scream any second.
But part of me was standing off to one side, LOOKING at the fear...
And then the penny dropped. Most of it wasn't MINE. It was his.

So I took the thing that he was most afraid of right out of his mind, and I threw it back to him.
SHE KEPT A DIARY.

SHIT! I KNEW IT! WHERE DID YOU FIND IT? WHERE IS IT NOW?
AT...AT THE SCHOOL. ROOM B-12.
IT'S BEHIND THE RADIATOR.

WE'LL TAKE UP THIS CONVERSATION WHEN I GET BACK. IF YOU'RE LYING YOU'LL HAVE THE OCCASION TO BE VERY SORRY.
BUT YOU'RE... YOU'RE GOING TO KILL ME ANY-WAY.
TRUE. BUT I'VE GOT A GREAT DEAL OF DISCRETION ABOUT HOW LONG IT TAKES.

I heard the door slam and the car start. Then every-thing went QUIET again.
The school was only about three miles away. I didn't have long.
MONA?

HE'S GOING TO KILL YOU TOO! CALL YOUR GRANDMAS, ELAINE. THEY CAN DO MAGIC ON HIM!
NO THEY CAN'T. THEY'RE JUST GHOSTS.
THEY CAN'T DO ANYTHING ANY-MORE EXCEPT TALK.

SO LET'S TALK, MONA. THE WAY WE USED TO. LET'S SHARE SECRETS.
TELL ME ABOUT YOUR DAD.

IT WASN'T THERE.

S...SOMEONE MUST'VE MOVED IT. THAT'S WHERE IT WAS. REALLY.
PERHAPS. OR PERHAPS YOU INVENTED THE DIARY SO I'D LET YOU LIVE A LITTLE LONGER.
IN WHICH CASE I HOPE YOU GOT THE MOST YOU COULD OUT OF THE LAST TWENTY MINUTES.

I DID.

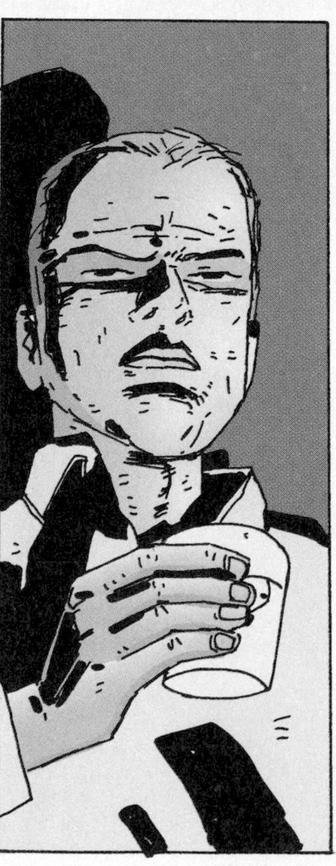

He ran out into the hall. But Mona said, with a ketamine overdose there's not much POINT calling a doctor.

You've got to make yourself throw up really quick before your LUNGS stop working.

He was trying to dial. He was saying "Ambulance! Ambulance!" over and over again.

But everything was looking really strange now-- like looking through a MARBLE. It felt like there was this big chunk of ice inside my chest.

And I thought, this isn't fair. It's HIS death, not mine.

But I must've swallowed too much of the stuff myself.
A little bit for each sachet I chewed open.
I got sucked in. I got sucked into his DEATH.
But there was someone ELSE there too.
Waiting for me.
NORMALLY WHEN PEOPLE LEARN TO JUGGLE THEY DON'T START WITH CHAIN-SAWS.
J...JUGGLE?
IT WAS BY WAY OF BEING A METAPHOR. NEVER MIND.

WHERE ARE WE?
HMM?
OH, YOU'RE INSIDE HIS MIND. THE TEACHER'S. THE MAN YOU'RE IN THE PROCESS OF MURDERING.
OXYGEN STARVATION SQUEEZES THE DRUG HIGH INTO SYNAESTHETIC SCREAMS. IT FEELS EVEN WORSE THAN IT LOOKS.
It just sort of came to me then. Even though he didn't have any HORNS or anything.
YOU'RE... YOU'RE HIM. THE DEVIL.
I SUMMONED THE DEVIL.
DON'T FLATTER YOURSELF, CHILD. I'M NOT HERE BECAUSE YOU CALLED ME.
BUT I DID HEAR YOUR VOICE, AND I WANTED TO SEE FOR MYSELF.
SOMEONE HAS BEEN WORKING FOR A VERY LONG TIME. CHANCE ALONE COULDN'T ACCOUNT FOR YOU.
WILL HE DIE SOON? MR. WADDINGTON, I MEAN?
HE SHOULD BE DEAD NOW. I'M THE ONE WHO'S HOLDING HIM BACK FROM THAT MERCIFUL RELEASE.
YOU? BUT WHY?
BECAUSE AS THINGS STAND, HE'LL TAKE YOU WITH HIM. A DECK OF CARDS I MET RECENTLY SUGGESTED THAT I SHOULD KEEP YOU ALIVE.
NOW TAKE WHAT YOU WANT AND BE QUICK ABOUT IT. I HAVE OTHER ENGAGE-MENTS.

I guess I knew what he meant. So I found it, Mona, and I took it. The TRUTH. About why Mr. Waddington KILLED you.
And even though the devil was in a hurry, I took a LONG time doing it. As long as I could.
That was our REVENGE, you see. That was how we got our own back on him.
It was stupid, really. HE was the one who was selling the drugs to your Dad.
Even went round to your flat a few years back.
MORE
He noticed you because you were reading MORE and Roundhey had just banned it.
When you started in year seven he RECOGNIZED you-- and he thought you recognized him, too. THAT'S why he killed you. To stop you from telling anyone.
And the crazy thing is, you DIDN'T remember him at all. He had nothing to be afraid of.
Until he met ME.
SATISFIED?
NO.
PITY. IT MAKES NO DIFFERENCE TO THE PRICE.
WH... WHERE ARE WE GOING?
WE? I AM GOING ON INTO THE REALMS OF PAIN.
YOU TO YOUR MORTAL BODY. BUT DON'T WORRY. I ALWAYS CALL IN WHAT'S OWED TO ME.

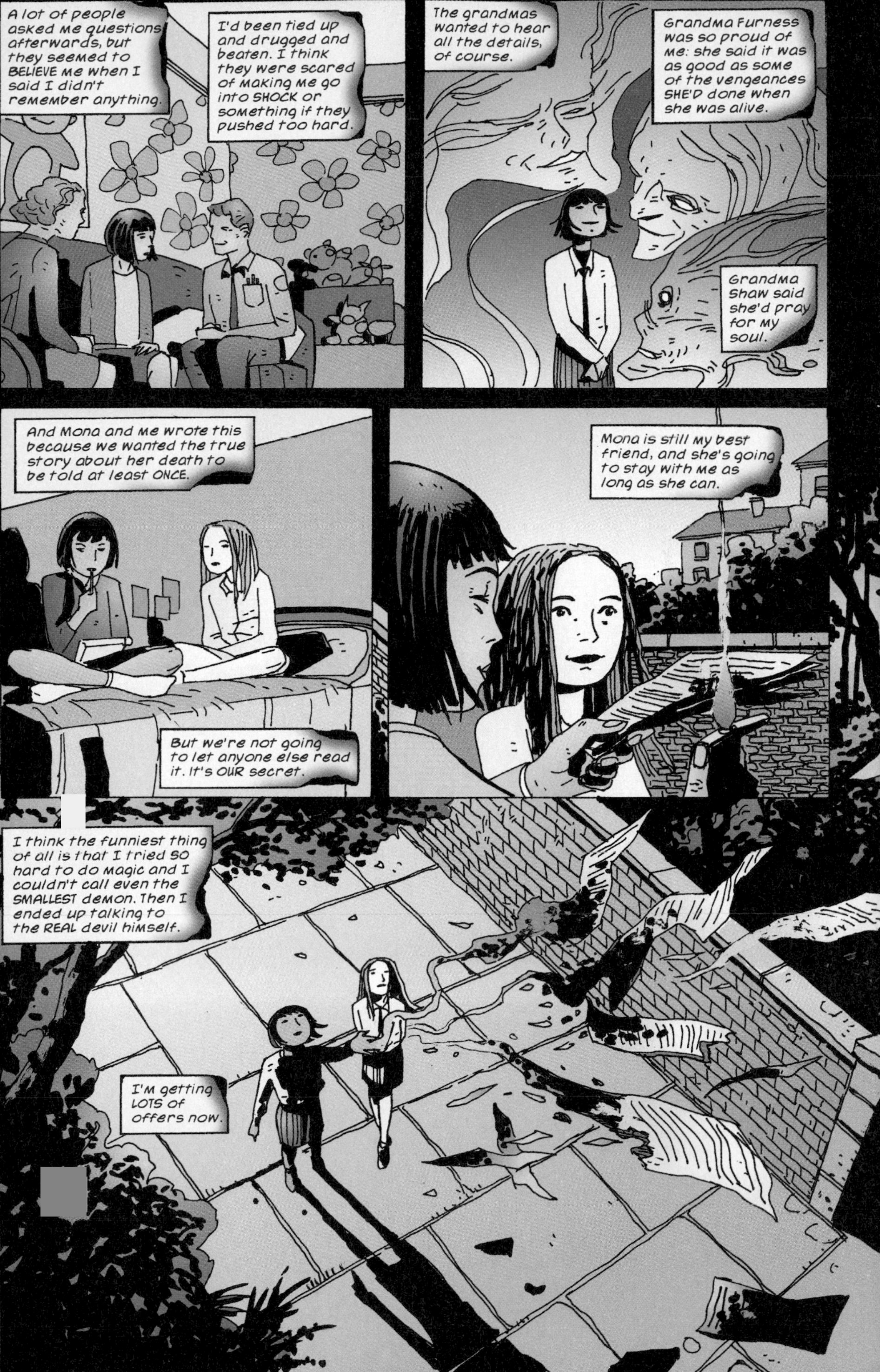
A lot of people asked me questions afterwards, but they seemed to BELIEVE me when I said I didn't remember anything.
I'd been tied up and drugged and beaten. I think they were scared of making me go into SHOCK or something if they pushed too hard.
The grandmas wanted to hear all the details, of course.
Grandma Furness was so proud of me: she said it was as good as some of the vengeances SHE'D done when she was alive.
Grandma Shaw said she'd pray for my soul.
And Mona and me wrote this because we wanted the true story about her death to be told at least ONCE.
But we're not going to let anyone else read it. It's OUR secret.
Mona is still my best friend, and she's going to stay with me as long as she can.
I think the funniest thing of all is that I tried SO hard to do magic and I couldn't call even the SMALLEST demon. Then I ended up talking to the REAL devil himself.
I'm getting LOTS of offers now.

FEGREDO

BONES.
FIVE.
HAH! I WIN. WHEN YOU HAVE NO BONES LEFT AT ALL, KIJO, I WILL DEVOUR YOU.
EYES.
THREE. IT IS YOUR CAST, RITSIME.
LOOK. OVER THERE. WHAT IS THAT THING THAT WALKS UPRIGHT, LIKE A MAN?
IT IS A MAN. OR SOMETHING LIKE. HOW PRESUMPTUOUS OF IT.
YOU COULD GO AND FETCH IT, RITSIME. IT HAS EYES AND TEETH AND BONES ENOUGH TO KEEP YOU IN THE GAME AWHILE.
I WILL DO SO. WAIT FOR ME.
IT WAS NOT A MAN, THEN.
EVIDENTLY NOT. BONES.
SEVEN.
BAH!

YOU COULD BE FORGIVEN FOR THINKING THAT THIS IS A DESERT. IT'S NOT.
BUT IT IS DRY ENOUGH, AND HOT ENOUGH. IT WILL SERVE.
HE HAS TO WALK BECAUSE IF HE STOPS THE GROUND WILL EAT HIM.
HE HAS TO BE NAKED BECAUSE NO CLOTH OR STONE OR METAL FROM THE REALMS OF LIGHT CAN EXIST HERE.
THESE ARE THE RULES. THEY ARE NOT HIS RULES.
THE BLOOD THAT HAS DRIED AND CRUSTED ON HIS SKIN IS THE BLOOD OF DEMONS. IT HAS ITS USES. THE FOUL SMELL OF IT DETERS OTHER PREDATORS.
HE IS LOOKING FOR THE HOUSE.
THE HOUSE OF IZANAMI, MISTRESS OF THE AFTERWORLD, WHERE THE IGNOBLE DEAD ARE PENNED FOR ALL ETERNITY BETWEEN EYELESS WALLS.
THE HOUSE THAT MAY NOT REST UPON THE EARTH.

LIGHT SPILLS FROM THE GROUND LIKE SWEAT, DISSIPATING AS IT RISES. A HEAT-HAZE OF DESPAIR SHIMMERS BETWEEN NOT-EARTH AND NOT-SKY.
LUCIFER HAS BEEN WALKING FOR NINE DAYS.
HE IS GOING TO HAVE SUPPER THERE.
The HOUSE of WINDOWLESS ROOMS Part One
Written by MIKE CAREY
Illustrated by PETER GROSS
Special Thanks to RYAN KELLY
Lettered by COMICRAFT
Colors & Separations DANIEL VOZZO
Assistant Edits WILL DENNIS
Edits SHELLY ROEBERG
Based on characters created by GAIMAN, KIETH and DRINGENBERG

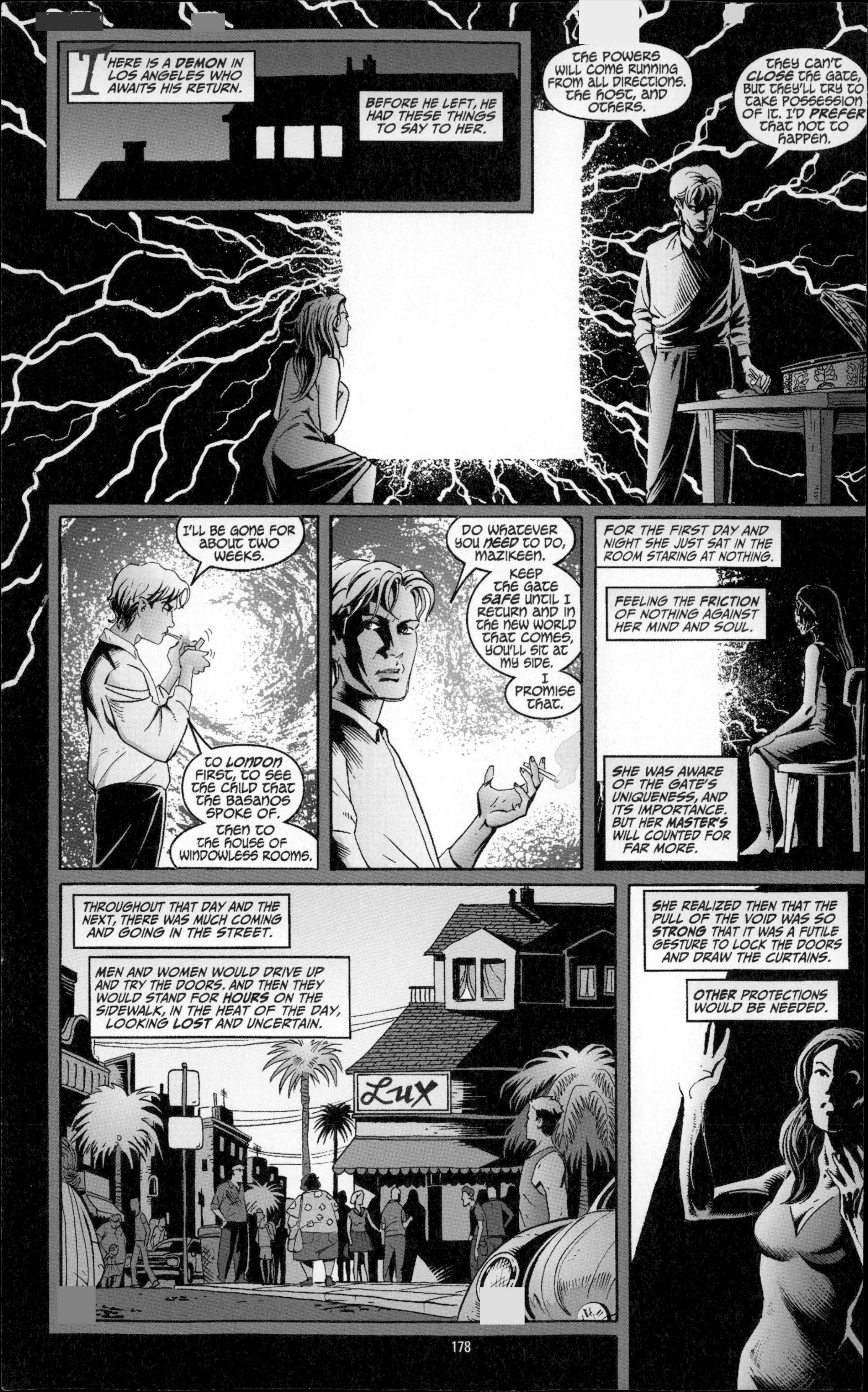

There is a demon in Los Angeles who awaits his return.

Before he left, he had these things to say to her.

The powers will come running from all directions. The host, and others.

They can't close the gate, but they'll try to take possession of it. I'd prefer that not to happen.

I'll be gone for about two weeks.

To London first, to see the child that the Basanos spoke of.

Then to the house of windowless rooms.

Do whatever you need to do, Mazikeen.

Keep the gate safe until I return and in the new world that comes, you'll sit at my side.

I promise that.

For the first day and night she just sat in the room staring at nothing.

Feeling the friction of nothing against her mind and soul.

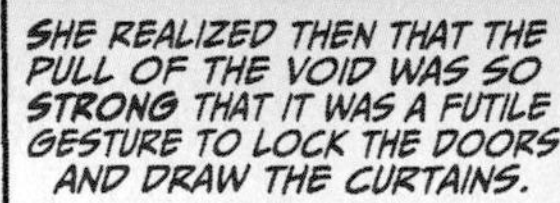

SHE WAS OF THE LILIM, SO THE MAGIC SHE KNEW WAS BLOOD-MAGIC: SIMPLE AND POWERFUL.
BUT THERE WERE NO BIRDS OR ANIMALS TO BE HAD.
HOWEVER THERE WERE ROACHES IN THE CELLAR.
SHE MADE A SOUL-WEAVING. A SLENDER MESH OUT OF ALL THOSE TINY SPIRITS.
SHE SUMMONED CHORONZON INTO THE MESH, AND ASKED WHAT THE PRICE WOULD BE FOR HIS HELP.
IF LUCIFER DIDN'T WANT FLIES AROUND, DEAREST, HE SHOULDN'T HAVE OPENED THE HONEYPOT.
ANYWAY, I'VE SWORN FEALTY TO REMIEL AND DUMA. I'M A GOOD BOY NOW.
I MIGHT FUCK YOU, FOR OLD TIMES' SAKE, IF YOU LET ME OUT OF THIS CAGE. BUT THAT'S AS FAR AS I'D GO.
SHE COULD NOT HIDE. SHE COULD NOT STAND ALONE.
THE SHATTERED CARAPACES OF COCKROACHES WERE A MANY-VOICED MEMENTO MORI BENEATH HER BARE FEET.
TO USE THE TELEPHONE DID NOT COME EASY TO HER.
BUT SHE MADE IT WORK AT LAST, AND SHE ISSUED HER SUMMONS, AND IN THE EVENING...
IN THE EVENING SHE OPENED FOR BUSINESS.

ELSEWHERE IN THE CITY, THE POWERS GATHERED.
SOME HAD COME FURTHER THAN OTHERS.
EXCUSE ME, SIR. WOULD YOU MIND PULLING YOUR FEET IN JUST FOR A MOMENT?
WHAT?
GATE 1
GATE 2

I WAS THINKING AND YOU DISTURBED MY TRAIN OF THOUGHT.
I'M SORRY, SIR. I JUST NEED TO...
AH, WELL. SORRY IS EASILY SAID.

THE RASH ON YOUR FACE MAKES YOU UNSERVICEABLE AS FOOD OR RAIMENT, SO I WILL GIVE YOU THIS GOLD COIN.
IT BEARS THE SIGIL CALX -- THE CLAW.
JEEZ! TH... THANK YOU, BUT I CAN'T...
OH.

YOU'LL LOOK AT IT FOR A LITTLE LONGER EACH DAY. THE PAIN AND THE PLEASURE WILL BECOME A LITTLE MORE INTENSE EACH TIME.
OH GOD!
JUDGING FROM YOUR BUILD, I'D GIVE YOU SIX MONTHS. A YEAR, PERHAPS. ENJOY.

THANK YOU, SIR. COME BACK SOON.
WELL, THAT'S A KIND OFFER, UNWISELY BUT IRREVOCABLY SPOKEN.
I'LL TAKE YOU UP ON IT BEFORE I MOVE ON.

BUT ON THE WHOLE I PREFER UNDOCUMENTED TRANSIENTS.
I LIKE TO KEEP MY RELATIONSHIPS SIMPLE.

GREETINGS, TRAVELER.
IF YOU WISH TO PASS THROUGH THIS GATEWAY, YOU MUST STOP AND PLAY A GAME WITH ME FIRST.
I'M REALLY NOT IN THE MOOD TO PLAY.
IT IS MY MISTRESS'S WILL. IT PAINS ME TO GIVE OFFENSE BUT SHE HAS DECREED IT, AND SO IT MUST BE.
SEE, HERE IS A CAULDRON OF MOLTEN LEAD. AT THE BOTTOM LIE THREE STONES OF DIFFERENT COLORS.
OH, IT IS A FINE GAME.

PUT IN YOUR HAND AND TAKE A STONE. I WILL REWARD YOU ACCORDING TO YOUR CHOICE.
RED WILL GAIN YOU ENTRY TO THIS PALACE. GREY WILL BRING MADNESS, AND WHITE INSTANT DEATH.
I'VE BEEN ON THE ROAD A LONG TIME. I WAS HOPING FOR A SHOWER BEFORE I ATE.
COULD WE WAIVE THE FORMALITIES?
YOU MUST CHOOSE AND I MUST ENACT YOUR FATE.
FATE'S A SLIPPERY SORT OF CONCEPT, THOUGH, ISN'T IT.
I MEAN, MOST OF THE TIME IT'S JUST AN EXCUSE FOR DOING WHAT YOU WANT TO DO ANYWAY.

NUUUH! IT BURNS! IT BURNS!
WELL THAT'S WHAT HAPPENS IF YOU PLAY WITH FIRE. HERE WE ARE.
THE RED STONE, I THINK YOU SAID.
AND THIS IS HOW HE COMES. UNANNOUNCED. WITH NO CEREMONIES OR TRUMPETS.
THE MORNINGSTAR, TO THE REALM THAT KNOWS NO MORNING.
THE APOSTATE PRINCE OF HELL, TO THE HELL WHICH HE HAS NEVER RULED.
KNK KNK
THE BLISTERS ON HIS PALMS BREAK AND WEEP.

YOU, TOO? WHAT ARE THE ODDS AGAINST THAT? THAT'S GOT TO BE AN AMAZING COINCIDENCE, HASN'T IT?
OH, WELL. NOT REALLY. I MEAN THIS IS LOS ANGELES.

PEOPLE COME HERE ALL THE TIME, DON'T THEY?

SURE THEY DO. TO DO THE HOLLYWOOD THING, OR WHATEVER. BUT THAT'S NOT WHY YOU CAME.
NO. I JUST FELT I HAD TO BE HERE. LIKE SOMETHING WAS CALLING TO ME.
IT WAS SO WEIRD.

AND I FELT IT TOO, LIKE THIS VOICE SINGING IN THE NEXT ROOM, OR SOMETHING.
ONLY IT'S NOT HERE, EXACTLY: IT'S JUST CLOSE.
LISTEN, DO YOU HAVE A PLACE TO STAY?

THIS ISN'T A COME-ON, I SWEAR. A FRIEND OF MINE HAS AN APARTMENT ON FIGUEROA. I'VE BEEN SACKING OUT DOWN THERE.
THERE'S ROOM FOR ONE MORE.
AND I PROMISE I WON'T TRY TO PUT ANY MOVES ON YOU.

WELL... MAYBE JUST FOR TONIGHT. THANKS.
NO PROBLEM.
PEOPLE ON THE ROAD HAVE TO WATCH OUT FOR EACH OTHER.
OTHERWISE THEY CAN GET INTO ALL KINDS OF DEEP SHIT.

DIVINE IZANAMI, QUEEN OF DEATH AND WHAT COMES AFTER DEATH, MISTRESS OF THE WINDOWLESS ROOMS...
I PRESENT MY COMPLIMENTS TO YOU WITH ALL DUE HUMILITY.
YOU ARE MOST WELCOME HERE, LUCIFER MORNINGSTAR. ALAS, MY MOTHER CANNOT GREET YOU HERSELF.
SHE SELDOM SPEAKS THESE DAYS, EVEN TO US.
THANK YOU, SUSANO-O-NO-MIKOTO. THAT'S UNFORTUNATE. THERE'S A LOT I NEED TO DISCUSS WITH HER.
AH. MOST REGRETTABLE.
BUT I THINK SHE SAYS WITHOUT WORDS HOW PROFOUND A PLEASURE SHE TAKES IN YOUR ARRIVAL.

I BEG YOUR LEAVE TO PRESENT MY BROTHERS, KAGUTSUCHI AND TSUKI-YOMI. AND OUR COUSIN, YAMA-NO-KAMI, THE GODDESS OF THE HUNT.
DELIGHTED.
PERHAPS WE MIGHT HUNT WHILE YOU ARE HERE, MY LORD.
IN THE MEANTIME YOU MUST REST FROM YOUR JOURNEY -- BATHE AND ROBE YOURSELF. I WILL ORDER SOME FOOD PREPARED.
TSUKI-YOMI, PLEASE ESCORT MY LORD LUCIFER TO A SUITE OF ROOMS CLOSE TO MY OWN.
YES, BROTHER.
IF TIME ALLOWS, CERTAINLY. BUT THERE'S SOME BUSINESS I'D LIKE TO ATTEND TO FIRST.
BUSINESS? PARDON ME, I DID NOT THINK THAT...
MY WINGS. I'VE COME TO COLLECT THEM.
YOUR... WINGS? BUT YOU LEFT THEM IN YOUR OWN REALM, DID YOU NOT?
YES, I DID. BUT THAT WAS A WHILE AGO.
THE ORACLE OF THE BASANOS TOLD ME THAT YOUR MOTHER HAS THEM NOW.
AAH. INDEED, IT MAY BE SO. I WILL ENDEAVOR TO ASK HER, BUT IT WILL INVOLVE COMPLEX AND PROTRACTED RITUALS.

THIS IS INCONVENIENT, IS IT NOT?
IT IS *INSUPPORTABLE.* WE MUST DEAL WITH IT.
MOTHER, IN YOUR REALM HE HAS NO POWER. HE IS *MORTAL.*
I WILL CHALLENGE HIM AND *KILL* HIM, IN YOUR NAME.
SHE DOES NOT WISH IT.
THE GESTURE IS AMBIGUOUS. IT *MIGHT* MEAN ONLY THAT HER NAME IS NOT TO BE ASSOCIATED WITH...
MORTAL OR NOT, HE IS *LUCIFER.*
IT IS FOLLY TO UNDERESTIMATE HIM.
YOU MAY *CHALLENGE* HIM, CERTAINLY, IF HE GIVES YOU CAUSE.
BUT HE KNOWS THIS AS WELL AS YOU DO.
AND IF YOU STRIKE HIM *OTHERWISE,* YOU ARE SHAMED.
ENOUGH! I CONCEDE IT. WHAT THEN?

I WILL SUMMON A DEMON OF THE *SHIKO-ME.* ONE OF THOSE YOU *BOUND* TO OUR SERVICE.
MUSUBI, I THINK.
A DEMON IS A DEMON, AFTER ALL. THEIR *VAGARIES* ARE WIDELY KNOWN.
AND OUR MOTHER'S HOSPITALITY IS NOT *TARNISHED* BY THEM.

MAYBE I'D BETTER GO IN AHEAD. PERSUADE THE BIGGER ROACHES TO *HIDE*, AND STUFF.
IT'S OKAY. I'VE SEEN ROACHES BEFORE.

WELL, HERE IT IS. NOT *MUCH*, BUT IT'S HOME.
IT'S FINE. REALLY.

YOU'RE WAITING FOR ME TO TURN MY *BACK*, AREN'T YOU?
TO TURN YOUR...? NO, NO. I WAS JUST LOOKING AT YOUR *EYES*. THEY'RE VERY...
YOU THINK I'M *HUMAN*.

WHAT? WHAT DO YOU MEAN?
WELL, HOW CAN I *BREAK* THIS TO YOU? YOU'RE NOT LOOKING AT *ME*.
YOU'RE LOOKING AT THE LAST THING I *ATE*.

YOU'VE LOST YOUR *EDGE*, SAUL. YOU WERE TRYING TO PREY ON YOUR OWN KIND.
I DON'T THINK I WOULD HAVE *AGREED* WITH YOU.

THE DARK PLACE SUCK YOUR EYES OUT! WHICH ONE ARE YOU? BERIM? CESTIS?
DOES IT MATTER?
YES. IT DOES. YOU'VE TRESPASSED ON MY TERRITORY. YOU'VE BROKEN THE PACT.
DON'T BE A FOOL. THERE IS A GATEWAY -- A DOOR INTO THE VOID.
THE PACT IS MEANINGLESS NOW.
I KNOW ABOUT THAT. I INTEND TO OWN IT SOON.
YOU CAN'T DO IT ALONE.
I CAN DO WHATEVER I LIKE. I'VE HUNTED AND KILLED UNDER THE MORNINGSTAR'S VERY EYES.
HE'S NEVER DARED TO CHALLENGE ME.

HE'S NEVER NEEDED TO. ANYWAY, IT'S NOT JUST LUCIFER. IT'S THE HOST.
DO YOU THINK YOU CAN TOPPLE HEAVEN ALL BY YOURSELF?
HEAVEN? WE WERE OLD BEFORE HEAVEN WAS BUILT!
DON'T LET'S FIGHT, SAUL. YOU'LL ONLY LOSE.
THIS IS A GREAT MOMENT. OUR FIRST BIG BREAK IN FIVE BILLION YEARS.
ZIP
BUT YOU'LL ONLY RUIN IT IF YOU TRY TO GO OUT ON YOUR OWN.

LOOK.
I BROUGHT YOUR SUMMER WARDROBE.

IS IT TRUE, LORD LUCIFER, THAT THE GOD OF THE COVENANT GAVE YOU A LETTER OF PASSAGE?
I THINK THE APPROPRIATE VERB IS "PAID." BUT THE LETTER EXISTS, YES.
IT HAS PUZZLED AND INTERESTED ME, HOW YOUR CREATOR CONTINUES TO EMPLOY YOU DESPITE THE FACT THAT YOU BETRAYED HIM.
IT IS A TESTAMENT TO YOUR SKILL AND YOUR INTELLECT.
AH, THIS IS A GREAT MARVEL. I CHOSE A PATH THAT WOULD TAKE US BY THE SEVEN-THROATED CHAMBER. HAVE YOU SEEN IT BEFORE?
I THINK NOT.
PLEASE, LET ME SHOW IT TO YOU.

I KNOW HOW YOUR MOTHER DISPOSES OF THE SOULS OF THE DEAD. SO THESE MUST BE --
THE SOULS OF THE LIVING. INDEED. YOU CANNOT GUESS, LUCIFER MORNINGSTAR, THE WONDERS THAT MY MOTHER HAS ACCOMPLISHED.
OR HOW CLEVERLY SHE PUTS THESE INNUMERABLE SPIRITS TO WORK.
SOMEDAY I SHOULD LIKE TO TRAVEL IN THE WORLD OF MEN, AND IN THE FURTHER REALMS. BUT I DOUBT THAT I SHALL EVER SEE A PLACE TO SURPASS MY MOTHER'S HOUSE.
SOMEDAY? IS THERE A PROBLEM?
I KILLED A WOMAN, A LONG TIME AGO. IT WAS PRACTICALLY AN ACCIDENT, BUT SHE WAS A GODDESS AND MY MOTHER AND SISTER WERE ANGRY.
I... SPEND MOST OF MY TIME HERE IN THE PALACE NOW.
BUT SEE, HERE ARE YOUR ROOMS. I LOOK FORWARD TO CONTINUING OUR CONVERSATION OVER SUPPER.
UNTIL THEN, TSUKI-YOMI. YOU HAVE BEEN A GRACIOUS GUIDE.
I LIVE IN YOUR PRAISE, LUCIFER MORNINGSTAR.
GREETINGS, MY LORD. I HAVE BROUGHT YOU HOT WATER AND SCENTED TOWELS.
I WILL WASH YOU, IF YOU WISH IT.
EVERYONE ELSE WILL CERTAINLY WISH IT.
THANK YOU.
THANKS ARE NOT NECESSARY. I HAVE BEEN SENT TO SERVE YOU.
I AM MUSUBI.

PLEASE. I NEED TO SPEAK WITH MR. LUX. IMMEDIATELY.
LUX
I'M SORRY, SIR. HE'S OUT OF TOWN RIGHT NOW.
BUT I HAVE MUCH EXPERIENCE OF THINGS THAT HAVE NO END. I AM BY MARRIAGE INTO THE RHODOCANAKIS FAMILY. YOU TELL HIM THIS.
YEAH, WELL I'D BE HAPPY TO TELL HIM, ONLY I'D HAVE TO SHOUT REAL LOUD.

PRISON HAS A WAY OF THROWING A MAN BACK ON HIS INNER RESOURCES.
YEAH. WELL. WHAT CAN I SAY?
IF I HADN'T BEEN SO BLEEDIN' SLOPPY I WOULDN'T HAVE BEEN THERE IN THE FIRST PLACE.

YOU WISH TO STAKE A CLAIM IN THIS GATEWAY, CONSTANTINE? THE LIGHTBRINGER IS NOT EASY TO DEAL WITH.
NAH, NO WAY. TOO MUCH BLOOD UNDER THE BRIDGE, MATE. I JUST FANCIED A QUICK LOOK AT THE FIELD.
WHAT ABOUT YOURSELF?

I HAVE INFORMATION TO TRADE. I HAD HOPED TO PUT A PROPOSITION TO LUCIFER.
SINCE THAT IS NOT POSSIBLE, I'LL BID YOU GOODNIGHT.
YEAH DON'T TAKE ANY WOODEN AES.

I TELL YOU HE WAS LOOKING AT US.
LET IT GO, SAUL. WE'RE HERE TO RECONNOITER, NOT TO PICK A FIGHT.

RECONNOITER! WE COULD TAKE THE GATE NOW! NOBODY HERE COULD STOP US.
WE'LL TAKE IT IN OUR OWN TIME. FOR NOW WE'LL SIT BACK AND SEE WHO ELSE IS INTERESTED.

DON'T GET ME WRONG, MAZIKEEN. I'M HAPPY TO BE WORKING AGAIN, WHAT WITH THE DIVORCE AND ALL.
BUT YOU'VE GOT TO ADMIT THEY'RE A FREAKY CROWD, EVEN FOR THIS PLACE.
HHHOW?

WELL, THERE'S TWO KINDS OF PEOPLE OUT THERE.
THE FIRST KIND ARE SORT OF DAZED -- LIKE THEY WALKED HERE IN THEIR SLEEP.
AND THE SECOND KIND ARE MAJOR LEAGUE CREEPS.
OH YEAH. AND THAT GUY IS BACK.

WHHO ISZ VHACK?
YOU KNOW. THE ASS-HOLE WHO SETS FIRE TO TABLES.

GOOD EVENING, MAZIKEEN OF THE LILIM. I'M HERE TO ACCEPT YOUR ATONEMENT.
AND YOUR SURRENDER.

THIS IS DEMON BLOOD, MY LORD. YOU MUST BE A MIGHTY WARRIOR.
MUST I? I COULD HAVE KILLED THEM IN THEIR SLEEP.
I DO NOT THINK SO. I THINK THAT MY LORD IS A GOD OF VENGEANCE.
A SCOURGE OF DEMON-KIND, LIKE KAGUTSUCHI OF THE THREE-NAMED SWORD.
AND TSUKI-YOMI? IS HE A MIGHTY WARRIOR TOO?
DOING HIS BIT TO MEET THE DEMON-SCOURGING QUOTA?
NO, MY LORD. TSUKI-YOMI IS A POET, AND A DREAMER, AND A LOVER OF WOMEN.
HE DOES NOT FIGHT.
WHAT ABOUT HIS COUSIN? THE HUNTRESS?
YAMA-NO-KAMI. AH, SHE IS FIERCE INDEED, MY LORD. SHE LIVES FOR THE HUNT, AND NO PREY HAS EVER ESCAPED HER.
WHAT'S HER FAVORED WEAPON?
SPEAR AND BOW ARE ALIKE TO HER, MY LORD. SHE IS MISTRESS OF ALL WEAPONS.
BUT SHE LIKES TO FINISH WITH A SHORT KNIFE, THEY SAY.

WILL YOU WEAR A SWORD, MY LORD? THERE ARE SEVERAL HERE, OF EXQUISITE WORKMANSHIP.
NO. NO SWORD.
THERE IS YET AN HOUR BEFORE DINNER.
IF MY LORD WISHES IT, I CAN MASSAGE HIS SHOULDERS AND BACK. MY TOUCH HAS BEEN PRAISED BY MANY.
A MASSAGE. WELL, WHY NOT? SINCE WE HAVE AN HOUR TO KILL.
AND SINCE SUSANO HAS SEEN FIT TO SEND ME A MAID WITH SUCH AN EXQUISITE TOUCH.
I'M ALL YOURS, MUSUBI. SHOW ME WHAT YOU CAN DO.
VERY WELL, MY LORD. SHALL I SING TO YOU WHILE I WORK?
NO. I DON'T THINK THAT WILL BE NECESSARY.

LET'S JUST CUT TO THE CHASE.

FEGREDO

MY POINT IS SIMPLE. A LETTER OF PASSAGE IN LUCIFER'S HANDS WAS TO A MARGINAL DEGREE ACCEPTABLE.
AN OPEN GATE IS NOT.
LUX
AMENADIEL OF THE THRONES.
APPEARANCES NOTWITHSTANDING, AN ANGEL.
THERE ARE TWO OF THE JIN EN MOK OUT THERE. CAN YOU IMAGINE WHAT THEY'D DO WITH A DOORWAY ONTO THE VOID?
AS LONG AS IT EXISTS, THERE'S A LOADED GUN POINTED AT ETERNITY.
DO YOU HEAR ME, CREATURE?
I COULD ASSEMBLE A HOST OF HEAVEN AND BURN THIS PLACE TO FINE ASH.
IS THAT WHAT YOU DESIRE?
VERY WELL, PIT-SPAWN. THIS IS THE ONLY DECLARATION OF WAR YOU'RE GOING TO GET.

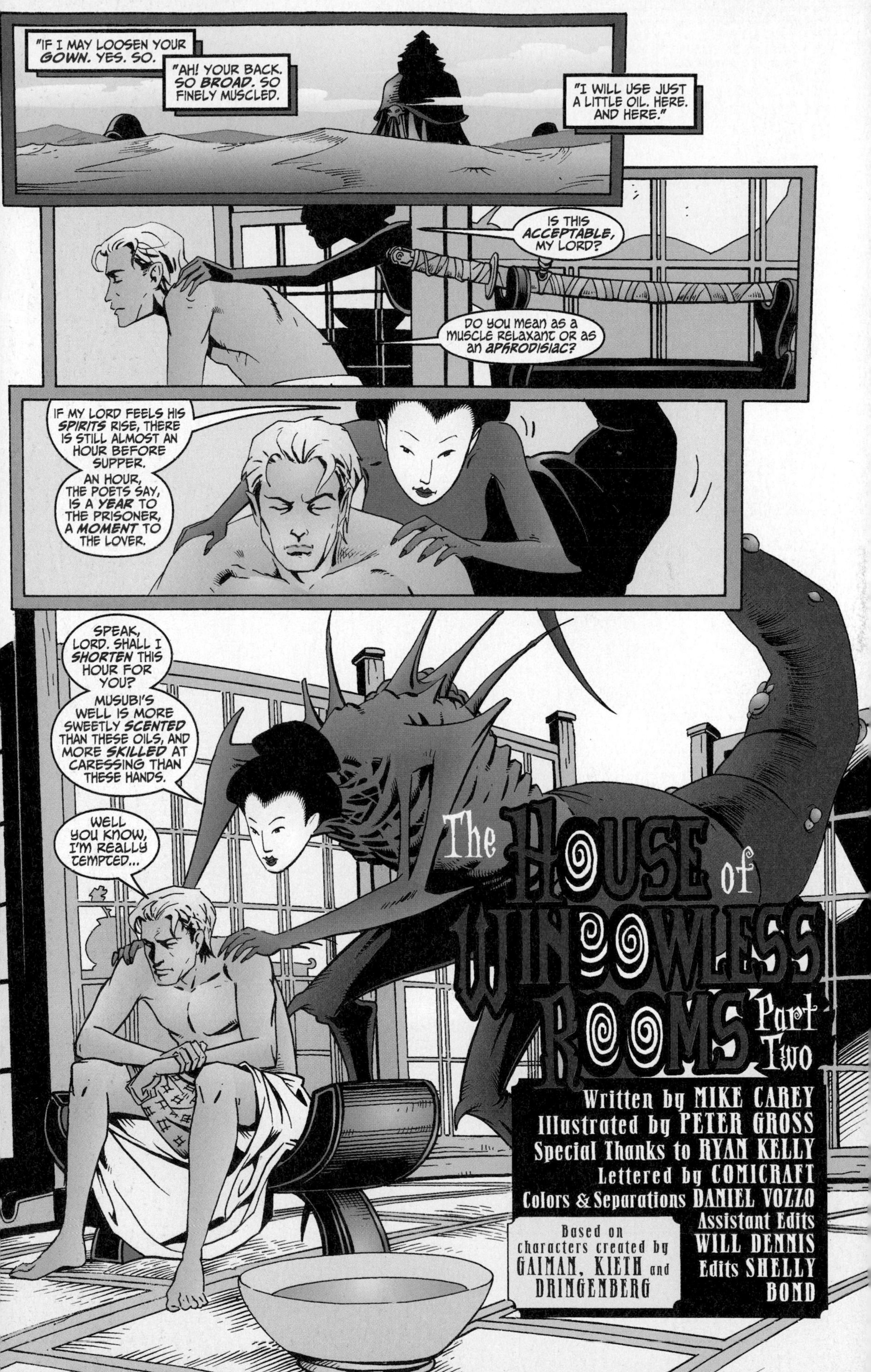
"IF I MAY LOOSEN YOUR GOWN. YES. SO.
"AH! YOUR BACK. SO BROAD. SO FINELY MUSCLED.
"I WILL USE JUST A LITTLE OIL. HERE. AND HERE."
IS THIS ACCEPTABLE, MY LORD?
DO YOU MEAN AS A MUSCLE RELAXANT OR AS AN APHRODISIAC?
IF MY LORD FEELS HIS SPIRITS RISE, THERE IS STILL ALMOST AN HOUR BEFORE SUPPER.
AN HOUR, THE POETS SAY, IS A YEAR TO THE PRISONER, A MOMENT TO THE LOVER.
SPEAK, LORD. SHALL I SHORTEN THIS HOUR FOR YOU?
MUSUBI'S WELL IS MORE SWEETLY SCENTED THAN THESE OILS, AND MORE SKILLED AT CARESSING THAN THESE HANDS.
WELL YOU KNOW, I'M REALLY TEMPTED...
The HOUSE of WINDOWLESS ROOMS Part Two
Written by MIKE CAREY
Illustrated by PETER GROSS
Special Thanks to RYAN KELLY
Lettered by COMICRAFT
Colors & Separations DANIEL VOZZO
Assistant Edits WILL DENNIS
Edits SHELLY BOND
Based on characters created by GAIMAN, KIETH and DRINGENBERG

... BUT TO SEE A DEMON OF THE SHIKO-ME WHORING HERSELF LIKE THAT... I THINK IT WOULD MAKE ME FEEL A LITTLE SICK.
GAAAAAHH!
YOU CALL ME WHORE, TOPPLED PRINCE? HERE, WHERE YOU ARE MORTAL?
THE SONS OF IZANAMI SENT YOU HERE TO WAVE YOUR SCENTED WELL UNDER MY NOSE.
WHAT WOULD YOU CALL IT?
I MIGHT HAVE KILLED YOU WITH MY TEETH AND CLAWS, BUT NOW I WILL USE MY STING.
THE VENOM WILL EAT YOU FROM THE INSIDE. YOUR BRAIN WILL LEAK AS TEARS OUT OF YOUR EYES.
THAT'S A PITY.
BECAUSE THEN YOU'LL ALWAYS WONDER WHAT MY OFFER WAS GOING TO BE.

THIS IS BECAUSE YOU ATE TOO FAST, SAUL.
THE BODY'S MEMORIES OF ITSELF RISE AGAINST YOU.
WELL, TO MOVE TOO FAST IS BETTER THAN STANDING STILL.
WHAT HAVE WE ACHIEVED TONIGHT? WE DIDN'T EVEN GET TO SEE THE GATE.
BUT WE DID GET TO SEE THE OTHER PLAYERS IN THE GAME.
ONLY THE HOST NEED TROUBLE US.
DO YOU REMEMBER ME AS I WAS BEFORE?
OF COURSE I DO.
WHEN I WAS BIGGER THAN WORLDS, AND BEAUTIFUL.
OLD MAN WITH A DOG. FORGET YOUR DOG.
THINK ABOUT THIS LIGHTED WINDOW, AND BE CURIOUS. COME AND SEE WHO'S HERE.

WE LIVE LIKE BEGGARS IN THIS PLACE. GRUBBING FOR SHAPE AND SUBSTANCE IN THE OFFAL OF A THIN UNIVERSE.
SAUL, WHAT DO YOU WANT THE GATEWAY FOR?
WHAT FOR?
AN EMERGENCY EXIT, WHAT ELSE? NONE OF THIS IS GOING TO LAST FOREVER.
MAYBE WE SHOULD BE THINKING BIGGER.
I'M TOO TIRED TO DANCE, CESTIS.
SPEAK IN STRAIGHT LINES, OR KEEP YOUR MOUTH SHUT.
OKAY. STRAIGHT LINES, THEN.
I'M TIRED OF IT. I'M SICK OF HOW COLORLESS AND CONSTRICTED IT ALL IS.
WE GOT PULLED IN BY THE BRIGHT LIGHTS AND WE END UP WEARING BODIES MADE OF MUD.
WE COULD PULL THE PLUG ON EVERYTHING. RIGHT NOW.
WE COULD GET OURSELVES FREE.
TAP TAP TAP
OOH. ROOM SERVICE.

I AM THE FAVORED OF PAIN. SHE DANCES IN MY HAIR AND IN THE PITS OF MY EYES.
MY KISS, MY TOUCH, MY VERY BREATH BRINGS ANGUISH AND DEATH.
SO THERE IS NOTHING YOU CAN OFFER ME IN EXCHANGE FOR YOUR LIFE.
BECAUSE THERE CAN BE NO JOY FOR ME SO GREAT AS TAKING IT.
SO YOU SAY, MUSUBI. BUT THAT'S ALL BULLSHIT, ISN'T IT?
YOU'VE KNOWN NO JOY AT ALL SINCE KAGUTSUCHI DRAGGED YOU HOME FROM THE BATTLEFIELD AND TRAINED YOU UP AS HIS SERVANT.
YOU... ARE FORFEIT. WHATEVER LIES YOU SPIN. WHATEVER PROMISES YOU MAKE.
YOU SPEAK WITHOUT RESPECT AND YOU WILL PAY FOR IT.
WELL, WHATEVER.
YOUR CONQUERORS WANT ME DEAD. THOSE WHO SLAUGHTERED YOUR SISTERS AND MADE A SLAVE OUT OF YOU.
THAT OUGHT TO BE WORTH A PAUSE FOR THOUGHT, NO?
BUT THEY SAY A DOG THAT'S BEEN WHIPPED OFTEN ENOUGH WILL BITE ANY HAND THAT OFFERS.
WHETHER IT'S HOLDING A STICK OR A STEAK.

WHAT IS IT, THEN, THAT YOU WOULD GIVE ME IF I FORSWEAR MY *ALLEGIANCE* TO THIS HOUSE?
BE *CONCISE*, AND *CONVINCING*.
DEATH.
HA HA HA HA HA HA HA HA HA HA HA HA HA!
WELL, I AM ANSWERED, AND YOU ARE A *FOOL*.
DEATH DELIVERS ME *AGAIN* INTO IZANAMI'S HANDS.
SHE IS MISTRESS OF THE AFTERWORLD, AND CAN CALL ME BACK INTO HER SERVICE AS OFTEN AS SHE *LIKES*.
TRUE AS FAR AS IT GOES.
OR THEN AGAIN, YOU COULD CHOOSE TO ENTER *MY* SERVICE.

I FEAR THAT OUR FIRST STRATAGEM HAS FAILED.
WHAT? YOU MEAN HE'S BEATEN HER? WITHOUT WEAPONS OR ARMOR?
SHE HAS NOT KILLED HIM.
HER BEST CHANCE OF SUCCESS WAS TO DO SO QUICKLY, BEFORE HE COULD SPEAK TO HER.
WELL, WE MUST GO ON AS WE AGREED.
I HAVE DESIGNED TWO OPPORTUNITIES DURING THE MEAL FOR YOU TO TAKE OFFENSE AND STRIKE HIM.
ONE IS ALL I REQUIRE.
BUT DOES IT NOT SEEM SAD, BROTHERS, TO KILL SO INTERESTING A GUEST?
I HAD HOPED TO HEAR MUCH ABOUT HIS PAST. HIS WAR WITH THE GOD OF THE COVENANT...
TSUKI-YOMI, IT IS OUR MOTHER'S WILL.
YOUR CONFINEMENT HERE LIES HEAVY ON YOU, I KNOW. BUT IF LUCIFER DOES NOT DIE, WE WILL BE OBLIGED TO RETURN HIS WINGS.
SO DIE HE MUST.
BUT PERHAPS WE MIGHT COMPOSE AN ODE TOGETHER, UPON THE OCCASION OF HIS DEATH.
OR A PLAY, BROTHER? WITH MYSELF, PERHAPS, IN LUCIFER'S ROLE?
EVEN BETTER.

THEY WILL WAIT FOR YOU TO SIT DOWN, AND THEN KAGUTSUCHI WILL CLAIM THAT YOU HAVE CHOSEN A PLACE ABOVE HIM.
AND HE WILL STRIKE YOU WITH THE THREE-NAMED SWORD, WHICH CANNOT BE WITHSTOOD.
IF THAT SHOULD MISFIRE, THEY WILL USE THE MEAL ITSELF TO ENTRAP YOU.
THE MEAL?
THE MEATS WILL BE FROM ANIMALS SACRED TO YAMA-NO-KAMI AS GODDESS OF THE HUNT.
TO EAT WILL OFFER INSULT TO HER -- TO REFUSE OFFENDS AGAINST HOSPITALITY.
EITHER WAY, KAGUTSUCHI WILL CHALLENGE YOU.
ARE YOU SURE YOU WANT TO DIE IN THIS BORROWED FORM?
IT IS EASIER TO KILL. ARE YOU SURE THAT YOU WILL KEEP YOUR PROMISE?
OF COURSE.
I AM A PSYCHOPOMP. IF YOU DIE AT MY HAND THE DESTINATION OF YOUR SPIRIT FALLS TO MY CHOOSING.
I WILL SEE YOU AGAIN, MUSUBI, IN ANOTHER PLACE.
SHHHKK
AND IN THE MEANTIME, LET'S SEE WHAT'S FOR SUPPER.

LIKE A SLINGSHOT STONE.
LIKE A SINGLE DROP OF WATER FALLING INTO THE IMMENSITY OF OCEAN.
AMENADIEL RETURNS TO THE BIRTHPLACE OF WILL, THE WOMB OF CONTEMPLATION.
SO LONG SINCE HE LAST WORE HIS OWN FACE AND FORM.
SO LONG SINCE HE BATHED IN THE RADIANCE OF THIS PLACE.
IT IS EASY TO FORGET THAT YOU ARE MADE OF UNSULLIED LIGHT.
EXCEPT FOR HERE.
IN THE SILVER CITY.

I HAVE ASKED THE DEMON TO SURRENDER THE GATE TO US.
SHE HAS *REFUSED.*
AND YET SOME OF US ARE UNEASY, AMENADIEL. GOD HAS NOT *SANCTIONED* THIS ACTION. INDEED, HE *GAVE* THE LETTER OF PASSAGE TO LUCIFER.
CAN WE BE *SURE* THAT WE DO HIS WILL?
AND WHEN DID GOD LAST SPEAK TO YOU, ZELAH?
THIS IS THE WAR AGAINST THE *ADVERSARY.* IT HAS NEVER ENDED.
I CALL A *VOTE.* WHO WILL SUPPORT ME?
AND AS THE HANDS RISE ON ALL SIDES, HE BOWS HIS HEAD TO HIDE THE SMILE OF SIMPLE JOY UPON HIS FACE.
HE IS MADE OF LIGHT. CLEAR AND PURE.
AND RED AS BLOOD.

GOOD EVENING, LORD LUCIFER.
YOUR PRESENCE GRACES THIS HOUSE, AND THIS COMPANY.
I HOPE THAT YOU ARE RESTED FROM YOUR JOURNEY.
RESTED, SUSANO-O-NO-MIKOTO? WHY, I'M PRACTICALLY COMATOSE.
HAVE YOU FOUND MY WINGS YET?
AS I SAID, MY LORD, IT WILL BE NECESSARY TO DISCUSS THAT MATTER WITH MY MOTHER WHEN NEXT SHE SPEAKS.
BUT YOU MUST BE HUNGRY. PLEASE. SIT DOWN.
DOES IT MATTER WHERE I SIT?
NOT IN THE SLIGHTEST. YOU ARE AMONG FRIENDS, STAR OF MORNING.
THAT'S GOOD TO HEAR.

THEN I'LL SIT AT THE FEET OF YOUR DIVINE MOTHER.
IT'S HER PARTY, AFTER ALL. I'D HATE TO BE RUDE.
YOUR COURTESY HUMBLES US ALL, LUCIFER MORNINGSTAR.
HAVE THE DISHES MOVED TO THE FLOOR.
THAT SWORD YOU WEAR, LORD KAGUTSUCHI.
WHAT OF IT?
I'VE HEARD THAT IT'S A HANDY LITTLE DEVICE.
"AS THE SPIDER SPINS, SO TAKAHAMA'S SWORD WEAVES WEBS OF AIR AND BLOOD."
OH! THAT IS BUSON! HE IS THE ONLY HAIKU-POET WHO CAN SPEAK MEANINGFULLY OF DEATH.
"IN THE DEEP FOREST, THE WOODSMAN..."
YES, THIS IS THE THREE-NAMED SWORD.
DURING YOUR VISIT HERE, LORD LUCIFER, I PROMISE I WILL LET YOU SEE IT.
YOU KNOW, THE SHEETS ARE CLEAN AND THE MAID SERVICE IS IMPECCABLE.
BUT IT'S THE WARM HOSPITALITY THAT'S GOING TO GET YOU YOUR FIVE STARS.

SHE KNOWS SHE'S WEAK. THAT'S WHY SHE DID IT.
TO TAKE THE MEASURE OF THEM, OBVIOUSLY. THE POWERS THAT ARE GATHERING.
BUT ALSO TO SHOW THEM EXACTLY HOW EXPOSED SHE IS. HOW HELPLESS.
NOW SHE CAN DO NOTHING BUT WAIT, AND SEE IF THEY TAKE THE BAIT.
OKAY, MAZ. I CLEARED OUT THE LAST FEW STRAGGLERS, AND LOCKED UP THE FRONT AND THE... UH...

OKAY, YOU'VE CUT YOUR HAND. YOU COULD'VE DONE THAT OPENING A BOTTLE, I GUESS.
AND YOU'RE PAINTING THE WINDOWS WITH YOUR BLOOD BECAUSE...

NO, YOU GOT ME ON THE BLOOD.
I'M JUST GOING TO PUT THAT DOWN AS ONE OF THOSE SCARY, PSYCHOPATHIC THINGS THAT MAKES YOU SPECIAL.
G'NIGHT.

VHEATRIZCH.

YEAH?

I RRHANT YOU TO SZHTAY.

THE CHANKO-NABE IS PARTICULARLY FINE, LORD LUCIFER.
THANKS. I'M SURE IT IS.

YOU HAVEN'T TOUCHED A THING, STAR OF MORNING.
PERHAPS THE FOOD IS NOT TO YOUR TASTE.

WELL, THANKS FOR YOUR SOLICITUDE, KAGUTSUCHI. BUT IT'S NOT THE FOOD.
IT'S A MATTER OF RESPECT.

RESPECT? IN WHAT SENSE COULD...?
YOU SEE, I CAN'T POSSIBLY EAT BEFORE MY HOST DOES.
YOUR... HOST?

YOUR MOTHER. "SHE WHOSE BLOOD IS WINE."
WHICH MAKES YOU THINK TWICE BEFORE ASKING FOR A *REFILL*, DOESN'T IT?

LUCIFER, I HAVE HEARD THAT YOUR CURRENT *BEDMATE* IS A DEMON.
TRULY YOU TAKE THE VICE OF *BESTIALITY* TO MAGNIFICENT EXCESS.
BUT EVEN HERE, KAGUTSUCHI, I FALL SHORT OF YOUR *HEROIC* EXAMPLE -- FOR AT THE TIME OF OUR COUPLING SHE WAS NEITHER *BOUND* NOR *DEAD*.
TSUKI-YOMI.
Y... YES, LORD LUCIFER?

I FIND I'M TIRED AFTER ALL. COULD YOU SEE ME BACK TO MY ROOMS?
OF COURSE, MY LORD.
THEN, I'LL SAY GOODNIGHT -- AND THANK YOU ALL.

GOODNIGHT, MY LORD.
KAGUTSUCHI, *HOLD*.

HOLD? WHY SHOULD I HOLD? YOU HEARD HIM INSULT ME!
IN RESPONSE TO A DIRECT INSULT FROM YOU. YOU HAVE ACTED MOST INDISCREETLY.
YOU YIELDED TO YOUR ANGER AND GAVE HIM AN EXCUSE TO LEAVE.

HONORED COUSIN, WHAT OF MY SUGGESTION? THE MORNINGSTAR SEEMED KEEN TO HUNT.
YES. IT IS POSSIBLE THAT A HUNT MIGHT PROVIDE COVER FOR A MORE DIRECT ATTEMPT.
SUSANO?
I WANT TO CHALLENGE HIM.
YOU CANNOT. YOUR CHANCE IS GONE.
VERY WELL, THEN.

I RENOUNCE ALL TIES OF BLOOD AND LOYALTY TO THIS HOUSE.
BROTHER, NO!
THE DISGRACE IS MINE -- AND I EMBRACE IT.

HE HAS HIS SWORD, AND HIS STRENGTH. AND THE ADVANTAGE OF FAMILIAR GROUND.
THAT IS SO. AND THE LIGHTBRINGER HAS NOTHING SAVE HIS WIT AND HIS WILL.

I FIND THAT THIS FAILS TO CONSOLE ME OVERMUCH.

HE TASTED STRINGY. AND HIS CLOTHES *STINK*.
BUT AT LEAST HE'S NOT GROWING SUPERNUMERY BODY PARTS.
SHE'S PUT *WARDS* ON THE WINDOWS.

YEAH, ON THE DOOR, TOO. HER OWN *BLOOD*.
SHE REALLY HASN'T DONE HER *HOMEWORK*, HAS SHE?

ARE YOU THERE YET? OR DO YOU WANT TO GO *DOWN* ON HER SOME MORE?
MAYBE LATER. THAT'LL DO JUST FINE FOR NOW.

KA-BOOM.

WHEN THE MUSIC OF DESCRUTION GIVES WAY TO UNEASY SILENCE, A FIGURE MOVES ON THE STAIRS.

THE KNIFE SHE HOLDS RINGS FAINTLY, LIKE STRUCK CRYSTAL.

VERHIEL SADIX IRDE SABAOTH REDOCTIN.
IN THE NAME OF CHRIST AND HIS HALLOWS I BIND THEE FAST.

IT'S A PENTAGRAM, SWEETHEART. SOLOMON'S SEAL.
SO MAKE YOURSELF COMFORTABLE.

I FEAR YOU ANGERED KAGUTSUCHI A GREAT DEAL.
I THOUGHT HE MIGHT CHALLENGE YOU THERE AND THEN, AT OUR MOTHER'S FEET.
HE WAS DEFINITELY THINKING ABOUT IT...
...BUT THE OFFICIAL LINE IS STILL PLAUSIBLE DENIABILITY, ISN'T IT?
PLAUSIBLE...?
NEVER MIND. I TAKE IT WE'RE HERE.
OH. YES.
THESE ARE THE WINDOWLESS ROOMS. THE CELLS IN WHICH THE IGNOBLE DEAD ENDURE ETERNITY.
THEY CANNOT MOVE OR SPEAK.
THEY EXIST FOREVER IN AN UNENDING MOMENT OF DREAD.
IT IS WONDERFUL, IS IT NOT? COMPACT, AND SIMPLE, AND UNIFORM.
VERY IMPRESSIVE, YES. BUT HOW DOES IT WORK?
WHAT IS IT THAT THEY'RE AFRAID OF?
THAT IS DISAPPOINTING. I THOUGHT YOU MIGHT HAVE GUESSED, SINCE I HAVE SHOWN YOU...
TSUKI-YOMI!

KAGUTSUCHI! I WAS JUST SHOWING LORD LUCIFER OUR MOTHER'S --
STAND AWAY FROM HIM, IMBECILE. OR SHARE HIS FATE.
WHAT FATE IS THAT, KAGUTSUCHI?
WHY, YOU DUNG-EATING KITE, YOU KNOW WELL ENOUGH WHAT YOU'VE DESERVED.
AND YOU KNOW THAT THIS WEAPON CANNOT BE STAYED NOR DEFLECTED.
IN WHICH IT MAKES A GOOD CONTRAST TO YOUR OTHER WEAPON.
UNLESS MUSUBI WAS JUST BEING UNKIND.
BROTHER, I BEG YOU! HE IS OUR GUEST! HE IS UNARMED!
KKKHH!

In the deep forest
The woodsman spits on his blade
The axe speaks, just once.

FEGREDO
2000

The House of Windowless Rooms
"IF LUCIFER DOES NOT DIE, WE WILL BE OBLIGED TO RETURN HIS WINGS...
Part Three
Written by MIKE CAREY
Illustrated by PETER GROSS
Finishes by RYAN KELLY and PETER GROSS
Lettered by COMICRAFT
Cover Art by DUNCAN FEGREDO
Colors & Separations DANIEL VOZZO
Assistant Edits WILL DENNIS
Edits SHELLY BOND
Based on characters created by GAIMAN, KIETH and DRINGENBERG
HHHHHHHUH...
TSO!
"SO DIE HE MUST."
YOU STILL STAND, PLAGUE SORE, BUT THIS BLOOD PROCLAIMS YOUR FALL.
NO MATTER HOW SHALLOW THE WOUND, YOU WILL DIE NOW.
SUCH IS THE VIRTUE OF THE THREE-NAMED SWORD.
INTERESTING.
THAT'S THE FIRST TIME I'VE EVER BLED FROM A WOUND TO THE LAPELS.
I FEAR... THAT IS MY BLOOD, MY BROTHER.

TSUKI-YOMI! IT IS IMPOSSIBLE.
MY AIM IS TOO SURE!
YOU TURNED THE BLADE AT THE END OF THE STROKE AND THE POINT GRAZED MY CHEST.
DID YOU... DID YOU NOT SEE ME?
MAGIC! YOU USED MAGIC TO TURN MY HAND!
WHY WOULD I NEED TO?
IT'S NOT AS THOUGH RAW STRENGTH AND STUPIDITY IS SUCH A HARD COMBINATION TO BEAT.
AAAAARRRHH!
IT WAS NOT I! IT WAS NOT! SOMEHOW YOU HAVE DONE THIS!
YOU HAVE KILLED MY BROTHER, TSUKI-YOMI, WHO OFFERED YOU NO HARM.
IT GETS BETTER, KAGUTSUCHI.
SHTANNG
I'VE KILLED YOU, TOO.

LUX. YOU'LL FIND IT EASILY ENOUGH, IF YOU WALK ALONG LA CIENEGA PAST THE MERIDIAN.
LUX
BUT YOU WON'T GO IN.
LIKE THE LOST SOULS WHO KEEP THEIR VIGIL DOWN THE BLOCK, YOU'LL SENSE THAT AURA OF INACCESSIBLE ELEGANCE AND YOU'LL KEEP YOUR DISTANCE.
UNLESS YOU'RE LOOKING FOR MORE THAN JUST GOOD FOOD AND AMBIENCE.
ALL CLEAR -- APART FROM THE CATTLE OUTSIDE.
THE SEERS AND THE SENSITIVES DRAWN BY THE GATEWAY. IGNORE THEM -- BUT CHECK UPSTAIRS.
THERE'S A HUMAN SCENT IN HERE.
DON'T TELL ME WHAT TO DO.
I WOULDN'T DREAM OF IT.
I THINK IT'S THE LITTLE WAITRESS, BUT YOU NEEDN'T TAKE HER UNLESS YOU'RE SURE YOU WANT TO.
THANK YOU.
POOR LITTLE CREATURE. THE GRIP OF THIS CIRCLE IS LIKE CHAINS OF IRON TO YOUR KIND, ISN'T IT?
BUT IT'S LIKE GOSSAMER TO MINE.
WHAT? DID YOU THINK WE WERE DEMONSPAWN, LIKE YOU?
I'M AFRAID NOT, SWEETHEART. WE'RE THE SHAPELESS. THE JIN EN MOK. YOUR ELDERS AND BETTERS.
SADIX
WHICH IS WHY THAT GATE YOU'VE OPENED BELONGS TO US.

AND WHAT WOULD YOUR LUCIFER DO OUT IN THE VOID, IN ANY CASE?
IS HE PLANNING TO LEAP OFF THE EDGE OF CREATION AND SHOUT "LET THERE BE LIGHT"?
ABSURD.
AFTER THE END OF THE FIRST COSMOS, WE FLOATED IN THE VOID FOR A TIME BEYOND IMAGINING. UNTIL WE LOST EVEN THE MEMORY OF OUR ORIGINAL FORM.
WE PAID FOR OUR IMMORTALITY. TOP DOLLAR IN ADVANCE.
HE BEGINS HIS SEARCH IN THE ROOM UPSTAIRS, BUT THE SEETHING NOTHINGNESS BEYOND THE GATE CONFUSES HIS SENSES.
SHE HAS BEEN HERE. RECENTLY. BUT...
AHH!
GONE TO GROUND.
BUT WE NEED THE GATE. THINGS HAVEN'T WORKED OUT FOR US HERE. NOT REALLY.
WE NEED TO GET OURSELVES UNSTUCK FROM ALL THIS TIME AND SPACE AND CAUSALITY SHIT.
WHAT'S THE MATTER, DEAR?
CAT GOT YOUR TONGUE?

YOU FOG MY EYES AND MY MIND... BUT YOU WILL NOT STOP ME.
THIS SWORD... THIS SWORD WILL NOT BE SHEATHED UNTIL IT HAS TASTED YOU.
THAT'S THE SPIRIT, KAGUTSUCHI. NEVER SAY DIE.
OF COURSE, ANGER AND EXERTION PROBABLY SPEED UP THE EFFECTS.
PERHAPS YOU SHOULD HAVE CULTIVATED CALM.
AKKKK!
"YOUR BRAIN WILL LEAK AS TEARS OUT OF YOUR EYES."
I THOUGHT THAT WAS POETIC LICENSE, BUT IT SEEMS SHE MEANT IT LITERALLY.
VERY NASTY. YOU CAN FALL ON YOUR SWORD --
-- IF YOU CAN REACH IT.

L... LUCIFER.
STILL WITH US, TSUKI-YOMI?
WHAT DID YOU DO TO HIM?
I CUT OUT MUSUBI'S POISON SACS AFTER I KILLED HER.
AND I SQUEEZED JUST A LITTLE INTO YOUR BROTHER'S WINE --
-- EACH TIME I FILLED HIS CUP.
OH, BASELY DONE! YOU REPAY MY MOTHER'S HOSPITALITY WITH TREACHERY!
NO SIN IS BLACKER THAN THAT!
YOU LIVE IN A WORLD OF YOUR OWN, DON'T YOU, BOY?
YOUR MOTHER'S HOSPITALITY CONSISTED OF TREACHERY. THIS IS HER HOUSE, AND SHE MAKES THE RULES.
TELL ME WHAT SHE'S DOING, TSUKI-YOMI. TELL ME WHY SHE BRINGS LIVING SOULS INTO THE HOUSE OF THE DEAD.
FIND OUT... FOR YOURSELF... DECEIVER.
YES. ALL RIGHT, THEN.

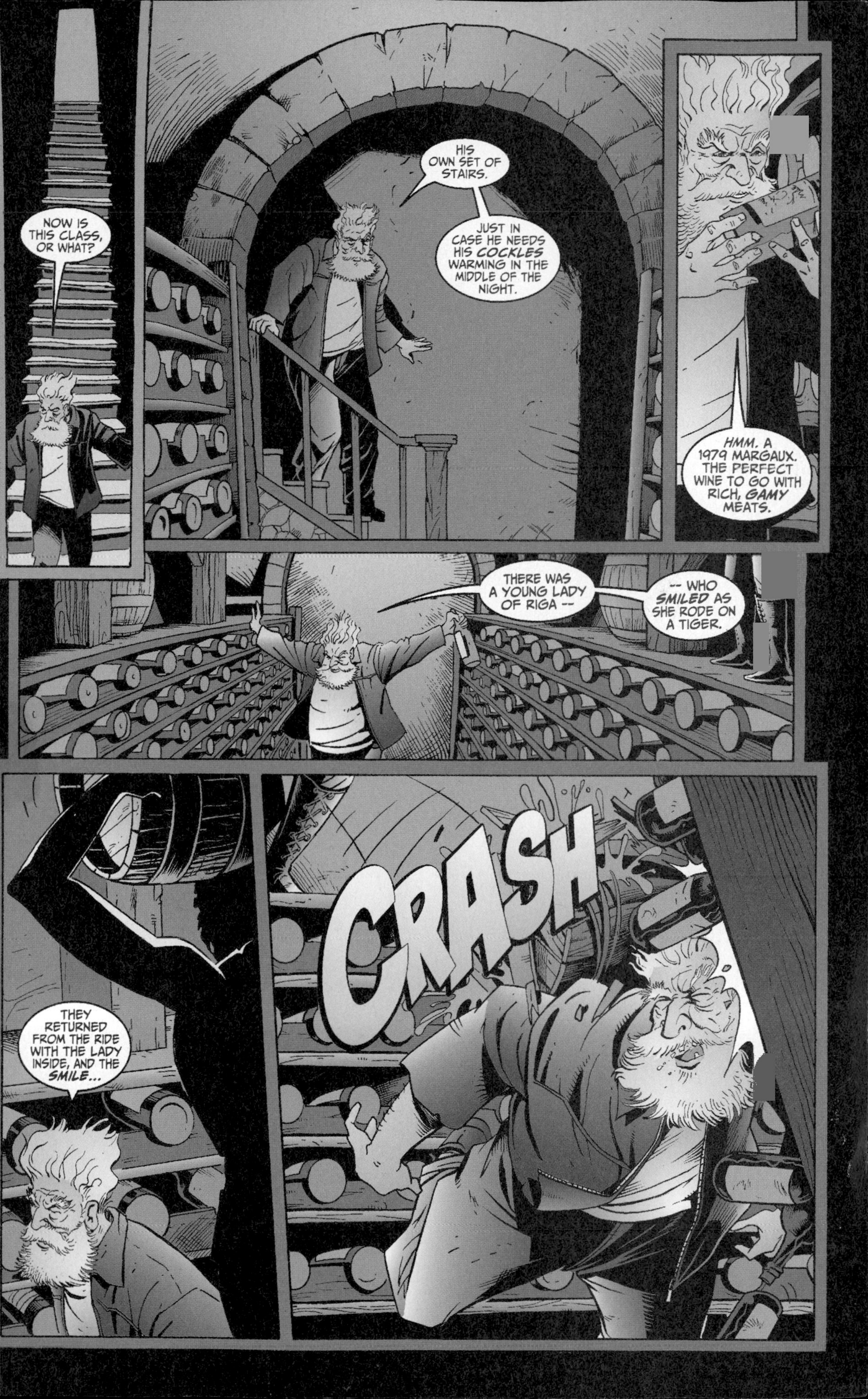

NOW IS THIS CLASS, OR WHAT?
HIS OWN SET OF STAIRS.
JUST IN CASE HE NEEDS HIS *COCKLES* WARMING IN THE MIDDLE OF THE NIGHT.
HMM. A 1979 MARGAUX. THE PERFECT WINE TO GO WITH RICH, *GAMY* MEATS.
THERE WAS A YOUNG LADY OF RIGA --
-- WHO *SMILED* AS SHE RODE ON A TIGER.
THEY RETURNED FROM THE RIDE WITH THE LADY INSIDE, AND THE *SMILE*...
CRASH

SAUL?
OH. I SEE.
NOW THAT... THAT WAS CLEVER.
LOOK, I JUST... I JUST WORK HERE, OKAY?
DON'T HURT ME. PLEASE.
YOU JUST WORK HERE? WELL THAT'S OKAY, SWEETHEART.
THIS IS ALL IN THE LINE OF BUSINESS, SO NO HARD FEELINGS.
BUT I HOPE THEY'RE PAYING YOU TIME AND A HALF.
KRACK

PTAHH! FHHH!
SO WE CAUGHT THE WRONG FISH.
THAT'S ALL RIGHT.
I LIKE SURPRISES.

I WARN YOU, MY MOTHER WILL NOT FORGIVE THIS TRESPASS.
SHE WILL KEEP YOU A MILLION YEARS DYING.
I CAN RELATE TO THAT.
I'M PRETTY POOR AT FORGIVENESS MYSELF.
LUCIFER. I AM... I AM AFRAID TO DIE.
I HAVE SCARCELY LIVED.
BUT THEY SAY THAT ALL LIVES, ALL WORLDS, ARE REPEATED ENDLESSLY. DO YOU THINK THIS IS SO?
I THINK IT'S GROTESQUE FOR SOMEONE WHO LIVES UPSTAIRS FROM HELL TO WANT COMFORTING LIES AS HE'S DYING.
AND I THINK...
I THINK I'VE FOUND A SMOKING PISTOL.

TEN THOUSAND MILLION CELLS, EACH WITH ITS OWN DAMNED SOUL. NOTHING TO SEE, OR DO, FOR THE REST OF ETERNITY.
IZANAMI'S HELL, SEVERE AND MINIMALIST.
BUT THE SCREAMING GHOSTS THAT POUR THROUGH THE WALLS AND THROUGH THE TERRIFIED INMATES ARE SOMETHING ELSE AGAIN. AN UNEXPECTED TOUCH OF GRAND GUIGNOL.
AND AT LAST HE UNDERSTANDS THEIR FUNCTION.

NOW DO YOU SEE?
I'M SAUL, OF THE SHAPELESS. MY FLESH IS JUST A MEMORY OF FLESH.
WOUNDS TRICKLE OFF ME LIKE WATER.
AS FOR YOU, YOU'RE JUST A LITTLE ANIMAL --
-- THAT LEARNED TO WALK ON ITS HIND LEGS.

SKUSH
BUT THE THING'S FLESH SHIFTS AND FLOWS BENEATH HER.
AND THE HEART IN HER HAND -- IT STILL BEATS.

AND THE CROWD IS REALLY LOVING THIS.
BRAVO, BRAVO.
CLAP
CLAP
CLAP
CLAP
CLAP

THAT'S WHAT I CALL GREAT LATERAL THINKING.
EVEN FOR THE JIN EN MOK, THERE'S NO BODILY RESURRECTION FROM THE LIMBO OF THE LARGE INTESTINE.

I LIKE THE WAY YOU FIGHT. NO SUBTLETY. JUST RAW ANIMAL STUFF.
I THINK I'D HAVE THE EDGE, MIND YOU. EVEN IF YOU WERE STILL FRESH.

BUT THEN WE'RE NEVER GOING TO FIND OUT, ARE WE?

LAX ALREADY. AND WHERE ARE THE MARCHING BANDS? THE HUNKY AIRPORT SECURITY GUYS? THE "WE LOVE YOU, JILL PRESTO" BANNERS?
I HAVE A CONNECTING FLIGHT TO MIAMI. WOULD THAT BE...?
TERMINAL FOUR.
THANKS.
BAGGA
US CITIZENS ONLY
LOOK, THERE'S NO FUCKING WAY I'M TRAVELING ON THE SAME FLIGHT AS YOU.
YOUR CONFRONTATION WITH YOUR MOTHER WILL HAVE TO WAIT. THERE IS SOMETHING THAT YOU MUST DO HERE FIRST.
WHAT? WHAT SORT OF SOMETHING?
GUESS.

GOOD MORNING TO YOU, MY LORD.
MY COUSIN WENT TO CALL ON YOU EARLY, BUT YOUR ROOM WAS EMPTY.
WILL YOU HUNT WITH US THIS MORNING? WE HAVE PICKED YOU OUT A SPIRITED MOUNT.
I REALLY ADMIRE YOUR SINGLE-MINDEDNESS, SUSANO.
YOU DON'T KNOW IF YOUR BROTHERS ARE ALIVE OR DEAD, BUT IT'S JUST BUSINESS AS USUAL, ISN'T IT?

SHNNNNG
BUT ENOUGH IS ENOUGH.
THIS IS KAGUTSUCHI'S SWORD. IF I EVEN PRICK YOUR SKIN, THERE'S NO COMING BACK.
NOBODY BUT YOU IS TO MOVE.
SHEATHE YOUR WEAPONS! I AM... I AM UNHARMED.
COUSIN, LET NO MAN STIR.
THEY'RE BOTH DEAD, IF YOU'RE INTERESTED. THE OLD BLOODLINE IS REALLY THINNING OUT.
SOMETHING TO BEAR IN MIND AS YOU STAND UP. SLOWLY.

YAMA-NO-KAMI, I'M TOLD YOU NEVER MISS WITH KNIFE OR BOW.
I TURN MY BACK ON YOU WITH FULL KNOWLEDGE OF THIS.

WHAT WILL YOU DO NOW, MORNINGSTAR? THIS IS A WASTED EFFORT. I HAVE NO POWER TO GRANT YOUR REQUEST.
THAT'S BEEN OBVIOUS FROM THE START.

YOU CAN COMMISSION ASSASSINS. LAY AMBUSHES. PULL CLOSE RELATIVES OUT OF YOUR SLEEVE LIKE CONCEALED WEAPONS.
BUT YOU DON'T HAVE ANY AUTHORITY EXCEPT WHAT SHE GIVES YOU.

"SO ALTHOUGH IT PAINS ME TO INTRUDE ON PRIVATE GRIEF...
"I'M GOING TO HAVE THIS OUT WITH YOUR MOTHER."

BEATRICE WECHSLER IS A WAITRESS.
THIS IS HER EVENING OFF, AND SHE HAS A HEAVY DATE LINED UP, THE FIRST SINCE HER MARRIAGE FELL APART.
BUT A LITTLE OVERTIME HELPS PAY THE BILLS.
IT DIDN'T TAKE HER LONG TO FIGURE OUT THAT THERE WAS SOMETHING PHONY ABOUT THE SETUP AT LUX.
HER PERSONAL MANTRA -- "IT'S JUST A JOB" -- HAS HELPED HER COPE WITH IT ALL.
BUT A COUPLE HOURS AGO, THE MANTRA FAILED HER.
WHEN SHE HEARD THE WORDS "I WANT YOU TO STAY" SPOKEN IN SLURRED, MOVIE MONSTER MAZIKEEN-SPEAK.
AND SOMETHING INSIDE HER WENT "YEAH, OKAY."
BUT "I WANT YOU TO STAY" TURNED OUT TO MEAN "I WANT YOU TO WEAR MY CLOTHES SO SOME HOMICIDAL SHAPE-CHANGING ZOMBIE-THINGS THINK YOU'RE ME."
AND HER FACE UNDER THE MASK...
EVEN FROM ONE GLIMPSE IN THE DARK, YOU COULD TELL. SCARRED, OR BURNED. REALLY FUCKED UP.
LUX
BUT YOU TAKE IT WHERE YOU FIND IT, THESE DAYS. THAT'S BEATRICE'S OTHER MANTRA.
IT HASN'T LET HER DOWN YET.

THE ONLY STRENGTH THAT MATTERS IS STRENGTH OF *MIND*. I'LL SHOW YOU.
KISS MY *SHOE*.
IT'S EXCITING ISN'T IT? BEING TAKEN SO *ROUGHLY*.
IT'S EVERYONE'S SECRET TURN-ON -- THE *FREEDOM* THAT COMES WITH TOTAL SURRENDER.
NOW PUT OUT YOUR EYE.
THE ONE ON THE *PRETTY* SIDE.
OKAY. GIVE ME THE KNIFE.
I'LL FINISH OFF.

HEY! BITCH!
THAT'S THE GOOD STUFF YOU'RE PADDLING AROUND IN. SIXTY PER CENT ABV.
NOW LEAVE HER ALONE OR WE'LL ALL BURN TOGETHER.
OOH. SOUNDS GREAT.

AH
WOOOM

KRESH
KRESH
KRESH
KRESH

YOU CAN QUIT LOOKING OVER MY *SHOULDER* NOW.
I'LL TAKE IT FROM HERE.

The House of Windowless Rooms Part Four

MIKE CAREY writer PETER GROSS layouts and finishes RYAN KELLY finishes DANIEL VOZZO colorist and separations COMICRAFT letterer WILL DENNIS assistant editor SHELLY BOND editor Lucifer is based on the character created by GAIMAN, KIETH AND DRINGENBERG

STILL... HHHH... SOMEONE.
I KNOW. LISTEN, YOU BETTER CALL 911. OR GET SOMEONE ELSE TO. THEY'LL HANDLE THE FIRE.

I'M HERE FOR THE THING IN THE BASEMENT.

TO TELL THE TRUTH, I DID THIS MAINLY FOR THE SAKE OF THE AMBIENCE.
THERE'S JUST SOMETHING ABOUT IT THAT WORKS FOR ME.
"FROM WHAT I'VE TASTED OF DESIRE, I HOLD WITH THOSE THAT FAVOR FIRE..."

IT'S THE END OF THE WORLD, mazikeen.
AREN'T YOU GLAD YOU WERE HERE TO SEE IT? TO BE A PART OF THE LAST BIG STORY?
EVEN IF IT WAS JUST A CAMEO?

THAK

THE FIRE CAN'T HURT YOU, CAN IT? YOU'RE NO MORE BOUND TO THAT MORTAL FORM THAN I AM.
YOU'RE PURE SPIRIT, AND THE SCARS ARE JUST FOR SHOW.

BUT I COMMAND YOU TO BE BOUND.
HEAR ME NOW.
FEEL YOUR SPIRIT SHRINK UNTIL THAT SOILED FLESH MEASURES THE LENGTH AND BREADTH OF YOU.
IT IS YOU.

AND IT'S FLAMMABLE.

YOU KNOW, PLAYING WITH YOU IS THE MOST FUN I'VE HAD IN AGES.
ESPECIALLY THE PART WHERE YOU ATE SAUL.

BUT I THINK IT'S TIME I GOT THE REAL FIRE STARTED.
I WANT TO GO HOME NOW.

YOU WERE JUST ONE OF THOSE HOLIDAY ROMANCES.

Izanami, I stand here at your feet with your son Susano on his knees beside me.
His life is forfeit to me, by your own codes of honor and hospitality.
And the sword that killed his brother, Tsuki-Yomi, stands ready at his throat.
Can I assume that I have your attention?
Excellent. You know, stone looks good on you.
All that fat hangs a lot better as architecture.
But let's be blunt.
Even carved in basalt you don't have much of a poker face.

YOUR WINDOWLESS ROOMS ARE FULL OF LIVING SPIRITS.
DREAMERS, BROUGHT HERE IN THEIR SLEEP. THEY TOUCH THE SHAME AND TERROR OF THE DAMNED AND THEY TAKE THE TAINT OF IT.
THEY'RE THE BLOOD IN THE VEINS OF YOUR HELL -- CARRYING TORMENT FROM ROOM TO ROOM, FROM LEVEL TO LEVEL.
IT'S A LOVELY SYSTEM -- REALLY. MINIMUM EFFORT, MAXIMUM OUTPUT. AN ERGONOMIC INFERNO.
"BUT TO DREAM OF THE ENDLESS, I IMAGINE IT WOULD LOOK LIKE POACHING, PURE AND SIMPLE.
"AND SINCE HE'S THE GAMEWARDEN HE WOULDN'T LIKE THAT AT ALL."
HE'LL DO IT. I WON'T EVEN NEED TO COMPEL HIM.
IF I SPEAK HIS NAME, HE'LL COME, AND HE'LL SEE WHAT YOU'VE MADE HERE. SO IT'S YOUR CALL, QUEEN OF DEATH. HEADS I WIN, AND TAILS --
-- TAILS IT ALL COMES DOWN.
SHE OFFERS ATONEMENT, LUCIFER MORNINGSTAR.
SHE OFFERS YOU YOUR WINGS.

THIS IS STAGE TWO. THE HIATUS BETWEEN THE STIMULUS AND THE RESPONSE, WHERE THE FIRE FEEDS UNCHECKED.
BEYOND A FAINT ACKNOWLEDGMENT OF KINSHIP, CESTIS PAYS IT NO HEED.

BUT THE VOID PULLS HER NOW LIKE THE MOON PULLS THE SEA.
OR LIKE THE HEAT PULLS VAPOR FROM THE LIQUID IN AN ALEMBIC, DRAWING AIRY SPIRIT FROM THE DULL HEAVINESS OF MATTER.
IT'S BEEN TOO LONG. SHE WANTS TO GET NAKED.

THE END OF CREATION IS JUST A SIDE EFFECT.
BUT IT'S A PRETTY FUNKY ONE, ALL THINGS CONSIDERED.

CRASH
OH, YEAHHHHH!

HALLELUJAH, LORD. I'M READY TO BE BORN AGAIN.

AND ALL OF THESE OBJECTS, YAMA-NO-KAMI, ARE POTENT FOCUSES OF BELIEF. THE LEAST OF THEM STILL HAS ITS HOLD ON MEN'S IMAGINATIONS.
YOU SEE IN THIS MY MOTHER'S EXTRAORDINARY WISDOM.
IN THIS WAY SHE PROTECTS US AGAINST THE VICISSITUDES OF FAITH. WEAVING THE DREAMS OF ALL HUMANITY INTO OUR ETERNAL PANTHEON --
-- SO THAT THEIR EVERY PRAYER OR FANTASY NOURISHES US.
SEE, HERE FOR EXAMPLE IS THE WEDDING GOWN OF LORD RAMA.
IMAGINE HOW MANY PICTURES SHADOW IT. HOW MANY THOUGHTS DWELL ON IT IN A SINGLE DAY.

AND IN THESE JARS --
THE ORGANS AND LIMBS OF DISMEMBERED GODS, OBTAINED IN TRADE FOR...

COUSIN, ARE YOU WELL?
DO YOU WISH ME TO FETCH THE WINGS?

MY BROTHERS.
MY BROTHERS ARE DEAD.

THE WINGS ARE HERE.
YOU SEE THAT THEY HAVE UNDERGONE A MOST FASCINATING TRANSFORMATION IN THEIR SEPARATION FROM --
FROM HIM. FROM LUCIFER.

THEY HAVE REMEMBERED THEIR FORMER STATE. THE FORM AND SUBSTANCE THAT THEY HAD BEFORE HIS FALL.
THEY HAVE HEALED THEMSELVES.

YOU -- CREATURE -- DO YOU HAVE ANY CONCEPTION OF HOW MUCH I CAN HURT YOU?
ON A SCALE OF ONE TO TEN? NOT REALLY.
GET OUT OF MY WAY.
FIND AN EMPTY TABLE DOWNSTAIRS AND SIT DOWN...
...AND SEE WHETHER THE SMOKE OR THE FIRE GETS YOU FIRST.
OH, YOU KNOW...
...MAYBE LATER.
SMACK
THAT MIND CONTROL CRAP MAY GO OVER REAL BIG WITH THE SAD LITTLE FUCKERS YOU NORMALLY SNACK ON.
BUT THE TRUTH IS, SWEETHEART, THE ODDS ARE SHIT. I'M CARRYING PASSENGERS.
AND THEY WROTE THE BOOK ON THAT MIND CONTROL SHIT.
SO HERE'S MY BEST OFFER: YOU GET UP ON YOUR FEET NOW --
-- OR ELSE YOU'RE GOING TO DIE LYING DOWN.

HERE, MOTHER. I CAN COMPLETE THE CONJUGATION OF MY SHAME BY TAKING THEM TO LUCIFER MYSELF.
BUT IF YOU WILL PERMIT, I WILL ENTRUST THAT TASK TO A SERVANT.
TO QUESTION YOUR JUDGMENT IS GROSS IMPIETY, BUT IT SITS ILL WITH ME TO SURRENDER TO HIM NOW...
...WHEN HE HAS HURT US SO RUINOUSLY.

OUR RUIN... IS NOT SO EASILY ENCOMPASSED.
DEATH IS AN OCEAN OF EXCREMENT, WITHIN WHICH YOUR BROTHERS' SOULS WILL SHINE LIKE PEARLS.
I WILL FIND THEM AGAIN.
THESE PINFEATHERS YOU WILL RETURN TO THEIR PLACES. THEY WILL QUICKEN AND TAKE ROOT AGAIN.
LUCIFER WILL NOT KNOW THEM FROM THEIR FELLOWS.
IN THE FULLNESS OF TIME, IT WILL COME.
HIS SCHEMES WILL FAIL. HIS FRIENDS WILL DESERT HIM. HIS FATE WILL FIND HIM UNPREPARED.
AND THEN, MY BABY, THE BRINGER OF LIGHT WILL LEARN WHAT DARKNESS IS.

THE THIRD STAGE IS EPIC. THE TAMING OF THE BEAST.
THE HUMAN STRUGGLE AGAINST THE BLIND MACHINERIES OF NATURE.
OH GOD! LOOK, PLEASE, I... I HAVE TO DO THIS. MY FRIEND IS STILL INSIDE.
NOT EVEN ON A BET, LADY. FIRST STORY COULD GO ANY SECOND.
'SIDES, ANYONE'S STILL IN THERE NOW...
...NOTHING YOU CAN DO FOR 'EM BUT PRAY.
GIRL, I AM CESTIS OF THE SHAPELESS.
CESTIS OF THE DANCING FLESH. WHAT ARE YOU, BESIDES MY LAST SUPPER?
WHAT AM I?
HELL, I'M JUST THE CABARET.

SEE, I'VE BEEN BRIEFED ON THIS.
YOU CALL YOURSELF SHAPELESS BECAUSE YOU COPY THE SHAPE OF THE THINGS YOU EAT, RIGHT?
BUT TO COPY IT YOU HAVE TO REMEMBER WHAT IT LOOKED LIKE.
AND SINCE YOU'RE OUT-NUMBERED SEVENTY-EIGHT-TO-ONE -- I THINK YOUR MEMORY'S GOING TO BE KIND OF RUSTY.
EURGHH! CREEPY STUFF!
ARRRRHH!
A TASTE OF YOUR OWN MEDICINE, BITCH.
CLOSE YOUR EYES AND SWALLOW.

TWO DAYS HE SOJOURNED IN THE REALMS OF PAIN.
TWO DAYS AND TWO NIGHTS.
BUT ON THE THIRD DAY HE ROSE, AND IN HIS RISING HE TORE APART THE VEILS OF ILLUSION WHICH ARE DISTANCE AND TIME.
HIS INVENTORY WAS ALMOST COMPLETE. HE HAD ACCESS TO THE VOID, AND A MEANS OF NAVIGATING WITHIN IT.
BRUSHWOOD AND KINDLING. ALL HE NEEDED NOW WAS A SPARK.
AND THE SPARK WOULD BE CHILD'S PLAY.

THE FINAL STAGE IS ALL SLAG AND SOUR MUD AND MELTED PLASTIC.
WHO NEEDS TO BE REMINDED THAT THE UNIVERSE IS OUT TO GET YOU.
WHO NEEDS TO SEE FEAR IN A HANDFUL OF SOOT?
FRIEND OF YOURS?
YEAH. SORT OF. SHE WAS MY... MY BOSS.
WHO THE FUCK KNOWS?
I WANTED TO HELP. I REALLY DID.
I DON'T UNDERSTAND ANY OF THIS SHIT ANYWAY. I THINK...
...I THINK I'M LOSING MY MIND.
YOU... YOU A DOCTOR?
IN THESE HEELS? HELL NO.
BUT IT NEVER HURTS TO LOOK, RIGHT?

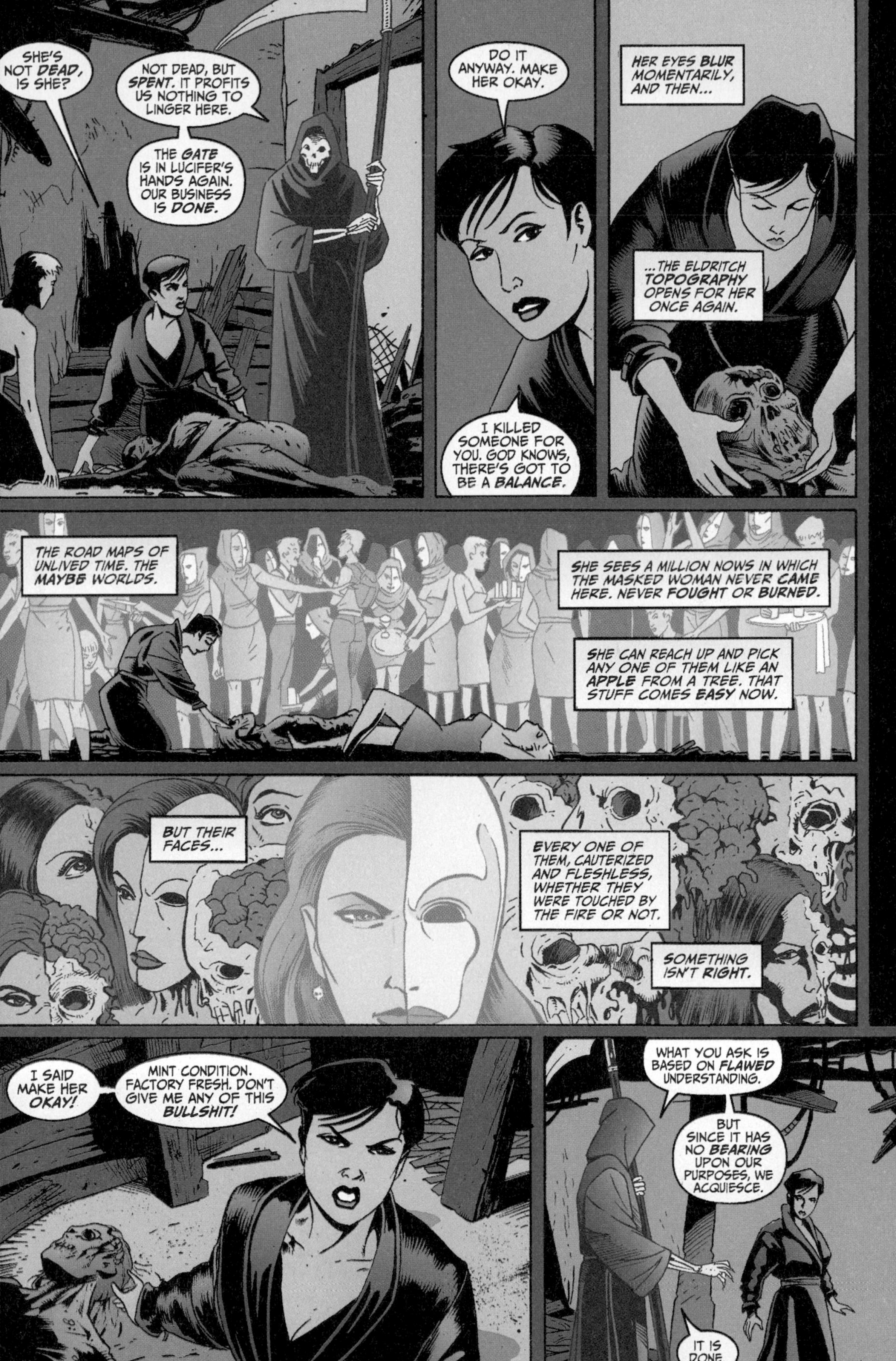
SHE'S NOT DEAD, IS SHE?
NOT DEAD, BUT SPENT. IT PROFITS US NOTHING TO LINGER HERE.
THE GATE IS IN LUCIFER'S HANDS AGAIN. OUR BUSINESS IS DONE.
DO IT ANYWAY. MAKE HER OKAY.
I KILLED SOMEONE FOR YOU. GOD KNOWS, THERE'S GOT TO BE A BALANCE.
HER EYES BLUR MOMENTARILY, AND THEN...
...THE ELDRITCH TOPOGRAPHY OPENS FOR HER ONCE AGAIN.
THE ROAD MAPS OF UNLIVED TIME. THE MAYBE WORLDS.
SHE SEES A MILLION NOWS IN WHICH THE MASKED WOMAN NEVER CAME HERE. NEVER FOUGHT OR BURNED.
SHE CAN REACH UP AND PICK ANY ONE OF THEM LIKE AN APPLE FROM A TREE. THAT STUFF COMES EASY NOW.
BUT THEIR FACES...
EVERY ONE OF THEM, CAUTERIZED AND FLESHLESS, WHETHER THEY WERE TOUCHED BY THE FIRE OR NOT.
SOMETHING ISN'T RIGHT.
I SAID MAKE HER OKAY!
MINT CONDITION. FACTORY FRESH. DON'T GIVE ME ANY OF THIS BULLSHIT!
WHAT YOU ASK IS BASED ON FLAWED UNDERSTANDING.
BUT SINCE IT HAS NO BEARING UPON OUR PURPOSES, WE ACQUIESCE.
IT IS DONE.

SAY, MISTER. DOES THIS PLACE BELONG TO YOU?
YES. IT DOES.
WELL, WE'RE GOING TO NEED TO LOOK AROUND. SEE WHAT STARTED THIS OFF.
TOMORROW.
WELL, SEE, I'M SUPPOSED TO...
TOMORROW. NOT NOW.
UMM... HI. WE MEET AGAIN, I GUESS.
IT WAS YOU IN HAMBURG, WASN'T IT?
YOUR WAITRESS JUST FAINTED, AND YOUR GIRLFRIEND... WELL, IT'S A LONG STORY.
IS IT?
I HAVE TOLD THE THINGS THAT RIDE YOU NOT TO INTERFERE IN MY AFFAIRS.
I DON'T NORMALLY GO TO THE TROUBLE OF REPEATING MYSELF.
WHAAAT?

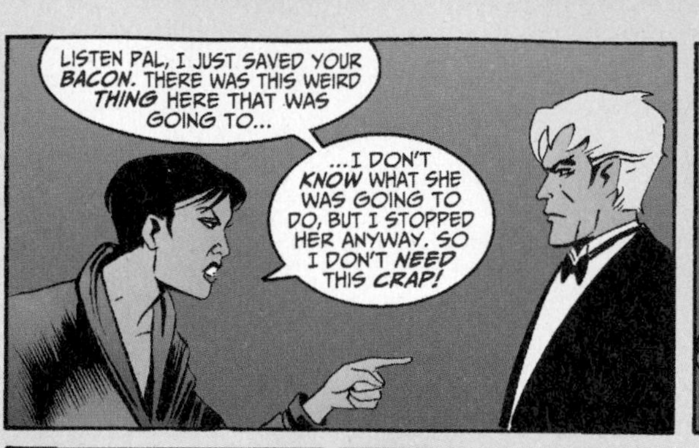
LISTEN PAL, I JUST SAVED YOUR **BACON**. THERE WAS THIS WEIRD **THING** HERE THAT WAS GOING TO...
...I DON'T **KNOW** WHAT SHE WAS GOING TO DO, BUT I STOPPED HER ANYWAY. SO I DON'T **NEED** THIS **CRAP!**

THEY... THEY SAY TO APOLOGIZE.
THEY SAY... THEY **PROMISE** THEY WON'T GET IN YOUR WAY AGAIN. THEY OFFER CONDIGN OBEISANCE.
WHATEVER **THAT** IS.

and what do **you** say, miss presto?

WELL... JUST SPEAKING FOR MYSELF...
...AND I'M GOING OUT ON A **LIMB** HERE.

I'D LIKE TO SAY THAT YOU'RE AN **ARROGANT**, UNGRATEFUL SON OF A BITCH ON A PERMANENT POWER TRIP.
ha! excellent. accurate on all counts.
but don't push your **luck**. my good humor could **evaporate** at any moment.
or mazikeen may **wake**...
...and realize what you've **done** to her.

BUT I...
...I MADE HER OKAY. I MADE HER BEAUTIFUL AGAIN.
YOUR PAROCHIAL AESTHETICS ARE A THING TO BE HIDDEN, NOT FLAUNTED.
AND BY REMAINING HERE YOU'RE RISKING THE ANGER OF THE CARDS AS WELL AS MINE.
I REALLY WOULD LEAVE NOW, IF I WERE YOU.
YEAH, WELL, DON'T MENTION IT. I BET THE FOOD HERE STINKS TOO.
AND I HOPE YOUR INSURANCE RAN OUT AT MIDNIGHT LAST FRIDAY.
SLAM
A FIRE, WHEN ALL IS SAID AND DONE, IS LIKE AN ANGEL.
A MESSENGER FROM ANOTHER PLACE, WHOSE TIDINGS WHETHER GOOD OR BAD MEAN THE SEVERING OF THE PAST, THE DEATH OF WHAT HAS BEEN KNOWN AND LIVED.
HE STANDS IN THE BURNED OUT SHELL AND INHALES THE SOUR REEK OF SPENT COMBUSTION LIKE INCENSE.
AND HE THINKS ABOUT THE FIRE THAT'S STILL TO COME.

THE SEA.
THE SEA IS OUR MOTHER.
THE HOME WE GREW TOO BIG FOR. THE WOMB FROM WHICH WE WOKE.
THIS IS WHAT THE WISE MEN SAY.
BUT THE WISE MEN LIE. WE BROUGHT THE SEA WITH US.
BECAUSE BLOOD IS SALT WATER, AND IN OUR HEARTS THERE IS A LIGHTLESS OCEAN.
HERE, NOW, IS THE TURNING OF THE TIDE.
HERE, NOW, THE BLOOD PAUSES--
FALLS IN UPON ITSELF--
AND IS RENEWED.
UHH!

WELL, ATHENS BEATS L.A. ON BOTH COUNTS--ITS MORE SCENIC AND MORE POLLUTED.
THANK YOU, CHARLES.
I KEPT THIS PLACE ON FOR TAX REASONS RATHER THAN SENTIMENTAL ONES.
SHALL I HAVE A LITTLE OF YOUR COMPANY TODAY, MY LOVE?
HMM? I'M SORRY, TONY. I WAS MILES AWAY.
WHAT DID YOU SAY?
I SAID, SHALL WE WASTE THE MORNING IN BED WITH MESSIEURS MOËT AND CHANDON?
OH, TONY, THIS IS MY MORNING TO SHOP.
YOU KNOW PERFECTLY WELL I DON'T HAVE A THING THAT'S FIT TO BE SEEN IN.
THIS AFTERNOON I'M YOURS. BUT RIGHT NOW I BELONG TO DIOR AND CARDIN.
MY DEAREST PAULINA, I'D LOVE YOU EVEN IN NO CLOTHES AT ALL!
À BIENTÔT, IDIOT. ANYWAY, YOU GET THE BEST OF THE DEAL.
YOU KNOW I'M NOT A MORNING PERSON.

MIKE CAREY • WRITER • DEAN ORMSTON • ARTIST
FIONA STEPHENSON • LETTERER • DANIEL VOZZO • COLORIST AND SEPARATOR • DUNCAN FEGREDO • COVER ARTIST
SPECIAL THANKS TO WILLIE SCHUBERT
WILL DENNIS • ASSISTANT EDITOR
SHELLY BOND • EDITOR
BASED ON CHARACTERS CREATED BY
GAIMAN, KIETH AND DRINGENBERG

WHAT... WHAT HAS HAPPENED HERE? WHO DID THIS?
THERE WAS A FIRE.
OBVIOUSLY THERE WAS A FIRE. I'M NOT SIMPLE!

THIS ISN'T POSSIBLE. MY DREAMS HAVE TOLD ME THAT I'D FIND IT HERE.
THE GATE.
WE'VE ALL BEEN DRAWN HERE, SISTER. WE'RE THE CHOSEN FEW. THE BLESSED.
SHARE BREAD WITH US. WEALTH IS AN ILLUSION. WE HAVE THE PEACE YOU SEEK.

GET AWAY FROM ME! YOU DON'T HAVE ANYTHING EXCEPT A SPARK OF THE TRUE SIGHT.
YOU DON'T EVEN KNOW WHAT IT WAS THAT DRAGGED YOU HERE!

THERE'S A SPECIAL PLACE IN HELL FOR THOSE WHO HEAR GOD'S CALL AND TURN AWAY.
NO, THERE ARE NO SPECIAL PLACES IN HELL. HELL IS A DEMOCRACY.
POLICE LINE

KEEP CLEAR

WHERE DO THEY DIG THESE PEOPLE UP FROM? A FUCKING VIGIL IN FRONT OF A BURNED-OUT RESTAURANT, FOR CHRIST'S SAKE!
MAYBE IT'S A CAMPAIGN FOR MORE FIRE ENGINES.

SHE THINKS FLEETINGLY OF THE NEAR-DEATH EXPERIENCES SHE'S READ ABOUT.

YOU JUST FOLLOW THE LIGHT...

YOU IGNORE THE FEAR THAT'S CLIMBING YOUR SPINE.
YOU JUST FOLLOW.

AND THERE IT IS.
NOTHING. NOTHING AT ALL.
CRACKLING WITH THE RAW ENERGY OF ITS OWN NEGATION.

THE BALM OF UNBEING, AT LAST WITHIN HER REACH.

THIS IS PRIVATE PROPERTY.
UNLIKE THE OPPOSITION, I DON'T HAVE ANY OBLIGATION TO FORGIVE TRESPASSERS.
LIGHT OF THE DAWN SKY, I PROSTRATE MYSELF BEFORE YOU. I BEG YOU. LET ME...
LET ME STEP THROUGH YOUR--
NO.
YOU'VE HAD A WASTED JOURNEY.
THE GATE LEADS TO THE VOID OUTSIDE OF CREATION. THAT'S NOT THE SAME AS NON-EXISTENCE.
THERE'S NOTHING FOR YOU HERE.
BUT YOU... YOU ARE HE WHO FELL. YOU CAN MAKE THIS STOP.
I'LL PAY ANYTHING!
YOUR DEATH IS NOT MY BUSINESS. I SUGGEST YOU TAKE IT UP WITH THE GODS THAT CURSED YOU.
DO YOU THINK I HAVEN'T DONE THAT?
FOR FOUR THOUSAND YEARS I'VE CALLED. THEY NEVER ANSWER.
WELL, TIME DISTILLS MOST THINGS DOWN TO THEIR ESSENCE. IF IT WERE ME, I'D BARGAIN FROM STRENGTH...
...IF YOU THINK YOU HAVE ANY.

LAST NAME IS A LUXURY IN ANY CASE. NOT SOMETHING SHE NEEDS.
SHE NEITHER TOILS NOR SPINS. THE MEN PROVIDE FOR HER, OFFERING UP THEIR WEALTH IN WILLING SACRIFICE.
AND IT'S ONLY HER FIRST NAME THAT THEY EVER USE.
OH, PAULINA! PAULINA, MY LOVE!
MY SWEET GIRL!
OHHHHH!
YOU'RE LOST IN THOUGHT, MY LOVE.
I'M FINE.
WHICH IS A LIE, OF COURSE. BUT LOST? NO.
IT'S HER THOUGHTS THAT TAKE HER HOME.
INTO A PAST FAR MORE IMMEDIATE THAN THE MEANINGLESS FARCE SHE JUST COLLUDED IN.

WHEN SHE REMEMBERS CHALDAEA SHE REMEMBERS THE CORN.
SO MUCH OF IT. SOIL SO RICH THAT EVERY SEED UNFOLDED AND THRUST UP ITS HEAD.
FIELDS SO WIDE THAT THERE WAS NO END TO THEM.
AND THE TEMPLE PRECINCTS THAT SMELLED OF BRIAR ROSES. THE STONE THAT WAS COOL BENEATH HER FEET, EVEN IN THE HEAT OF NOONDAY.
IN CHALDAEA. WHEN THE GODS STILL LOVED HER.
WHEN THE KING'S GUARDS CAME FOR HER, THEY MARCHED HER THROUGH THE FIELDS WITH HER HANDS BOUND.
THE GLEANERS STOPPED THEIR WORK TO WATCH THE GREAT PRODIGY--A PRIESTESS BROUGHT SO LOW.
SHE AVOIDED THEIR EYES.
BUT THE EYES OF THE GOD-KING HELD HER SO THAT SHE COULD NOT LOOK AWAY.
YOU ARE ERISHAD, OF URUK.
OF WHOM THE GODS REQUIRED BOTH CHASTITY AND OBEDIENCE.
MAJESTY, I AM SHE. BUT I REPENT MY SIN AND WOULD FIND THE GODS' FAVOR AGAIN AT ANY COST.
INDEED?
THEN REJOICE, ERISHAD. FOR THE GODS WILL PARDON YOU.
PROVIDING ONLY THAT YOU TAKE YOUR OWN LIFE IN THE TEMPLE GROUNDS.

TAKE MY LIFE? BUT MAJESTY--
"AT ANY COST," YOU SAID.
AYE, ANY COST TO ME.
BUT I AM PREGNANT! I CANNOT KILL MY BABY! IF YOU WOULD STAY MY SENTENCE FOR JUST A FEW--
I CANNOT.
YOU KNOW I CANNOT!
ENOUGH! THE GODS OFFERED YOU DEATH AND YOU WOULD NOT TAKE IT.
TAKE THEIR CURSE INSTEAD. YOU ARE A SICKNESS HEAVED FROM THEIR AFFRONTED GORGE.
DEATH WILL NOT TOUCH YOU NOW.
"WHEN URUK SHALL BE DUST, AND THE DUST BAKED AND BUILT INTO CITIES STILL UNTHOUGHT-OF...
"...THE SUN WILL STILL LOOK DOWN UPON YOUR SHAME."

MY DEAR MISS ERISHAD!
I AM DOWN HERE.
NARAMSIN. IT WAS GOOD OF YOU TO COME.
NOT AT ALL, DEAR LADY. WE ARE OLD FRIENDS, ARE WE NOT? BY THE WAY, IT IS RAVI AT THE MOMENT.
TELL ME, HAVE YOU EVER EATEN JELLIED EELS?
THEY HAVE A MOST UNPLEASANT CONSISTENCY, AND A SMELL WHICH CAN ONLY BE DESCRIBED AS INSIDIOUS.
THEIR PRESENCE IN MY HAMPER DISTRESSES ME GREATLY.
I WANT TO SPEAK TO THE HOLY NAMES AGAIN. TO THE GODS.
YOU WERE ALWAYS ON BETTER TERMS WITH THEM THAN I WAS. WILL YOU HELP ME?
HELP YOU TO MAKE YOUR SKITTISH DEITIES SIT STILL WHILE YOU MAKE THE SPEECH THAT THEY HAVE IGNORED A HUNDRED TIMES.
HA, HA. THAT IS NOT AMUSING. CAN YOU NOT RESIGN YOURSELF TO LIFE, ERISHAD? IS IT SO TERRIBLE?
DID I EVER TELL YOU, SAGACIOUS ONE, THE NATURE OF MY IMMORTALITY?

IT IS THE RECYCLING OF A SINGLE DAY, IS IT NOT?
YES, IT IS. EVERY MORNING MY BODY FORGETS ALL WOUNDS, ALL HURTS.
AND MAKES ITSELF AGAIN EXACTLY AS IT WAS WHEN THE GODS FIRST CURSED ME.

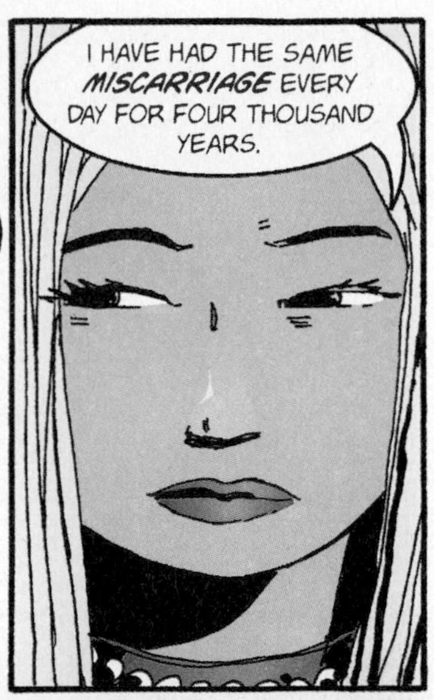
I HAVE HAD THE SAME MISCARRIAGE EVERY DAY FOR FOUR THOUSAND YEARS.

THEY ARE VERY OLD, YOUR GODS. IT MAY BE THAT YOUNG MAGIC WILL TAKE THEM BY SURPRISE. NEW WORLD MAGIC.
THERE IS A PRIEST OF VOUDUN WHO LIVES VERY NEAR HERE-- MAMBO PAWOL ANPIL PA LEVE LE MO.
THANK YOU. AND HOW WILL HE KNOW TO TRUST ME?

YOU ASK FOR TOO MUCH, DEAR LADY.
IT IS YOUR ONLY FAULT.

TO BARGAIN FROM STRENGTH...
THE STRENGTH THAT TIME DISTILLS.
A THOUGHT FORMS IN HER MIND-- SO TERRIBLE THAT EVEN LIFE MAY BE PREFERABLE.

DAWN TAKES HER BY SURPRISE, STILL WRESTLING WITH TEMPTATION.
HER GUTS CLENCH ONCE AGAIN.
THE TIDE TURNS, AND SPILLS DOWN BETWEEN HER LEGS.

TONY KEEPS VERY LITTLE MONEY ON HAND, BUT IN THE WALL SAFE THERE ARE MANY THINGS WHICH CAN BECOME MONEY VERY QUICKLY.
SHE TAKES ONLY THOSE WHICH ARE COMPLETELY UNTRACEABLE.

THE BED'S GRISLY LADING IS ALL THE FAREWELL SHE LEAVES HIM.
WHY SHOULD HE DESERVE ANY MORE? SHE HAS PAID WELL FOR HER BOARD AND LODGING.
BUT SHE KISSES HIS CHEEK, AND HE MURMURS SOMETHING WHICH MIGHT BE HER NAME.

THERE IS A DRUMMING INSIDE HER THAT ISN'T HER HEART.
SOMEONE ELSE'S HEART, PERHAPS. HER HANDS SHAKE ON THE WHEEL OF THE CAR, AND HER EYES ARE WET ALTHOUGH SHE DOES NOT WEEP.

SALT WATER REMINDS HER TOO MUCH OF BLOOD.
NOK NOK

YOU SHOULDN'A BROUGHT THAT CAR ROUN' HERE, MISSY. IT JUST BE A PUDDLE OF OIL BY MORNIN'.
I DON'T CARE ABOUT THE CAR. YOU KNOW WHY I'M HERE? WHAT I WANT?

YEAH, I HEAR. YOU WANNA GO FOR CATCH SOME GHOSTS.
YOU COME INTO MY PARLOR, MISSY.
WE GONNA DO SOME FUCKIN' BIG-TIME MAGIC THIS NIGHT. PROMISE YOU DAT.

NARAMSIN SAID THAT YOU'RE A MAN OF POWER. WHY DO YOU LIVE IN SUCH SQUALOR?
MAITRESSE URZULIE BRING ME, THREE YEAR GO. SOMEONE BIG COME BY HERE SOON.
THEY BE NEW GHOSTS OR OLD GHOSTS, MISSY? OLD GHOSTS BE HARDER TO CATCH.

THEY'RE GODS.

HAHAHAHAHAHA! THAT BE FUCKIN' WONDERFUL!
WE MAKE A CATCH-CATCH FOR GODS, SURE!

HNN. YOU GOT SOME MONEY FOR ME, YES?
NO MONEY. SOME BEARER BONDS. GEMSTONES. KRUGERRANDS.
THE CAR TOO, IF YOU WANT IT.
I LIKE TO WALK. LOTTA STRENGTH IN THE GROUND, YOU KNOW.
BUT NEGOTIABLE FINANCIAL INSTRUMENTS, THEY ALWAYS WELCOME.
WE MAKE MAGIC NOW.
"YOUNG MAGIC." THERE IS A SMELL OF RANK SWEAT IN THE AIR THAT FEELS AS OLD AS THE PIT.
BUT HER WHITE ROBE IS HER ARMOR AND HER DECLARATION OF WAR.
OKAY, BEL FAM. YOU BRING 'EM, I KEEP 'EM. OR IF THEY BE BIG, STRONG GODS THEY EAT US UP.
WE FIND OUT.
SHE MIXED WATER AND SEMEN IN A CRACKED SAUCER, AND ANOINTED HERSELF.
SHE CALLED OUT TO THEM IN HALTING CHALDAEAN.
AND THE BLACK MAN COMMENCED TO HUM, VERY QUIETLY.

MASTERS OF ALL, YOUR SERVANT CALLS! LORDS OF THE HARVEST, STEP THROUGH THE WORLD! UTTERERS OF LIFE, SPEAK TO US NOW!
MAP TRAVAY POU VE DE TE YO, M PA BEZWENN LAJAN. O! LANE A BOUT O, MAP PARET TAN YO.
SHE REPEATED THE WORDS AGAIN AND AGAIN, TO THE MAMBO'S COUNTERPOINT, AND ONLY SILENCE ANSWERED HER.

BUT THEN SHE HEARD THE WHISPER OF THE CORN IN THOSE DEAD FIELDS, AND THE SCENT OF THE BRIAR ROSE LIFTED THE SOUR STENCH OF THE ROOM.
THE GODS WERE THERE, AND THE WORDS DIED IN HER MOUTH.

SE LI KE WA, SE LI KAP KOMANDE! DOS LES BONDYE, TONBE NAN LA BOUTYE!
MANO!

GOT 'EM ALL, BEL FAM. THEY BE REAL LICKLE GODS. NO TROUBLE AT ALL.
SET IT DOWN. AND STAND AWAY.
HOLY NAMES, YOUR SERVANT SPEAKS TO YOU.
ERISHAD OF URUK ASKS YOUR FORGIVENESS.
PLEASE?
BUT YOUR SIN... IS GREAT... ERISHAD.
AND NOT YET... EXPIATED.
IT IS... SACRILEGE... FOR YOU... EVEN TO CALL ON US.
YOU CANNOT IMAGINE HOW LITTLE I CARE ABOUT SACRILEGE NOW.
I ASK AGAIN.
WILL YOU REMOVE YOUR CURSE, AND LET ME DIE?
NOT... YET.
IN A THOUSAND YEARS' SPACE... WE WILL... CONSIDER.
AND YOU MAY... ASK... AGAIN.

IT WILL NOT WAIT A THOUSAND YEARS. IT WILL NOT WAIT ANOTHER DAY.
LET ME SHOW YOU WHAT WILL HAPPEN IF YOU REFUSE ME.

THERE'S ANOTHER SPIRIT HERE. YOU KNOW IT. YOU FEEL IT.
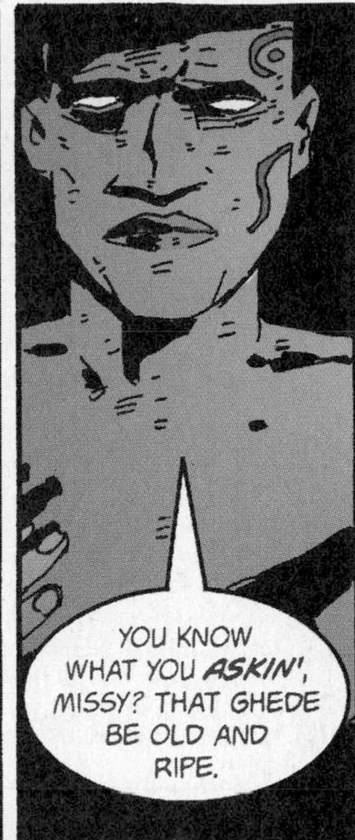
YOU KNOW WHAT YOU ASKIN', MISSY? THAT GHEDE BE OLD AND RIPE.
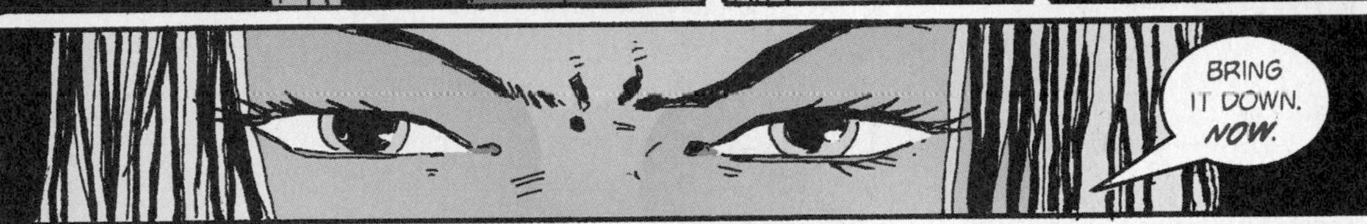
BRING IT DOWN. NOW.

YEAH. YEAH, I CALL 'IM. BUT NOT FOR YOU.
HE THE ONE, I THINK. LA DOUCE MAITRESSE SEND ME HERE FOR THIS.
YOU WANT HIM FOR TO RIDE ME?

NO. PUT IT INTO THE BOTTLE.

DLO KWALA MANYAN, NAN PEYI SA MAMAN PA KONN PETIT LI. MAP FE ECLAME POU LE BEBE.

YO PRALE WE KI JAN YAP MET A JENOU. MAP FE ECLAME POU LE BEBE.
UHH!

ERISHAD... HOLD!
YOU MUST... NOT... DO THIS.
WE DO NOT... PERMIT IT.
MAP FE ECLAME POU LE BEBE. MARE TET OU, MARE VANT OU, MARE REN OU!
ARE YOU FRIGHTENED, SMALL GODS? ISN'T DEATH YOUR CREATURE, TO STRIKE OR STAY AS YOU WHISTLE?
GIVE ME WHAT I ASK!
CALLED INTO FLESH A MILLION TIMES. EXPELLED A MILLION TIMES FROM THE WARM DARK.

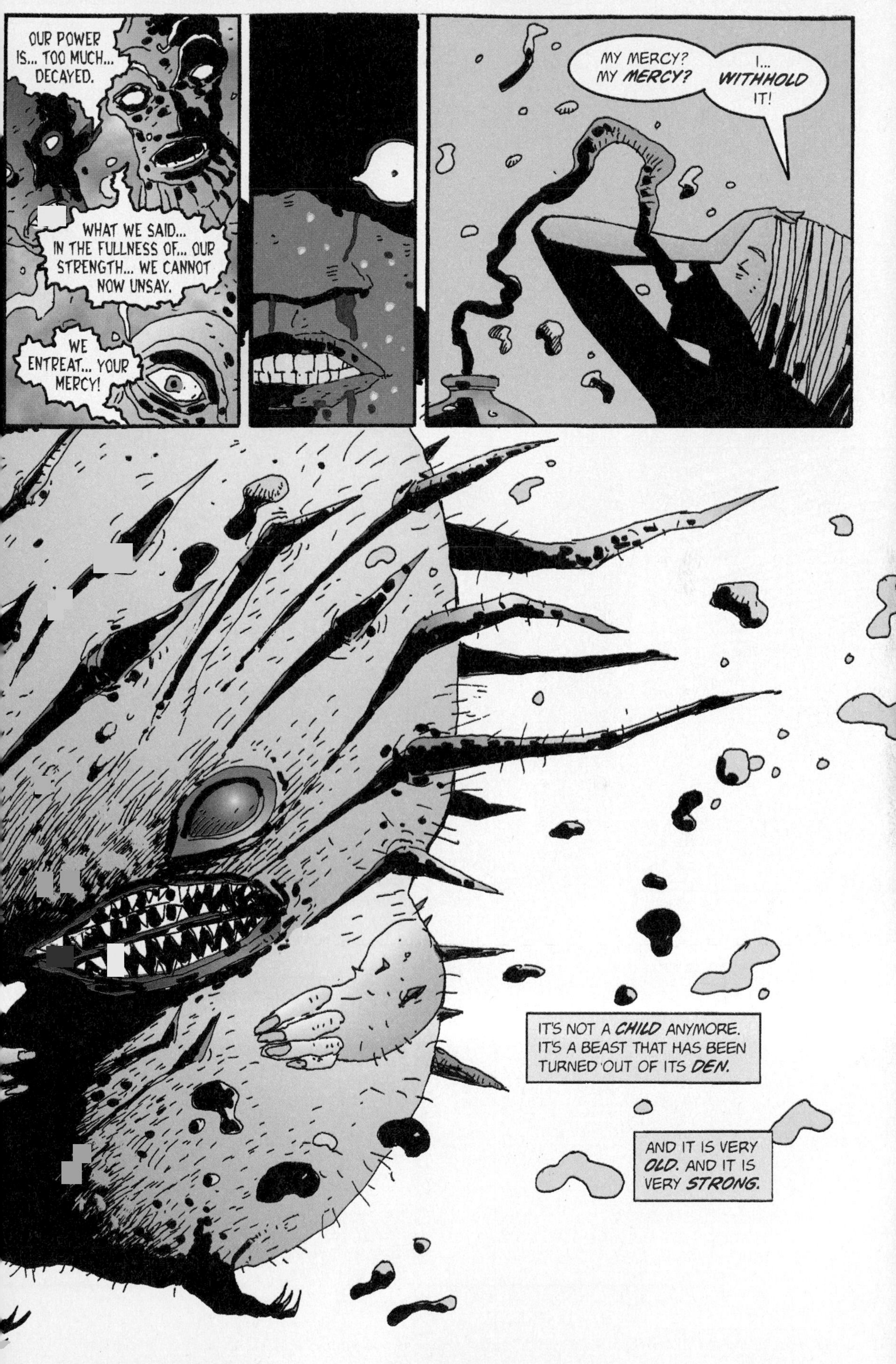
OUR POWER IS... TOO MUCH... DECAYED.
WHAT WE SAID... IN THE FULLNESS OF... OUR STRENGTH... WE CANNOT NOW UNSAY.
WE ENTREAT... YOUR MERCY!
MY MERCY? MY MERCY?
I... WITHHOLD IT!
IT'S NOT A CHILD ANYMORE. IT'S A BEAST THAT HAS BEEN TURNED OUT OF ITS DEN.
AND IT IS VERY OLD. AND IT IS VERY STRONG.

IT TAKES A LONG TIME.
EVEN IN DECAY, THE GODS DON'T DIE EASILY.
THE CONTENTS OF THE BOTTLE ROIL AND PITCH IN SILENT TURMOIL.
WHEN IT'S OVER, THE ANGRY LITTLE CLOUD SWIRLS ALONE IN ITS NEW HOME.
PUSHES AGAINST THE WALLS OF THE COLD, GLASS WOMB.
THE ROOM IS FULL OF DEATH, AND NONE OF IT IS HERS.
SHE STANDS WITH THE SEETHING BOTTLE IN HER HAND, LIKE A BRIDESMAID CLUTCHING THE BOUQUET.
WHILE THE WEDDING CAR RECEDES INTO UNREACHABLE DISTANCE.
AND SHE KNOWS IN THE STONY FASTNESS OF HER HEART THAT HER TURN WILL NEVER COME.
THIS IS MY BABY, SHE THINKS AS SHE WALKS AWAY. WHAT IS INSIDE ME NOW IS JUST A DOLL-- MADE OF FLESH.
A SHARP DOUBT PIERCES THE DULLNESS. PERHAPS AFTER ALL--
THERE ARE SPECIAL PLACES IN HELL.

OTHER NAMES FOLLOWED, AND OTHER CITIES.
ROME. OSLO. LA PAZ. IT MADE NO DIFFERENCE. THE TIDE STILL TURNED IN THE *DARK* BEFORE EACH DAY'S DAWNING.
AND DEATH WAS STILL *CLOSED* TO HER.

IN PARIS SHE DRANK TEPID ESPRESSO AT A PAVEMENT CAFÉ IN THE MARAIS.
WHERE AFTER A WHILE A *MAN* CAME AND JOINED HER.

I DIDN'T THINK YOU'D DO ANYTHING SO *JEJUNE* AS TO GLOAT.
OR IS *TORTURE* STILL YOUR STOCK IN TRADE?
MERCI. RIEN POUR MOI.

NO, TODAY MY STOCK IN TRADE IS DEATH.
ASSUMING YOU'RE STILL IN THE *MARKET* FOR SUCH A THING.

DEATH? *MY* DEATH? BUT... BUT YOU REFUSED ME! YOU SAID--
I SAID YOU HAD NOTHING I *WANTED*.
WHICH WAS PERFECTLY TRUE. AT THE TIME--

THE *BOTTLE*, PRIESTESS.
IT HAS A GREAT MANY USES--PARTICULARLY IF GIVEN *FREELY*.

MY BABY? YOU THINK I'D LET YOU USE MY BABY?
WHY NOT? YOU DID.
REVENGE MAY BE A SWEET DISH, BUT IT'S NOT GENERALLY FOUND ON THE CHILDREN'S MENU.
IT WOULD FEED ONE MORE TIME. A MEAL OF MY CHOOSING, AT MY DISCRETION.
AND THEN IT, TOO, WOULD BE RELEASED INTO DEATH.
I HAVE OTHER MATTERS TO ATTEND TO. IF YOU AGREE, TOUCH MY HAND.
OH GODS! I CAN'T... I CAN'T JUST GIVE YOU...
WHAT WOULD YOU DO WITH IT? WOULD IT BE DAMNED?
THE SPRING WIND BLEW A SCATTERING OF DUST ALONG THE RUE DANTE TOWARDS NOTRE DAME.
THE OTHER PATRONS RUBBED THEIR EYES, AND THE WAITER CURSED WHEN HE SAW THAT THE CORNER TABLE WAS EMPTY.
THE SMELL OF BRIAR ROSE HE TOOK TO BE THE LADY'S PERFUME.
BUT LUCIFER WALKED BACK ALONG THE BOUQUINISTES, UNTOUCHED BY THE SCURRYING DUST.
REFLECTING, NOT ON DEATH, BUT ON THE PROFIT THAT CAN BE TURNED FROM THE LEAST PROMISING OF TRANSACTIONS.
AND HE CONSIDERED HIS DAY WELL SPENT.
NEXT: CHILDREN AND MONSTERS, PART ONE

crayons
Fegredo

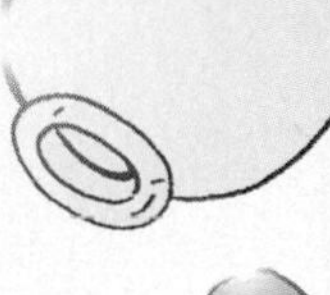

Children & Monsters

Written by MIKE CAREY Layouts by PETER GROSS Finishes by RYAN KELLY and PETER GROSS
Lettered by COMICRAFT Colored and Separated by DANIEL VOZZO
Assistant Editor WILL DENNIS
Editor SHELLY BOND

Based on characters created by GAIMAN, KIETH and DRINGENBERG

THE SILVER CITY.
AFRAID? OF LUCIFER?
AS ALWAYS, AMENADIEL, YOU THINK LOOSELY AND SPEAK COARSELY.
THEN WHY DO WE SIT AND DEBATE STRATEGY INSTEAD OF FIGHTING HIM?
WHY DO WE WATCH HIS COMINGS AND GOINGS LIKE GOSSIPS PEERING FROM BEHIND OUR CURTAINS?
URIEL.
LET US BE BLUNT.
HE HAS OPENED A GATEWAY INTO THE VOID BEYOND CREATION. HE HAS A PLAN ALREADY AFOOT, AND WE DON'T KNOW WHAT IT IS.
TO ACT IN IGNORANCE IS TO RISK MUCH.
ZELAH.
MY CONCERN IS THIS: LUCIFER CONSULTED THE ORACLE OF THE BASANOS, IN THE HUMAN CITY OF HAMBURG.
DOES THIS NOT MEAN HE KNOWS OUR INTENTIONS?
THAT WHATEVER WE DECIDE TODAY, HE HAS ANTICIPATED?

RAPHAEL.
THE LIGHTBRINGER DOES NOT COW ME, AS HE MAY OTHERS. BUT I AM THINKING ABOUT THE CHILD HE SAW WHEN HE WENT TO LONDON.
THE ADVERSARY, AND A HUMAN CHILD. I FEAR THE CORRUPTION THAT HE WEAVES, AND THE FOULNESS OF HIS SELF-LOVE.
CASOR.
A CERTAIN MEASURE OF FEAR IS WISDOM. HE WENT DOWN TO THE AFTERWORLD OF IZANAMI, SURRENDERING HIS IMMORTALITY AT THE GATE.
HE FACED THE GODS OF THAT PLACE, POWERLESS AND ALONE.
IT IS NOT KNOWN WHAT PASSED BETWEEN THEM, BUT HE RETURNED WITH HIS WINGS ONCE MORE UPON HIS BACK.
HE IS AS MIGHTY AS HE EVER WAS.
MAY I REMIND YOU -- AGAIN -- THAT WE DEFEATED HIM ONCE.
AYE. WITH MICHAEL AT OUR SIDE.
WITHOUT HIM, THE OUTCOME MAY BE DIFFERENT.
AMENADIEL.
ON THAT OCCASION LUCIFER HAD A THIRD OF THE HOST UNDER HIS BANNER.
NOW A SINGLE DAUGHTER OF LILITH IS ALL HE CAN MUSTER.
WHILE OUR OWN NUMBERS ARE ALL BUT INFINITE.

IN FACT, THIS PRESENTS US WITH SOMETHING OF A LOGISTICAL PROBLEM.
BRINGING SUCH A FORCE TO BEAR AGAINST SO SMALL A TARGET IS LIKE ASKING THEM TO *DANCE* ON THE HEAD OF A PIN.

"IT IS NO MATTER. WE MUST *ACCEPT* THAT OUR CASUALTIES WILL BE HEAVY.
"IF WE POUR THRONES AND SERAPHS ON HIM LIKE *RAIN*--"

You see? You can't harm me.
Your mother gave you to me. So you're bound by her word and my will.
Learn my face, and my smell. Remember my voice.
I'm your master.
Anyone else you find here comes under the heading of food.
Now stay.
Until I whistle.
Come in, Mazikeen.
I'm available now if it's something quick.

THERE'S NO NEED TO KNEEL.
COME TO THINK OF IT, THERE'S NO NEED TO WEAR THE MASK ANYMORE, EITHER.
IS THAT THE POINT?

THIS... IS NOT MY VOICE, LORD.
THIS IS NOT... MY FACE.
THEY ARE WOUNDS... THAT OPEN AGAIN... EVERY TIME I SPEAK.

IRONICALLY, THEY WERE INTENDED AS BLESSINGS.
BUT IN THE HANDS OF A WILLFUL CHILD, EVEN THE POWER OF THE BASANOS IS LIMITED.
JILL PRESTO REBUILT YOUR FACE BY GUESSWORK.

I WILL... KILL HER... WHEN I SEE HER NEXT. HER MOTIVES DO NOT... MATTER TO ME.
BUT MY LORD... THIS THING...
IT RESISTS... MY WILL. IT DOES NOT CHANGE.
MMM.

I UNDERSTAND. YOU'VE BEEN ACCUSTOMED TO CHOOSE YOUR APPEARANCE, AS YOUR KIND DO.
BUT THE MOLD OF THE BASANOS IS ALMOST INDELIBLE.
THE POWER NEEDED TO REMOVE IT WILL BE ENORMOUS.

WE'LL PUT THIS DISCUSSION OFF UNTIL LATER.
WE HAVE A GUEST COMING OVER --
-- AND HE DOESN'T HAVE ANY DIRECTIONS.

NORTH LONDON.
C M S E
RO_ _A_ _
K_ _AI!
"FOR HE SCORES IT IN SCARLET HIMSELF ON HIS OWN BESPOKEN."
BISHOP LAUD
ROMAN CATHOLIC SECONDARY SCHOOL
FOR GIRLS AND BOYS
YOU SEE WHAT HE'S DOING HERE? SCORES IT IN SCARLET. THE ALLITERATION ON THE "S" AGAIN.
UMMM... ELAINE. TRY STANZA THIRTY-FOUR.
OH! STANZA THIRTY-FOUR.
SORRY, MISS. I'VE LOST THE --
OH YEAH.
"NOW BURN, NEW-BORN TO THE WORLD, DOUBLE-NATURED NAME. THE HEAVEN FLUNG, HEART-FURLED, MAIDEN-FLESHED MIRACLE OF MARY IN FLAME."
"MID... MID-NUMBERED..."
THANK YOU. WELL READ.
NOW YOU WON'T GET MUCH SENSE OUT OF THAT, BUT LISTEN TO THE SOUNDS OF IT.
EVERY LINE STIFF WITH ALLITERATION.
HE'S TALKING ABOUT THE MESSIAH, OF COURSE.
BRRRING
TRY IT FOR YOURSELF FOR HOMEWORK.
AN EIGHT-LINE POEM WITH SOME ALLITERATION ON EVERY LINE.

IT WAS RONAN KEATING.

I *KNOW* IT WAS. I WAS GOING TO GUESS THE "N" NEXT.

ELAINE. *ELAIIIIIIIIIINE!*

LIFE IS A BOWL OF TOE-JAM, JUST GOTTA BI-ITE IT.

UHH... I'LL CATCH YOU UP, OKAY?

HELLO? WHO'S THERE?

COME ON, I HEARD YOU CALLING ME.

I KNOW YOU'RE HERE.

IS THIS SOME KIND OF A JOKE?

OR DID YOU WANT TO TALK TO ME?

YES.

LET'S *TALK.*

IF THIS IS SOMETHING THAT COULD WAIT...

...LIKE MAYBE 'TIL BREAK?

NO, WE'VE GOT TO HAVE A WORD, POPPET.
IT'S FAMILY BUSINESS, AS YOU MIGHT SAY.
GRANDMAS, YOU SHOULDN'T BE OUT IN DAYLIGHT!
I'M LATE FOR PHYSICS. YOU'RE GOING TO GET ME INTO TROUBLE.
AYE, WELL...
TROUBLE IS ALREADY SNIFFING AFTER YOU, GRANDDAUGHTER. THAT'S WHY WE'RE HERE.
WHAT SORT OF TROUBLE?
THE WORST SORT, DEAREST. THE SORT THAT SNEAKS UP ON YOU SIDELONG, COAXING AND COSSETING.
LOOK AROUND YOU. WHEN DID YOU EVER KNOW US ALL TO COME IN CONCLAVE LIKE THIS?
WE'VE A WARNING FOR YOU, POPPET -- AND ANSWERS, TOO, IF YOU'VE GOT QUESTIONS AS NEEDS ANSWERING.
QUESTIONS? ABOUT WHAT?
YOUR NAME. YOUR NATURE. THE LITTLE KNACKS THAT MAKES YOU DIFFERENT.

THERE'S THINGS YOU NEED TO KNOW. BUT RULES IS RULES.
YOU GOT TO ASK THE RIGHT QUESTIONS, AND THEN WE'LL ANSWER.

I TOLD YOU, I'M LATE FOR PHYSICS.
OKAY. OKAY, BUT NOT NOW.
JUST GIVE ME THE WARNING, PLEASE, GRANDMAS.

VERY WELL. THE ONE WHO MADE YOU CAN STILL BREAK YOU.
DON'T DEFY HIM, OR GIVE HIM CAUSE FOR ANGER.
TRUST NOBODY EXCEPT FOR CHILDREN -- AND MONSTERS.

ER... ELAINE? MR. FISHER TOLD ME TO COME AND GET YOU.
ARE YOU... ARE YOU OKAY?
OF COURSE I'M OKAY, BARRY. I'M DOING VOICE EXERCISES. YOU KNOW, FOR THE CHOIR.

OH, RIGHT.

"BEWARE OF THE EVERYTHING."
GREAT.

"AND IN A WHOLE DIFFERENT TIME ZONE, WAY ACROSS THE OCEAN IN NYC, I WOKE UP WITH A START.
"NOT KNOWING WHERE I WAS, OR EVEN, FOR A MOMENT, WHO.
"NOTHING UNUSUAL. MY CATALEPSY WAS SO BAD BACK THEN, IT WOULD HAPPEN TO ME THREE OR FOUR TIMES A DAY.
"THE ONLY REASON I DIDN'T MISS MY STATION THAT DAY IS BECAUSE SOMEONE JUMPED UNDER THE TRAIN AT 101ST STREET.
"HOW CAN PEOPLE WANT TO SEE SOMETHING LIKE THAT?
"FOR SOME REASON I THOUGHT ABOUT THAT GAME I USED TO PLAY WITH JUDE, WHERE SHE'D THINK OF AN APPALLING PRODUCT, AND I'D COME BACK WITH A SLOGAN FOR IT.
"SO HOW WOULD YOU MARKET DEATH?
"'LITERALLY THE ULTIMATE EXPERIENCE.'
"'NO INSURANCE! NO TRAVEL SICKNESS! IT'S A HASSLE-FREE ONE-WAY TRIP!'
"IT'S NOT EVEN AS THOUGH DEATH IS SO BAD, I THOUGHT. SOME OF THE ALTERNATIVES... WELL, JEEZ.
"NOT THE TRAIN, THOUGH. THAT'S WAY TOO MESSY. AND NO SLASHED WRISTS.
"YOU WOULDN'T WANT TO BE SITTING THERE, PUMPING LIKE A FIRE HYDRANT AND THINKING 'I'VE CHANGED MY MIND!'
"THERE ARE ALWAYS GUNS, OF COURSE, BUT WHAT DO YOU NEED TO GET ONE?
"FILL IN FORMS? SHOW A CLEAN BILL OF MENTAL HEATH? HAH.
"AND AROUND ABOUT THEN, I REALIZED WHAT I WAS DOING.
"'DEAD MAN WALKING,' I THOUGHT. AND I LAUGHED, LIKE YOUR TYPICAL NEW YORK CRAZY PERSON GETTING OFF ON HIS OWN INNER VOICES.
"AND THEN I WENT HOME.
"TO KILL MYSELF."

Thank you, Mazikeen.
A certain amount of REDUNDANCY is going to be necessary here.
REDUNDANCY?
CHARCOAL FROM THE DOORPOSTS. EARTH FROM THE THRESHOLD.
TAKE PLENTY.
WE NEED TO BE ABSOLUTELY CERTAIN THAT HE'LL FIND US.
THIS IS A LITTLE LIKE USING A SUPERNOVA AS A SIGNAL FLARE, BUT WHEN SUBTLETY'S NOT GOING TO DO THE JOB --
-- YOU MIGHT AS WELL GO FOR GLORIOUS, TASTELESS EXCESS.
THERE. IT'S DONE.
I'D LIKE TO SEE HIM LOSE HIS WAY NOW.

THE DREAMING
HOW COME I GOTTA STAND OUT HERE LIKE SOME KINDA POTTED SHRUB?
IT SMELLS LIKE FRIED BILE, MERVYN. FRIED BILE LEFT TO SOUR.
IT'S JUST A CIGAR.
IT DOES NOT.
A GOOD CIGAR IS LIKE A GOOD WOMAN, YA KNOW? SMOOTH, AND ROUND, AND --
AND --
SAY WHAT?
HEY, LOOK, LOOSH. IT'S RAININ' DOORS.
WHADDYA MAKE OF THAT?
HMM.
I'D SAY THAT SOMEONE IS SENDING OUT AN INVITATION.
SOMEONE WHO DOESN'T CARE ABOUT INCURRING OUR LORD'S ANGER.
TOSS A COIN.

IT WAS SLAUGHTER.
BLOOD AND HAIR ON THE WALLS.
I MEAN, LOOK. THIRTY-SIX PERCENT YIELD OVER THREE YEARS, AND A GUARANTEED OPTION AT TERM.
EXCELLENT. GRAN CANARIA IS *ON*, THEN.
OH YES.
MILK. MOTHER. MOSS. MOOSE. MOUSE.
GIRL. GOD. GHOST. GOOD. GRIEF.
DAD, WHAT ELSE BEGINS WITH G?
WHAT'S THAT, SQUEAK?
YOU KNOW. FOR ***ALLITERATION.*** LIKE GERALD HOPKINS DOES.
JESUS! THEY'VE GOT YOU READING ***HOPKINS*** IN YEAR SEVEN?
I DIDN'T TOUCH THAT STUFF UNTIL MY ***A LEVELS.***
HERE YOU GO, ELAINE. THE SHORTER OXFORD DICTIONARY.
ALL THE G WORDS YOU CAN HANDLE.

IP, DIP, DOO, THE CAT GOT THE FLU. THE DOG CAUGHT SIXTY-THREE HENS --
MONA! WHAT ARE YOU A-DOING OF, GIRL?
OOP!
THAT'S NOT FAIR, GRANDMA FURNESS!
I WAS UP TO SIXTY-THREE AND NOW I'VE GOT TO START AGAIN.
GAMES, IS IT? WELL, THIS ISN'T NO TIME TO BE FOOLING WITH RHYMES AND HOOPLAS.
CAN'T YOU SMELL THE BURNIN'? CAN'T YOU TASTE THE BLOOD?
NO. I CAN'T. I CAN'T TASTE ANYTHING ANYMORE, THANKS VERY MUCH.
NOT SINCE I GOT KILLED.
AYE, WELL, DEATH'S NO GREAT MATTER, ONCE YOU'RE USED TO IT.
BUT THERE'S SOMETHING OUT THERE THAT'S WAITING TO BE BORN, AND THAT I DO FEAR.
IT OPENS ITS MOUTH AND THERE'S NOTHING INSIDE.
AND OUR LAINIE'S RIGHT IN THE PATH OF IT.

"OKAY, SO WINTERSON SUFFERED AS A GAY TEEN IN A FUNDAMENTAL RELIGION. BUT NOW SHE'S THE ONE WITH THE CROSS AND THE NAILS, AND THIS REVIEWER ISN'T LOOKING TO BE PUT UP FOR THE EASTER HOLIDAYS."
THAT'S GOOD, MATT. I *LIKE* THAT.
OKAY, SQUEAK, LET'S SEE WHAT YOU'VE GOT.
UHH? I DIDN'T...
I DIDN'T FIND ANYTHING YET.
"AND I SAW A NEW HEAVEN, AND A NEW EARTH, FOR THE FIRST HEAVEN AND THE FIRST EARTH WERE PASSED AWAY."
THAT'S NOT HOPKINS. THAT'S JOHN THE DIVINE.
DAD, WHAT ARE YOU *ON* ABOUT?
IT'S OKAY, SQUEAK. I ALWAYS LOVED THAT BIBLICAL BLOOD AND THUNDER TOO -- BUT DON'T TRY TO *SNOW* ME BECAUSE I KNOW YOUR HANDWRITING.
YEAH.
SO DO I.

"SO I DIDN'T HAVE A CAR AND A HOSEPIPE, OR A PENTHOUSE APARTMENT I COULD CONVENIENTLY JUMP OUT OF.
"BUT PILLS -- THOSE I HAD. THREE BOTTLES OF TEMAZEPAM THAT JUDE LEFT BEHIND.
"SLEEPING PILLS. A PRESENT FROM THE GOD OF CHEAP SHOTS.
"I DIDN'T BOTHER WITH A NOTE. SOME SUICIDES ARE JUST PURELY SELF-EXPLANATORY.
"'I LOST MY WIFE. I LOST MY JOB. YOU NEED A PICTURE?'
"I COUNTED DOWN FROM A HUNDRED. BY EIGHTY I COULDN'T LIFT MY HAND UP.
"MY EYES WERE STARTING TO DEFOCUS, TOO. THIS WAS SO EASY. I SHOULD'VE DONE IT YEARS AGO.
"BUT SOMEHOW THE LONG BLACK CLOUD REFUSED TO COME DOWN.
"AT ZERO I WAS STILL AWAKE. STILL ALIVE.
"A CHILD WAS CRYING SOMEWHERE, A LONG WAY AWAY, AND THE NOISE WOULDN'T LET ME SLEEP.
"SO FINALLY, RELUCTANTLY, I HAULED MYSELF OUT OF BED.
"AND SET OFF TO LOOK FOR THAT SAD LITTLE KID."

"I PASSED GIRLS WITH STA-FRESH™ SMILES. THE BEEF-CUBE MAN. CAPTAIN CODFISH GAVE ME THE BREADED FINGER.
"I KEPT RIGHT ON GOING. I'M NOT IN ADVERTISING ANYMORE, NOT SINCE THIS MORNING. I DON'T HAVE TO SOCIALIZE WITH THESE PEOPLE.
"THE SUNSPLASH RAISINS WERE DOING THEIR WAR DANCE ON A GIANT KITCHEN WORKTOP.
"THERE WAS A RAVEN THERE, TOO, BUT I FIGURED HE WAS JUST A TYPO.
ORANGE JUICE
ORANGE JUICE
KNOW WHAT A FISH ON A HOOK FEELS LIKE, PAL?
NO.
YOU SHOULD.
"FINALLY I FOUND MYSELF IN A STARLIT RUIN, AND ALL SOUND DIED AT ONCE.
"EXCEPT THAT THERE WAS SOMEONE PLAYING A PIANO. SOMETHING BAROQUE, I THINK. MAYBE PACHELBEL'S CANON.

HELP YOURSELF TO A DRINK.
IT'S A LUSSAC ST. EMILION. BETTER THAN AVERAGE.

AM I... AM I DREAMING ALL THIS?
NO.

YOU WALKED THROUGH A DREAM TO GET HERE, BUT THIS PLACE IS IN THE WAKING WORLD.
OUR DISCUSSION CALLS FOR PRIVACY, AND THE DREAMING IS A VERY PUBLIC PLACE.

THERE WAS A CHILD. A CHILD CRYING. WAS THAT REAL TOO?
NOT EXACTLY. THAT WAS THE THREAD THAT LED YOU THROUGH THE MAZE, SO TO SPEAK.
BUT IN A DEEPER SENSE, YES. THE CHILD IS REAL. WAS REAL.
I DIDN'T MANUFACTURE THE SOUND. I FOUND IT IN THE ABYSS OF THINGS PAST AND BROUGHT IT HERE.
SO THAT YOU COULD HEAR IT.
I DON'T UNDERSTAND.
THINK OF IT AS THE ANSWER TO A QUESTION YOU HAVEN'T ASKED ME YET.
OH MY GOD! ARE YOU TELLING ME...?
WHAT I SAW THAT NIGHT! WHEN JUDE --
HOLY CHRIST! DID IT REALLY HAPPEN?
YOU SAW WHAT YOU THOUGHT YOU SAW. YOU WERE VISITED BY AN ANGEL.
YOUR WIFE WAS THE VICTIM OF A ROBBERY, TO WHICH YOU WERE THE ONLY WITNESS.
GOODBYE, MR. EASTERMAN.
"I WAS LYING ON MY OWN BED. UNDER MY HAND THERE WAS A PIECE OF PAPER...
"I MADE IT TO THE BATHROOM AND STUCK MY FINGERS DOWN MY THROAT.
"I CARRIED ON UNTIL I WAS HEAVING NOTHING BUT AIR.
"DEATH WASN'T AN OPTION ANYMORE."

HAS HE GONE?
YES, HE HAS. I THOUGHT HE HANDLED RATHER *WELL*. EASY TO AIM, AND EASY TO FIRE.
YOU SAID THAT WE WOULD *TALK*. AFTERWARDS. ABOUT MY FACE.

YOUR FACE... IT HAS A MOST *RELENTLESS* SYMMETRY, NOW.
A CIRCULAR, SELF-REFERENTIAL PERFECTION.
IT IS... INTERESTING.

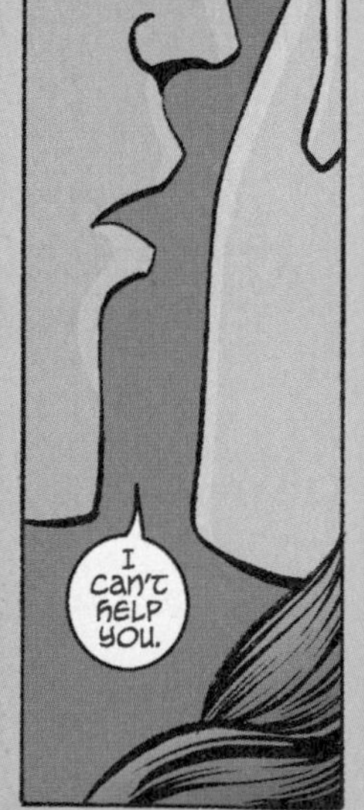

"I TRIED TO CALL JUDE BUT I JUST GOT HER BOYFRIEND'S ANSWERING MACHINE. NO TIME TO WAIT. I THREW SOME CLOTHES INTO A BAG AND WENT OUT TO JFK.
"THINKING UP SLOGANS FOR SHITTY STICKS. CANNED EYEBALLS. SPEW-U-LIKE.
"THE PIECE OF PAPER IN MY POCKET BURNING AGAINST MY HAND LIKE A BRANDING IRON.
LONDON, PLEASE. GOING OUT TODAY. AS SOON AS POSSIBLE.
CERTAINLY, SIR. AND COMING BACK...?
I'M NOT... I'M NOT ACTUALLY SURE. JUST GIVE ME A ONE-WAY TICKET.
AND MAKE IT A WINDOW SEAT, PLEASE.
"I DIDN'T NEED TO BUY A BOOK BECAUSE I'D PROBABLY SLEEP THE WHOLE WAY.
"HENCE THE WINDOW SEAT. IT MEANS PEOPLE DON'T HAVE TO STEP OVER ME ALL THE TIME.
"THEY USED TO CALL THE DEVIL THE FATHER OF LIES.
"BUT FOR SOMEONE WHOSE SIN IS MEANT TO BE PRIDE, YOU'D THINK THAT LYING WOULD LEAVE SOMETHING OF A SOUR TASTE.
"TOO EASY. TOO SLEAZY. TOO MUCH OF A COWARD'S TOOL.
"SO MY THEORY IS THAT WHEN THE DEVIL WANTS TO GET SOMETHING OUT OF YOU, HE DOESN'T LIE AT ALL.
"HE TELLS YOU THE EXACT, LITERAL TRUTH.

"AND HE LETS YOU FIND YOUR *OWN* WAY TO HELL."

LONDON.
AND THEN SHE GOES, SOMETHING IS GOING TO BE BORN, RIGHT?

AND I'M LIKE. WHAT SORT OF SOMETHING, GRANDMA F.?
AND SHE COMES BACK WITH, "OH, YOU KNOW, SOMETHING BIG AND AWFUL WITH ITS MOUTH WIDE OPEN."
THAT WAS ALL SHE SAID?
YEAH. OH, AND SHE ASKED ME IF I COULD SMELL SOMETHING ON FIRE.
GREAT. SO I JUST HAVE TO LOOK OUT FOR BURNING BABIES WITH BIG MOUTHS.

CAN'T YOU JUST ASK HER WHAT'S GOING TO HAPPEN TO YOU?
I THOUGHT THE GRANDMAS SAID THEY'D TELL YOU ANYTHING YOU WANT TO KNOW.

IT'S NOT THAT EASY, MONA.
HOW COME?
BECAUSE WHAT THEY WANT TO TALK ABOUT IS ME.
THEY WANT TO EXPLAIN HOW COME I CAN DO ALL THE WEIRD STUFF.

OH... IS THAT BAD?
YES! YES IT IS!
I DON'T WANT TO KNOW!

IT'S LIKE... THE ONLY WAY I CAN GO ON PRETENDING TO BE NORMAL IS IF EVERYONE ELSE PRETENDS, TOO.
I WANT TO KNOW WHAT THIS DANGER IS THAT'S COMING.
I DON'T WANT TO BE GIVEN A... A SECRET ORIGIN OR SOMETHING.

I GUESS WE JUST HAVE TO WAIT AND SEE.
HOW BAD CAN IT BE, ANYWAY?
THANKS, MONA. SPOKEN LIKE A DEAD PERSON.

"I USED TO WORRY ABOUT SO MANY THINGS THAT DON'T MATTER NOW.
"JOB. BILLS. RELATIONSHIPS. ALL THE USUAL SHIT.
"SORRY. I SHOULDN'T TALK LIKE THAT TO YOU, BUT YOU KNOW WHAT I MEAN.
"I'M AMAZED NOW, LOOKING BACK, AT HOW MUCH OF MY LIFE I SPENT BEING AFRAID.
YOU SEE? NO ONE'S GONNA BUST A PISS-PIT LIKE THIS. IT'S A PRIVATE ROOM, MAN.
I SUPPOSE. COME ON THEN. COOK UP.
HEY, SEAN. YOU BEEN RIDIN' BAREBACK, JUS' LATELY?
PISS OFF. IF YOU DON'T WANNA SHARE MY STUFF, YOU DON'T SODDING WELL 'AVE TO.
"IT'S NOT AS THOUGH FEAR EVEN HELPS.
"IT DOESN'T KEEP THE WOLF FROM THE DOOR.
"OR MAKE THE TRUCK ON THE FREEWAY SWERVE AND MISS YOU, OR WHATEVER.
"IT'S JUST A WASTE OF EFFORT. A WASTE OF TIME.
"MENTAL POLLUTION.
FUCK ME! THIS PLACE IS HUGE.
"AND IN THE END...
"...THE TRUCK IS GOING TO HIT YOU JUST THE SAME."
I MEAN, LIKE THE FRIGGIN' TARDIS. YOU GOTTA COME AND --

WHAT? I CAN'T HEAR YOU.
THUK
FOR FUCK'S SAKE MARK, IT'LL BE READY IN HALF A --
KLUDD
UNCLE S... SANDALPHON?
THE P... PERIMETER IS S... SEC... SECURE.
GOOD.
NOW CLEAN UP THE MESS, CAL.
THERE'S A GOOD BOY.
Children & MONSTERS
Part Two
Written by MIKE CAREY Layouts by PETER GROSS
Finishes by RYAN KELLY and PETER GROSS Colors MARGUERITE VAN COOK Separations JAMISON
Lettered by COMICRAFT Assistant Editor WILL DENNIS Editor SHELLY BOND
Based on characters created by GAIMAN, KIETH and DRINGENBERG

Los Angeles.
I am the resurrection, and the life.
In this instance at least. Welcome back, Musubi.
I am... alive. You were as good as your word, Lucifer Morningstar.
You're not a resource to be so lightly thrown away.
And now you're considering how best to kill me, and how soon.
A word to the wise:
This is not the house of windowless rooms.
I'm in my place of power and the gauge shows full.
One bite -- one scratch and I'll snap my fingers and put you among the things that were.

YOU MISUNDERSTAND ME, LORD LUCIFER. I OWE YOU MY LIFE AND MY FREEDOM.
I PLEDGE MY FEALTY TO YOU, FREELY AND FOREVER.
AS YOU DID TO KAGUTSUCHI?
KAGUTSUCHI TOOK ME AS THE SPOILS OF BATTLE. HE HAD AS MUCH OF MY LOYALTY AS HE COULD ENFORCE.
THIS IS MOST CURIOUS. WHERE DOES IT LEAD?
IT LEADS NOWHERE.
COSMICALLY SPEAKING, THE GROUND FLOOR.
THE HOST OF HEAVEN WOULD CHEW THEIR ARMS OFF AT THE ELBOWS TO CLOSE IT.
ANGELS.
MMM. ANGELS ARE A LITTLE LIKE GODS, I THINK.
THAT SOUR SELF-RIGHTEOUSNESS THAT STICKS IN THE TEETH LIKE FINE BONES.
WHICH BRINGS ME TO THE POINT.
THE DEMON WHO WAS TO HAVE GUARDED THE GATE IS OFF LOOKING FOR HER FACE. AND I HAVE ONE LAST ERRAND TO RUN BEFORE THE FIREWORKS START.
DO YOU THINK YOU CAN KEEP THE ARMY OF HEAVEN ENTERTAINED UNTIL I GET BACK?
OH YESSSS. MOST CERTAINLY. EVEN IF YOU WERE NOT THE LORD OF MY DUTY...
...THAT WOULD BE MY PLEASURE.

THE SILVER CITY.
THERE WERE NO DISSENTING VOICES.
EVEN RAPHAEL, SPEAKING FOR THE ARCHANGELS, AGREED TO THIS ACTION.
AS OF NOW, HEAVEN IS ON A WAR FOOTING.

YOU UNDERSTAND ME? IT IS NO LONGER A QUESTION OF WHETHER WE WIN OR LOSE.
THE HOST IS A SINGLE SWORD, UNSHEATHED AND PLACED IN MY HAND.

WHAT IS STILL AT ISSUE IS HOW MANY MORE MUST DIE, BESIDES THE MORNINGSTAR.
AND IT IS THERE, NOBLE CHERUBIM, THAT YOU CAN HELP ME.

UNCERTAINTY. AMBIVALENCE. WILLINGNESS TO LISTEN.
SUSPENSION OF JUDGMENT. CONTINUED ATTENTION.
THE THEATRE OF WAR WILL BE NOT HEAVEN, BUT EARTH.

HE HAS BUILT HIMSELF A HOUSE IN A POPULOUS CITY. MORTAL MEN AND WOMEN TEEM AROUND HIM.
NO DOUBT HE FLATTERS HIMSELF THAT WE DARE NOT STRIKE HIM WHERE SO MANY INNOCENTS MUST WITHER IN THE BLAST.

WRONG, SERPENT.
WRONG ON EVERY COUNT.

WHAT DO YOU SAY, SQUEAK? YOU WANT TO GO FOR A NEW WORLD RECORD?
UMM. I DUNNO, DAD. I'M NOT REALLY ON GAME FORM THIS MORNING.
MAYBE ONE ROUND.

O-O-OKAY. JUST FOR A CHANGE, START FROM GERMANIUM --
-- AND GO BACKWARDS.

GERMANIUM, GALLIUM, ZINC, COPPER, NICKEL...
SLIDING DOORS. CONVEYOR BELT. CUDDLY TOY.
...COBALT, IRON, MANGANESE... STOP PUTTING ME OFF, THAT'S NOT FAIR!

BONG CLANG
STOP THE CLOCK. FIVE-MINUTE TIMEOUT.
IT'S OKAY, I'LL GET IT.

BONGCLANG CLANG
I'M COMING, JESUS.

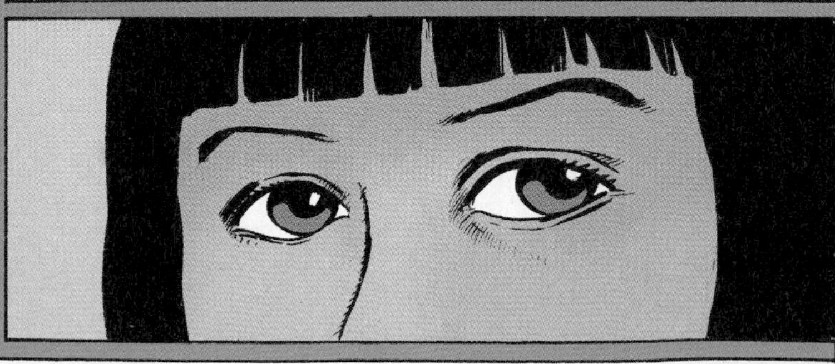

ER. HI. GOOD MORNING. I WAS WONDERING --
COULD I SPEAK WITH ELAINE BELLOC, PLEASE?

ELAINE?
I'M SORRY, I DON'T UNDERSTAND. WHY DO YOU NEED TO SPEAK TO MY DAUGHTER?

WELL THAT'S JUST IT. SHE'S NOT YOUR DAUGHTER, SHE'S MY DAUGHTER.

BUT I GUESS YOU ALREADY KNOW THAT.

BABS, GET ELAINE BACK IN THE KITCHEN. NOW.
MATT, DON'T --

YOU BASTARD! YOU SICK BASTARD!

I DON'T KNOW WHO YOU THINK YOU ARE --
I THINK... I'M ELAINE'S FATHER.

-- YOU COME NEAR MY FAMILY AGAIN...
...I'M GOING TO RIP YOUR FUCKING THROAT OUT!
I JUST... I JUST WANT TO SEE HER!

I'M CALLING THE POLICE.

PLEASE.

SLAM
AARH!

DAD, WHO WAS THAT? HE SOUNDED AMERICAN.
SOME SORT OF LUNATIC. GO BACK INTO THE KITCHEN, ELAINE.
HELLO? POLICE, PLEASE.

OH GOD, MATT. THIS IS AWFUL.
WHAT'S HAPPENING? WHAT DID HE SAY?
WE'LL TALK ABOUT IT LATER, BABS NOT NOW.

HELLO? YES, MY NAME IS MATTHEW BELLOC. I'M CALLING FROM THIRTY-THREE CRESCENT, KENSAL RISE.
I WANT TO REPORT A STALKER. HE'S BEEN FOLLOWING MY DAUGHTER AND WE THINK HE MAY BE VIOLENT.

GO AND GET YOUR SATCHEL, ELAINE. WE'D BEST GET YOU TO SCHOOL.
BUT HE HASN'T BEEN FOLLOWING ME, HAS HE? I'VE NEVER SEEN HIM BEFORE!
YES. YES, THANK YOU, THAT WOULD BE VERY WELCOME.

WHAT ARE WE GOING TO DO?
WHAT ELSE CAN WE DO? WE'RE GOING TO LIE.
THERE'S NOTHING ON PAPER ANYWHERE. NOBODY CAN PROVE ANY OF THIS.

SHE'S OURS, BABS. OUR LITTLE GIRL.
ALWAYS.

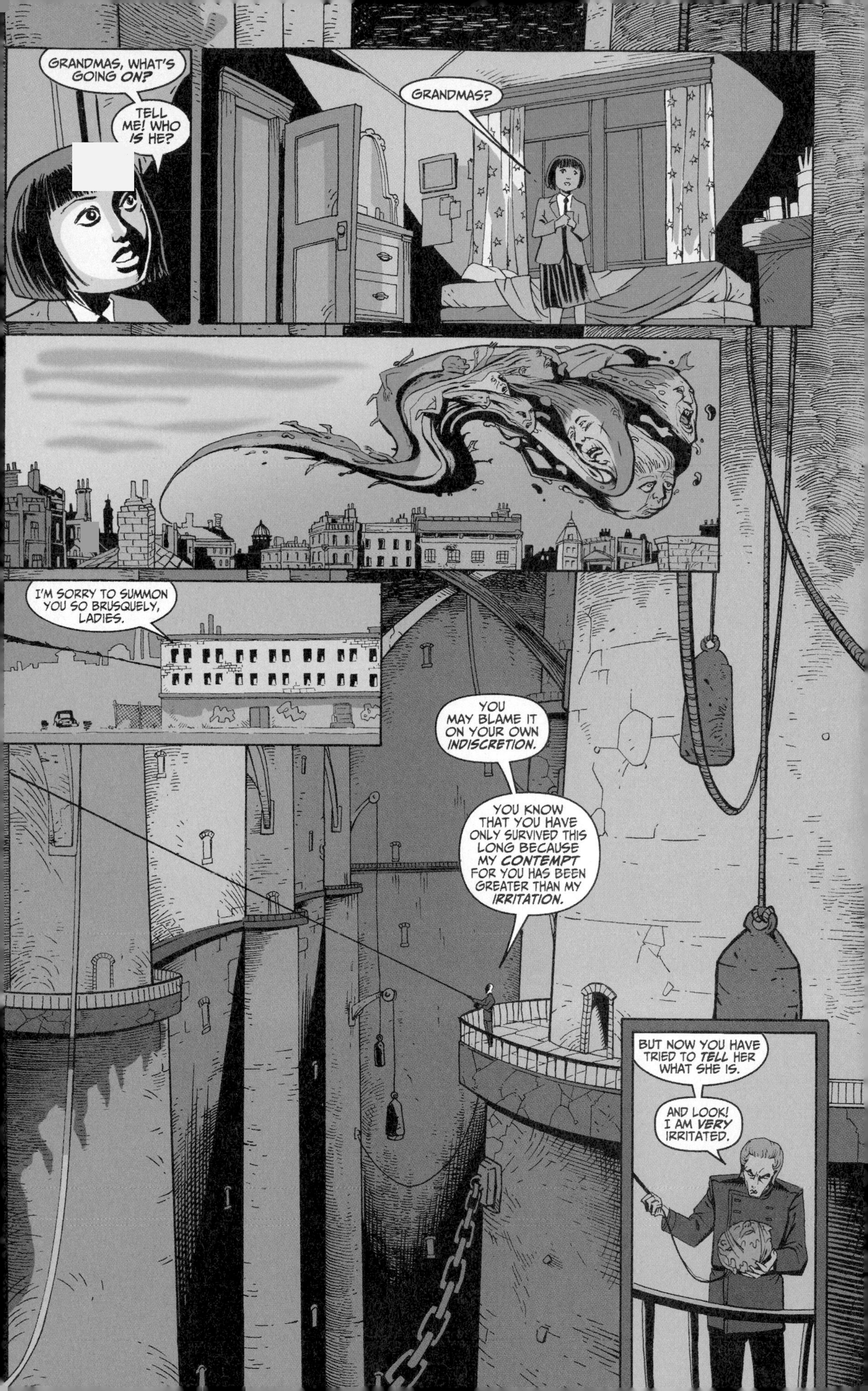
GRANDMAS, WHAT'S GOING *ON?*
TELL ME! WHO *IS* HE?
GRANDMAS?
I'M SORRY TO SUMMON YOU SO BRUSQUELY, LADIES.
YOU MAY BLAME IT ON YOUR OWN *INDISCRETION.*
YOU KNOW THAT YOU HAVE ONLY SURVIVED THIS LONG BECAUSE MY *CONTEMPT* FOR YOU HAS BEEN GREATER THAN MY *IRRITATION.*
BUT NOW YOU HAVE TRIED TO *TELL* HER WHAT SHE IS.
AND LOOK! I AM *VERY* IRRITATED.

I'VE F... FED THE NON-V... VIABLES, UNCLE. AND SCRUBBED THE FL... THE FLOORS.
COME HERE, CAL.
I'VE ALWAYS RELIED ON YOU TO PROTECT THE LITTLE ONES. YOU KNOW THAT?
Y... Y... YES, UNCLE.
WELL SOMEONE IS TRYING TO HURT THEM, CAL.
SOMEONE WANTS TO STEAL THEM AWAY FROM US FOREVER.
HE M... MUSTN'T, UNCLE. HE MUSTN'T!
CLOSE YOUR EYES. THERE. YOU SEE HIS FACE?
Y... YES. I SEE HIM.
DO WHAT YOU HAVE TO DO. THE LITTLE ONES HAVE NO ONE ELSE TO LOOK AFTER THEM.
ANOTHER NECESSARY EVIL?
I SEE NO EVIL IN IT. IT'S THE HUMAN SOUL THAT'S SACRED, NOT LIFE.
LIFE IS A SPARK IN A FORGE. IT DIES AS IT RISES.

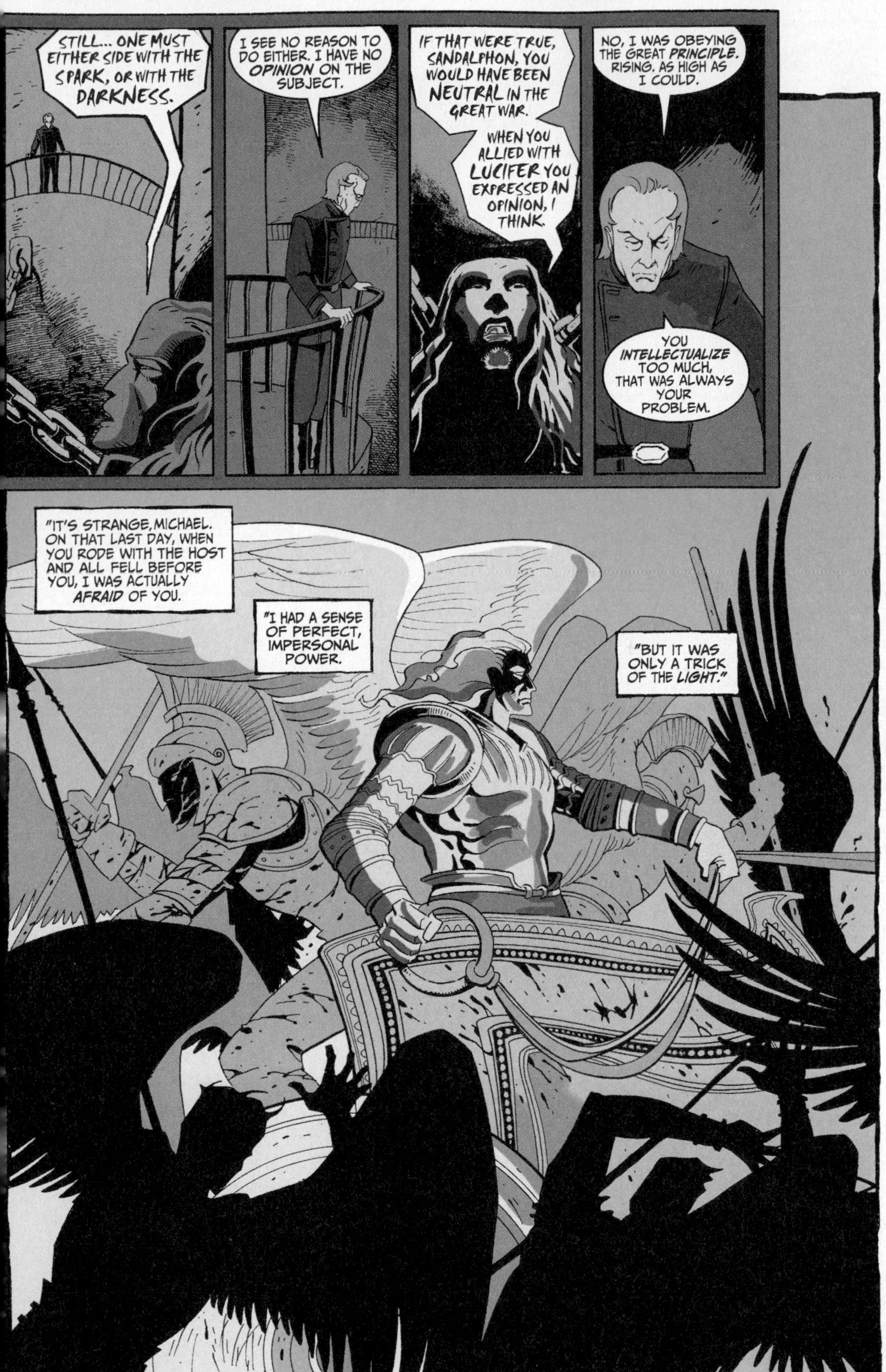
STILL... ONE MUST EITHER SIDE WITH THE SPARK, OR WITH THE DARKNESS.
I SEE NO REASON TO DO EITHER. I HAVE NO OPINION ON THE SUBJECT.
IF THAT WERE TRUE, SANDALPHON, YOU WOULD HAVE BEEN NEUTRAL IN THE GREAT WAR.
WHEN YOU ALLIED WITH LUCIFER YOU EXPRESSED AN OPINION, I THINK.
NO, I WAS OBEYING THE GREAT PRINCIPLE. RISING. AS HIGH AS I COULD.
YOU INTELLECTUALIZE TOO MUCH, THAT WAS ALWAYS YOUR PROBLEM.
"IT'S STRANGE, MICHAEL. ON THAT LAST DAY, WHEN YOU RODE WITH THE HOST AND ALL FELL BEFORE YOU, I WAS ACTUALLY AFRAID OF YOU.
"I HAD A SENSE OF PERFECT, IMPERSONAL POWER.
"BUT IT WAS ONLY A TRICK OF THE LIGHT."

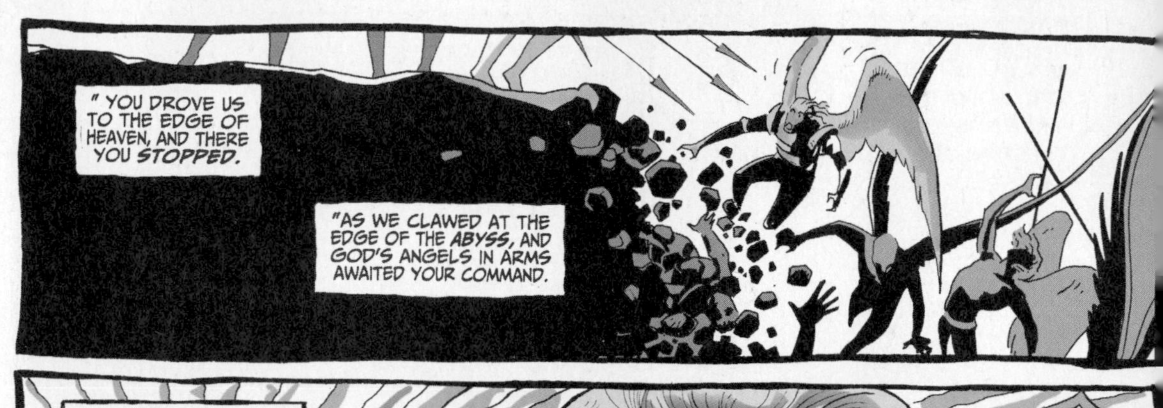

"BUT YOU HESITATED -- AND IN THAT MOMENT I STRUCK YOU DOWN.

"THERE IS A MORAL HERE, IF YOU CAN BEAR TO PURSUE IT."

SANDALPON, SPARE ME THE MORAL. YOU KNOW WHAT I AM, AND WHAT I CONTAIN.

BY TORTURING ME, YOU PUT THE WHOLE OF CREATION AT TERRIBLE RISK.

I DO NOT TORTURE YOU. YOU ARE A PRISONER OF WAR.

BUT I'M SURE YOU RECALL THE PARABLE OF THE TALENTS, MICHAEL.

I CAN'T LET YOUR POWER LIE IDLE, CAN I?

THAT WOULD BE A SIN.

BISHOP LAUD
THIS IS WAY WEIRD, ELAINE. WHY WOULD YOUR DAD GO OFF THE DEEP END LIKE THAT?
MAYBE THIS AMERICAN GEEZER WAS A PERVERT OR SOMETHING.
MAYBE HE WAS A PEDOPHILE.
BUT HOW WOULD DAD KNOW THAT JUST BY LOOKING AT HIM?
YEAH. HE WOULDN'T GO AROUND WEARING A SMILE-IF-YOU'RE-A-PEDOPHILE BADGE, WOULD HE?
THERE'S A LOOK THEY'VE GOT. YOU CAN JUST TELL.
WAS THIS GUY SKINNY WITH SCRUFFY HAIR AND A LONG MAC?
YEAH, HOW DID YOU --
OVER THERE.
I'M GONNA GO TALK TO HIM.
IF HE TRIES TO GRAB YOU, DON'T BITE HIM. HE COULD BE HIV POSITIVE.
OH SHUT UP, BARRY!

HI.
YOU FOLLOWED ME. YOU'RE GOING TO GET YOURSELF IN A LOT OF TROUBLE, MISTER.
I DON'T CARE.
ARE YOU A PEDOPHILE?
NO. I'M NOT.
THIS IS FOR YOU.
TAKE IT.
I WON'T TRY TO TOUCH YOU.
OKAY, I GIVE UP.
WHAT IS THIS? A BABY?
IT'S AN ULTRASOUND SCAN. MY WIFE'S STOMACH, THIRTEEN WEEKS AFTER SHE... AFTER WE CONCEIVED.
IT'S THE ONLY PICTURE I HAVE OF YOU, ELAINE.
YOU'RE CRAZY! I'M NOT ADOPTED! MY MUM AND DAD WOULD HAVE TOLD ME IF I WAS!
NOT ADOPTED. STOLEN. YOU SHOULD ASK YOUR PARENTS HOW --
EXCUSE ME, SIR.

IS THERE A PROBLEM, OFFICER?
I WAS JUST WONDERING WHAT BROUGHT YOU TO THE SCHOOL THIS TIME OF DAY.
FAMILY BUSINESS, IS IT?

YEAH, THAT'S RIGHT.
I WAS PASSING BY AND I WANTED TO SAY HI TO MY --

ALL RIGHT NOW, SIR. TAKE IT EASY.
WE JUST NEED TO ASK YOU A FEW QUESTIONS.
HEY! WHAT IS THIS?

UUUUF!
CHRIST! GET A GRIP ON HIM!

LET GO OF ME! I HAVEN'T DONE ANYTHING!
BUGGER IT!

THIS IS UNIT FORTY-ONE REQUESTING BACK-UP AT BISHOP LAUD'S SCHOOL, WEMBLEY.
FUCKING NOW!

YOU KNOW THE OBJECTIVE, AND YOU KNOW THE ORDER OF BATTLE.
ONE FINAL WORD, BEFORE WE SPREAD OUR WINGS.
THE MORNINGSTAR WILL FIGHT WITHOUT HONOR, AND WITHOUT MERCY. THAT IS A GIVEN.
THOSE OF YOU WHO FOUGHT HIM BEFORE WILL REMEMBER, AND KNOW I SPEAK THE TRUTH.
NOW IT MAY BE THAT IN THE TIDE OF BATTLE SOME OPPORTUNITY WILL PRESENT ITSELF.
BUT THAT ONE OF YOUR COMRADES STANDS IN THE PATH OF YOUR BLOW.
DO NOT HESITATE, BUT STRIKE HOME.
IF THE ADVERSARY COULD BE DROWNED WITH OUR BLOOD, EVERY SOLDIER HERE WOULD SLIT HIS OWN VEINS AND SING AS HE EMPTIED THEM.
NOW GO FORTH --
-- AND END THIS!

THEY'RE COMING, MUSUBI.
PREPARE YOURSELF.
EVERYTHING COMES TO A HEAD AT ONCE. WHICHEVER WAY IT GOES, THIS WILL BE *DECISIVE*.
WILL THERE BE A *BOUNTY* FOR THOSE I KILL, LORD LUCIFER?
NO. YOU FIGHT FOR THE HONOR OF THE SHIKO-ME.
THE ONLY BOUNTY IS THE *MEMORY* YOU'LL LEAVE BEHIND.
THE SWORDS ARE VERY FINE.
YOU KNOW HOW IT IS. YOU PUT THINGS AWAY FOR A RAINY DAY.
...THEN YOU LOOK UP ONE DAY AND IT'S RAINING *ANGELS*.
I'LL BE BACK IN AN HOUR OR TWO IF ALL GOES WELL. GOOD LUCK.
THERE IS NO NEED FOR UNDUE HASTE.
COME, CHILDREN OF HEAVEN.
COME *DANCE* WITH MUSUBI!

"WE WERE TALKING ABOUT FEAR, WEREN'T WE? WELL JUST FOR ONCE I WASN'T AFRAID.
"NONE OF THIS SEEMED LIKE LIFE OR DEATH, YOU KNOW?
"ALL I'D DONE WAS SAY HELLO TO YOU. THEY CAN'T ARREST A GUY FOR THAT.
POLICE
"IF THEY CAUGHT ME I'D DEMAND A DNA TEST.
"THEN THE SHIT WOULD BE HITTING SOMEONE ELSE'S FAN.
HHF! HHF! HHF!
"I WAS THINKING ANY MOMENT NOW, I'M GOING TO TAKE THE INITIATIVE. I'M GOING TO SORT THIS MESS OUT.
"THEN I LOOKED DOWN AT MY HAND.
"AND I HEARD THIS SOUND.
"LIKE A FLAG CRACKING IN THE WIND, BUT FAST.
"AND GETTING LOUDER."

J... JESUS.
JESUS CHRIST!
UUUUHH!
YOU. YOU'RE A VERY B... BAD MAN.
AND YOU'RE GOING TO D... D... DIE.

WELL DID HE THREATEN YOU AT ALL?
OR ASK YOU TO DO ANYTHING TO HIM?
NO.
NO. NOTHING.
HE SAID THAT HE WAS REALLY MY DAD. AND THAT I GOT STOLEN WHEN I WAS A BABY OR SOMETHING.
AND HE LOOKED LIKE HE WAS GOING TO CRY.
...MOST LIKELY...
...PHRENIC RATHER THAN...
...SHOULDN'T MINIMIZE...
...PARENTS WILL HAVE TO BE...
ALL RIGHT, ELAINE. THE OFFICER DOESN'T NEED YOU ANYMORE RIGHT NOW. YOU CAN GO TO YOUR LESSON.
BUT COME BACK HERE AFTER SCHOOL. I'M GOING TO CALL YOUR MOTHER AND ASK HER TO COLLECT YOU.
YES, MR. PATMORE...
THERE'S NO SUCH THING AS A HARMLESS SCHIZOPHRENIC, SIR.
NO, IF HE'S GENUINELY FIXATED ON THE GIRL, THE DANGER IS REAL ENOUGH.

KRESHH
UHHH!
P... PLEASE! YOU'RE MAKING A MISTAKE! I'M NOT BAD. I PROMISE YOU. I'VE NEVER KILLED ANYONE OR --
SNAP
OH GOD! OH MY GOD!
WHY ARE YOU DOING THIS TO ME?
B... BECAUSE YOU WOULDN'T LEAVE HER ALONE.
YOU W... W... W... WANTED TO HURT HER.
YOU WANTED TO HURT MY LITTLE S... SISTER.

"YOU KNOW THAT LINE ABOUT HOW WE HAVE TO SEE EVERYTHING THROUGH A GLASS, DARKLY? I THINK IT'S IN THE BIBLE.
"WELL, IT DOESN'T APPLY TO ME ANYMORE. I'VE PASSED THROUGH THE VEIL, LIKE YOUR GRANDMAS SAID, AND FROM THIS SIDE IT ALL LOOKS AS CLEAR AS DAYLIGHT.
"HE NEEDED A VANTAGE POINT-- A PLACE TO WATCH FROM.
"AND NATURALLY HE CHOSE THE BEST ONE IN THE ENTIRE UNIVERSE.
"HE DOESN'T THINK TWICE ABOUT STUFF LIKE THAT.
"SO HE WENT TO THE EDGE OF EVERYTHING. THERE'S SOMETHING OUT THERE CALLED THE SOURCE, BUT THAT'S NOT WHAT HE WAS AFTER.
"IN FACT HE IGNORED IT.
"WHAT HE WANTED WAS THE ALEPH.
"YOU HOLD YOUR HEAD IN THIS ONE PLACE, AND YOU CAN SEE EVERY-THING IN THE UNIVERSE, ALL AT ONCE.
"SO HE SAT THERE, WAITING FOR THE PERFECT MOMENT TO MAKE HIS MOVE.
"AND WHILE HE WAITED... MAYBE FOR DIVERSION, OR MAYBE OUT OF A SORT OF PROFESSIONAL INTEREST-- "

"HE WATCHED THE INVASION.
Children & MONSTERS
Part Three
Writer MIKE CAREY Layouts pp2-4,10-11, 14-15,18-22 PETER GROSS Finishes RYAN KELLY & GROSS
Art pp1,5-9, 12-13,16-17 DEAN ORMSTON Colored by DANIEL VOZZO Separations by JAMISON
Lettered by COMICRAFT Assistant Editor WILL DENNIS Editor SHELLY BOND
Based on characters created by GAIMAN, KIETH and DRINGENBERG

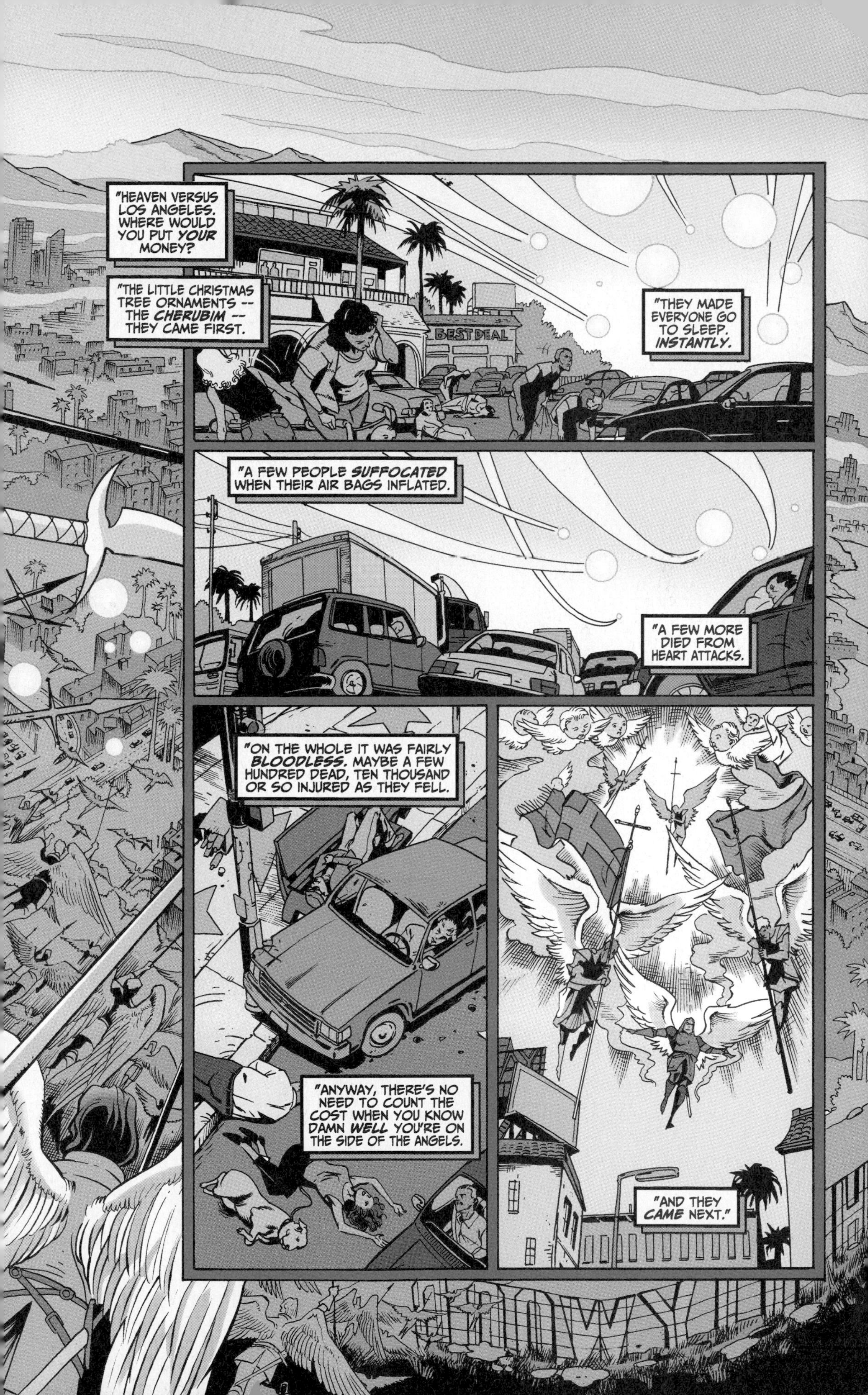
"HEAVEN VERSUS LOS ANGELES. WHERE WOULD YOU PUT YOUR MONEY?
"THE LITTLE CHRISTMAS TREE ORNAMENTS -- THE CHERUBIM -- THEY CAME FIRST.
BEST DEAL
"THEY MADE EVERYONE GO TO SLEEP. INSTANTLY.
"A FEW PEOPLE SUFFOCATED WHEN THEIR AIR BAGS INFLATED.
"A FEW MORE DIED FROM HEART ATTACKS.
"ON THE WHOLE IT WAS FAIRLY BLOODLESS. MAYBE A FEW HUNDRED DEAD, TEN THOUSAND OR SO INJURED AS THEY FELL.
"ANYWAY, THERE'S NO NEED TO COUNT THE COST WHEN YOU KNOW DAMN WELL YOU'RE ON THE SIDE OF THE ANGELS.
"AND THEY CAME NEXT."

YOU'VE DONE WELL, CHERUBIM. SOME OF THESE MAY STILL DIE, IF THE FIGHTING SPILLS OUT FROM THE GATEWAY, BUT MOST WILL BE SPARED.
GRATITUDE RELIEF INQUIETUDE.
BUT YOU'D BEST WITHDRAW. YOU'RE ILL-SUITED FOR WHAT COMES NEXT.
KEEP TEN THOUSAND SERAPHS CIRCLING ABOVE THE GATE AT ALL TIMES. IF THE ADVERSARY ATTEMPTS TO ESCAPE, HE MUST BE CONTAINED.
YES, GENERAL.
AMENADIEL--
THE THRONES ARE IN POSITION AROUND THE RUINED BUILDING.
THEY ARE READY TO MOVE ON YOU ORDER.
GOOD. AND LUCIFER?
HE HAS NOT RESPONDED. INDEED, HE HAS NOT SHOWN HIMSELF AT ALL.
SHOULD WE WAIT FOR SOME CONFIRMATION OF HIS PRESENCE BEFORE WE--
BY NO MEANS. THE INITIATIVE IS OURS, ZELAH. LET'S USE IT WHILE WE CAN.
GO IN AND SECURE THE GATE.
THANKS TO THE CHERUBIM, YOU CAN KILL ANYTHING THAT MOVES.
WITH A CLEAR CONSCIENCE.

"I KNEW NOTHING ABOUT THIS THEN, OF COURSE. AND I WOULDN'T HAVE CARED IN ANY CASE. FEAR MAKES YOU *SELFISH*.
"YOUR WHOLE WORLD *CONTRACTS* TO A SINGLE IMPERATIVE."
PLEASE, DON'T KILL ME!
I'M NOT TRYING TO *HURT* ANYONE.

L... L... LIAR! DO YOU WANT TO GO TO GOD WITH A... *LIE* IN YOUR MOUTH?
BUT IT'S TRUE. ELAINE IS MY --

DON'T YOU *DARE SP*... SPEAK HER NAME!
YOU DON'T HAVE THE *RIGHT!*
THIS IS TO KEEP HER SAFE. YOUR D... DEATH *BELONGS* TO HER.
I D... *DEDICATE* IT TO HER!
KKKkkhh

LEAVE HIM *ALONE!*

LOOK WHAT YOU'VE *DONE* TO HIM, YOU *MONSTER!*
GET *AWAY* FROM HIM!
N... NO, ELAINE. DON'T SAY... DON'T SAY THAT! PL... PLEASE!

SHIT, THAT HURTS! HOW'D YOU... FIND US?

THE PICTURE. I FOLLOWED ITS TRAIL BACK TO YOU.
MR. EASTERMAN, YOU HAVE TO TELL ME WHY YOU THINK THIS IS ME.
I WAS JUST MUGGED BY AN ANGEL. CAN THIS WAIT UNTIL I'VE BEEN TO CASUALTY?

NOW, PLEASE.

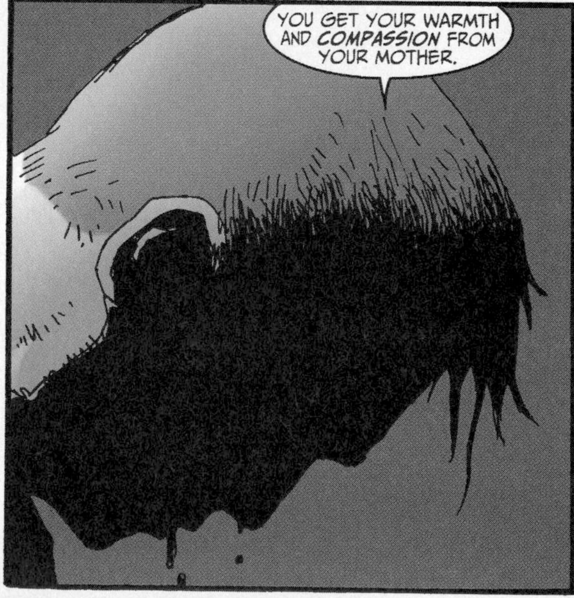
YOU GET YOUR WARMTH AND COMPASSION FROM YOUR MOTHER.

OKAY. PARTS OF THIS ARE GOING TO SOUND INSANE, BUT YOU'RE JUST GOING TO HAVE TO HEAR ME OUT AND SAVE ALL YOUR QUESTIONS 'TIL THE END.

"YOUR MOTHER'S NAME IS JUDE. SHE CONCEIVED YOU ON THE TWENTY-FIFTH OF FEBRUARY, 1988.
"AND IT'S NOT LIKE IT CAME EASY, EITHER.

"WE WENT A LITTLE CRAZY, I GUESS.
"WE'D BEEN TRYING FOR SO LONG. DID THE WHOLE THING WITH THE THERMOMETER AND THE TICKCHART, SO WE COULD MAKE LOVE JUST AFTER SHE'D--
"UHH, YOU ALREADY KNOW ABOUT THE BIRDS AND THE BEES, RIGHT?

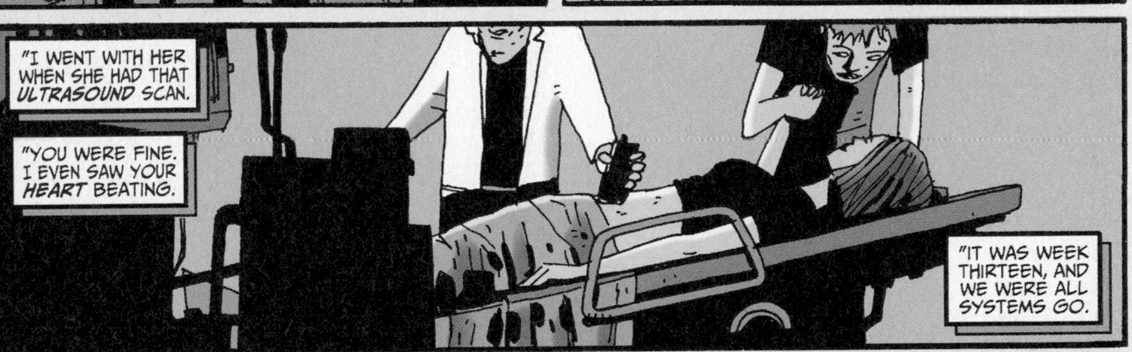
"I WENT WITH HER WHEN SHE HAD THAT ULTRASOUND SCAN.
"YOU WERE FINE. I EVEN SAW YOUR HEART BEATING.
"IT WAS WEEK THIRTEEN, AND WE WERE ALL SYSTEMS GO.

"I CELEBRATED WITH A BOTTLE OF MERLOT, JUDE ATE A BOX OF GODIVA. OUR DRUGS OF FIRST CHOICE.
"AND WE FELL ASLEEP NESTED LIKE SPOONS.

"BUT SOMETHING WOKE ME UP AROUND 2:00 AM. I REMEMBERED I'D TURNED THE LIGHT OFF -- BUT NOW THE ROOM WAS LIT UP BRIGHTER THAN DAYLIGHT.

"THERE WAS -- I SWEAR, THERE WAS A MAN LEANING OVER THE BED.
"AND HE HAD HIS HANDS... ON JUDE'S STOMACH.

"I TRIED FOR THE MACHO TONE."
GET THE HELL AWAY FROM MY WIFE!
"BUT I SWEAR, ELAINE, THE WORDS DRIED UP AS HE LOOKED AT ME.

"IT WAS LIKE HE HADN'T EVEN BOTHERED TO NOTICE ME UNTIL I SPOKE.
"AND NOW HE WAS JUST LOOKING AROUND FOR SOMETHING TO SWAT ME WITH."

SLEEP. NOW.

"AND THEN-- IT WAS MORNING. AND THE BED WAS COLD.
"IT WAS LIKE, 'WHAT IS WRONG WITH THIS PICTURE?'

"SHE WAS IN THE BATHROOM. SCARED. CRAZY. ALREADY OUT OF TEARS.
"SHE WAS MAKING THIS SOUND. THIS WHIMPERING SOUND.
"THE BABY WAS GONE."

GONE?
YEAH. NO BLOOD, NO MESS, NO RECEIPT. JUST GONE.

THE OBSTETRICIAN SAID SPONTANEOUS ABORTION. WHAT ELSE WAS SHE GOING TO SAY?
AND JUDE WOULDN'T TALK ABOUT IT AT ALL.

IT SPLIT US UP IN THE END. WELL, THAT AND MY CATALEPSY.
EVER SINCE THAT BASTARD TOLD ME TO SLEEP I'VE BEEN DOING NOTHING ELSE.
FEB 17.

THAT'S A REALLY SAD AND STRANGE STORY, MR. EASTERMAN.
BUT YOU STILL DIDN'T SAY WHY YOU THINK THE PICTURE IS A PICTURE OF ME.

YEAH, WELL I WAS HOPING THAT WOULD GET LOST IN THE SHUFFLE.
OKAY, SOME GUY TOLD ME IN A DREAM. THERE YOU GO.

A MAN IN A DREAM? A MAN WITH BLOND HAIR?
UH... YEAH.
AND HE WAS DRESSED IN BLACK AND WHITE?
NOW THAT YOU MENTION IT...

THAT WASN'T A MAN, MR. EASTERMAN.
THAT WAS THE DEVIL.
THERE'S A CHEMIST'S ROUND THE CORNER WHERE WE CAN GET YOU FIXED UP.

"AND I FOLLOWED YOU, MEEK AS A KITTEN."

LUX.
HE IS NOT HERE, CASOR.
IS HE NOT? GOOD, THEN.
TO DEFEAT THE LIGHTBRINGER WOULD HAVE BEEN GLORIOUS.
BUT I CONFESS I'D AS SOON TAKE THE GATE WITHOUT A STRUGGLE... AND LIVE TO TELL THE STORY OF HOW HE FLED FROM US.
EHURIEL, SIMODECH, YOU CAN BRING UP YOUR COHORTS NOW. GEDIEL, IT WOULD BE BEST IF THE SERAPHS STAND WATCH OUTSIDE IN CASE LUCIFER SHOULD --
WHAT WAS THAT SOUND?
ONLY ME, LITTLE SPARROWS.
ONLY MUSUBI.

THRONES, TO ME!
THE GATE IS *GUARDED* AFTER ALL! SOUND THE --
NOT SO FAST, LITTLE BIRD.
HOW *MANY* ARE YOU?
COUNTLESS THOUSANDS, PITSPAWN. ENOUGH TO SEND YOUR RACE TO *EXTINCTION* IF YOU OPPOSE US.
I *AM* MY RACE.
RRIP
BUT LET ME SEE IF I CAN *RETURN* THE FAVOR.

PHONE

WHAT DID THEY SAY?
NOT MUCH. THEY JUST CRIED A LOT.
THEY WERE GOING TO TELL ME WHEN I WAS SIXTEEN.

BUT DID YOU ASK THEM WHERE THEY GOT YOU FROM?
I MEAN WE'RE NOT TALKING ABOUT A LEGAL ADOPTION HERE.
I KNOW.

THEY'D ALREADY BEEN TOLD THEY COULDN'T ADOPT.
THEN THIS MAN CAME AND TOLD THEM THEY COULD, IF THEY... KEPT IT A SECRET.
JESUS! HOW SICK IS THIS?

MR. EASTERMAN, SOMEONE JUST JOINED US.
AND YOU'RE NOT GOING TO BE ABLE TO SEE HER UNLESS WE HOLD HANDS.
WHAT?

HI, MR. EASTERMAN. I'M MONA DOYLE, ELAINE'S BEST FRIEND.
LISTEN, I CAME TO TELL YOU THAT--
AAH!

WHAT WAS THAT?
DON'T BE RUDE, MR. EASTERMAN. THERE'S NOTHING TO BE SCARED OF.
SHE'S JUST A GHOST.

YOU KNOW, MY LIFE STOPPED MAKING SENSE YESTERDAY.
I'VE BEEN WAITING FOR IT TO CLICK BACK ON TRACK AGAIN, BUT I'M STARTING TO GIVE UP HOPE.

HELLO, MONA. I'M ELAINE'S FATHER. I'M VERY PLEASED TO MEET YOU.
YEAH, LIKEWISE.

ELAINE, I CAN'T FIND THEM!
WHAT?

WHO CAN'T YOU FIND?
MONA, THIS IS STUPID. THEY'RE ALWAYS WHERE I AM.
I KNOW. BUT NOW THEY'RE GONE. I CAN'T EVEN FEEL THEM.

WHO ARE --?
MY GRANDMAS. THEY'RE DEAD, TOO, BUT THEY SORT OF LOOK AFTER ME.

WE HAVE TO FIND OUT WHAT'S GOING ON.
"YOU TOLD YOUR FRIEND TO GO HOME AND WAIT FOR YOU.
"I THINK YOU WANTED TO PROTECT HER FROM WHAT WAS ABOUT TO HAPPEN.

"AND THEN YOU SAT AND WATCHED ME FINISH MY COFFEE. WHICH I SPUN OUT AS LONG AS I COULD.
"LIKE THE COWARD I WAS."

"SENATE TO DEBATE THIRD WORLD DEBT."
THIS ON PAGE ONE. I BELIEVE TODAY IS WHAT IS CALLED A SLOW NEWS DAY.

GENERAL, THERE IS A *DEMON* GUARDING THE GATE.
AND...?
THE THRONES ARE ENDEAVORING TO ***SUBDUE*** HER, BUT SHE IS OF THE SHIKO-ME.
SHE HAS KILLED MANY OF US.

SHIKO-ME. A ***SOUVENIR*** FROM HIS RECENT TRIP, THEN.
WELL, ONE OF THE THINGS I WAS AFRAID OF WAS COMPLETE *ANTICLIMAX...*

"...AT LEAST WE'VE BEEN SPARED THAT."

TELL ME HOW MANY I KILLED... ANGEL.
NOT ENOUGH.
IT IS OVER. THE GATE IS OURS.
WE HAVE DEFEATED LUCIFER.

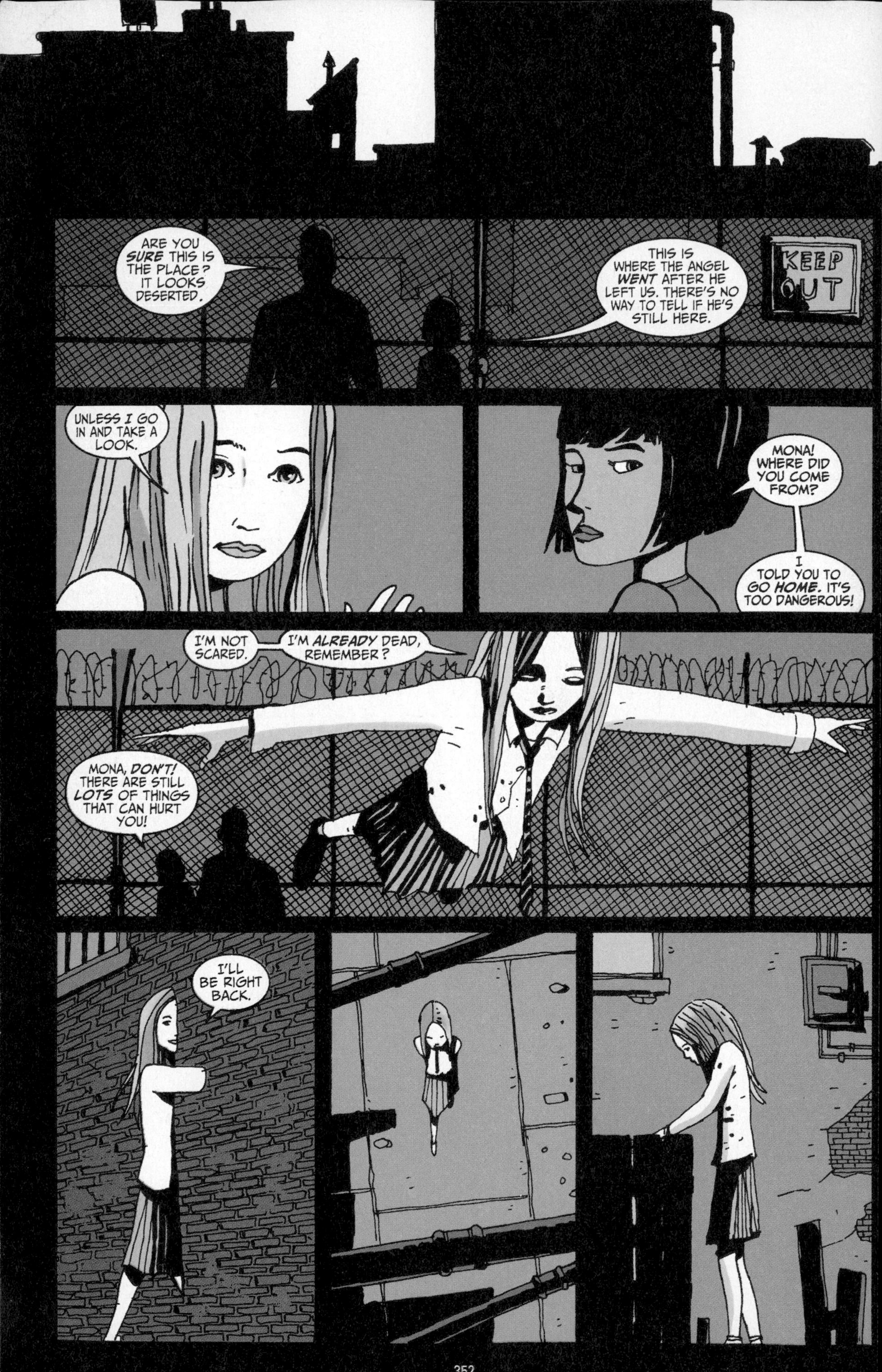
ARE YOU SURE THIS IS THE PLACE? IT LOOKS DESERTED.
THIS IS WHERE THE ANGEL WENT AFTER HE LEFT US. THERE'S NO WAY TO TELL IF HE'S STILL HERE.
KEEP OUT
UNLESS I GO IN AND TAKE A LOOK.
MONA! WHERE DID YOU COME FROM?
I TOLD YOU TO GO HOME. IT'S TOO DANGEROUS!
I'M NOT SCARED.
I'M ALREADY DEAD, REMEMBER?
MONA, DON'T! THERE ARE STILL LOTS OF THINGS THAT CAN HURT YOU!
I'LL BE RIGHT BACK.

OOLLP!
I'D ASK YOU TO EXPLAIN YOUR PRESENCE HERE...
WH...WHAT?
...BUT I'M AFRAID IT SPEAKS FOR ITSELF.
I...UH... I WAS JUST GOING TO...
...I HAVE TO-- HEY!
TO LEAVE? NO. NOT NOW.
YOUR TIME HERE HAS EXPIRED. THERE IS NO LONGER A PLACE FOR YOU IN THIS WORLD
TRY THE NEXT.

LOS ANGELES.
WE WILL NOT COMPROMISE OUR DIGNITY BY FILING THROUGH ONE OR TWO AT A TIME.
RAPHAEL. URIEL. MAKE US A WAY.
NOW MARCH--
--AND ADD THE VOID TO HEAVEN'S DEMESNES.

SERAPHS, TAKE UP DEFENSIVE POSITIONS. AND BE WARY OF *ANYTHING* THAT --

I DON'T LIKE THIS PLACE.
IT FEELS WRONG.
WELL, YOU CAN'T SEE YOUR HAND IN FRONT OF YOUR FACE, FOR ONE THING.
HERE, LET ME... DAMN!
CLICK CLICK CLICK
THAT SHOULD SHED SOME LIGHT ON --
ELAINE, I CAN'T SEE YOU.
MONA! OH MY GOD!
PLEASE HELP ME! I FEEL LIKE I'M...
MONAAA!

"AT THE EDGE OF CREATION, HE STOOD POISED.
"THE WINDOW WOULD BE NO WIDER THAN A HEARTBEAT. BETWEEN THE MOMENT WHEN ACTION BECAME POSSIBLE...
"...AND THE MOMENT WHEN IT BECAME POINTLESS."
YOUR FRIEND IS DEAD. I HELPED HER TO COME TO TERMS WITH THAT FACT.
YOU BRING HER BACK RIGHT NOW OR I'LL --
-- I'LL KILL YOU!
HAVE A CARE, CHILD. THE ABYSS GAPES AT YOUR FEET.
TAKE YOUR HANDS OFF MY DAUGHTER, BUDDY. I MEAN IT, I'LL --
-- JESUS! IT'S YOU!
YOUR DAUGHTER? YOU DELUDE YOURSELF.
YOU WERE ONLY THE JOSEPH.
THAT IS HER FATHER!
IF YOU'VE COME HERE FOR REVELATIONS, THEN HELP YOURSELF.

OH CHRIST! SWEET CHRIST!
YOU ARE HERE. IT IS... ALMOST OVER, THEN.
I AM SORRY, ELAINE BELLOC. FOR WHAT YOU HAVE LOST...
AND WHAT YOU STILL MUST LOSE.

"HE'D JUST SPOKEN. LIKE THE VOICE OF SOME INSTRUMENT THAT THEY NEVER CAGED IN AN ORCHESTRA.
"SO NATURALLY I LOOKED AT HIS FACE.
"THEN I LOOKED DOWN AND SAW THE GREAT SLABS OF IRON, BIG ENOUGH TO CRUSH A MAN TO DEATH.
"AND I THOUGHT, 'HOW COULD YOU CHAIN SOMETHING THAT LOOKS LIKE THAT?'
"THE CHAINS WERE OBSCENE.
"BUT THEY WERE NOTHING COMPARED TO HIS WOUNDS. HIS WHOLE TORSO WAS LAID OPEN, SCARRED AND BLEEDING.
"THOUSANDS OF YEARS OF TORTURE, LIKE GEOLOGICAL STRATA.
"MY EYES HURT FROM LOOKING AT HIM.
"I WAS DUMBSTRUCK. I'D NEVER SEEN SO MUCH BEAUTY, OR SO MUCH UGLINESS. BUT YOU RECOVERED PRETTY QUICKLY, ALL THINGS CONSIDERED.
DOES IT HURT?
"I GUESS YOU'RE MORE USED TO ANGELS THAN I AM."
NO. IT DOES NOT HURT. BUT IT EVENTUALLY KILLS.
AS WITH SO MANY THINGS IN YOUR WORLD.
Children & MONSTERS
Written by MIKE CAREY Layouts by PETER GROSS Part Four
Finishes by RYAN KELLY Colored by DANIEL VOZZO Separated by JAMISON
Lettered by COMICRAFT Associate Editor WILL DENNIS Editor SHELLY BOND
Based on characters created by GAIMAN, KIETH and DRINGENBERG

I'M MAKING ANGELS.

THAT'S... THAT'S STUPID! I'M NOT AN ANGEL.
I HAVEN'T GOT ANY WINGS OR ANYTHING.
WE ARE STERILE, YOU SEE. ALL EXCEPT FOR HIM. MICHAEL.
HE HAS THE DEMIURGIC POWER, BEQUEATHED BY GOD HIMSELF.
I USED THAT POWER TO QUICKEN HUMAN WOMBS. THEN I TOOK THE UNBORN CHILDREN AND USED HIS BODY TO INCUBATE THEM.
AND THINGS HAVE GONE WELL. TRUE, CAL HAS NO GENITALIA, AND IS A LITTLE... IMPAIRED IN OTHER WAYS.
BUT THEN THERE'S YOU. AFTER ONLY FOUR THOUSAND GENERATIONS.
OR MORE TO THE POINT, THERE'S YOUR OVARIES. PERFECT AND FULLY FUNCTIONAL.
BELIEVE ME WHEN I SAY THAT I TAKE NO PLEASURE IN THIS.
TO HARVEST IN SPRINGTIME IS SOMEHOW INTENSELY UNAESTHETIC.

YOU BASTARD! YOU FUCKING PSYCHOPATHIC BASTARD!
IF YOU THINK YOU'RE TOUCHING ONE HAIR ON HER HEAD --

YOU ARE UTTERLY IRRELEVANT TO ALL THIS. SHE IS NOT YOUR CHILD.
THE HUMAN SIDE OF HER HERITAGE IS YOUR WIFE'S -- WHILE MICHAEL BOTH SIRED AND ULTIMATELY BIRTHED HER.

YOU SHOULD HAVE STAYED AT HOME, LITTLE MAN.
FOR IN TRUTH, YOU HAD NOTHING TO GAIN HERE.

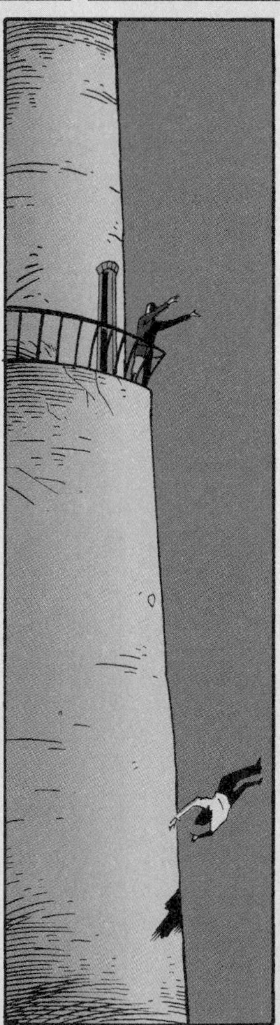

NO PLEASURE? THEN WHAT CAUSE WAS SERVED BY HIS DEATH?
ONLY NEATNESS. NOTHING MORE.

"OTHERS WERE DYING TOO. THE ANGELIC EXPEDITIONARY FORCE, STEPPING INTO THE VOID, HAD MET A SPIRIT THERE.
"SOMETHING THEY COULDN'T *DEAL* WITH.
"IT'S A BIT PETTY OF ME, I KNOW.
"BUT *THINKING* ABOUT THIS PART GIVES ME A CERTAIN KICK.
"ANGELS ARE SUCH *SCUMBAGS*. IT'S GOOD TO SEE THEM TAKEN APART ONCE IN A WHILE."
AMENADIEL --
THERE IS RESISTANCE. A SINGLE CREATURE.
ANOTHER DEMON?
NO, NO. I FOUND THIS BOTTLE. THE TWO ARE CONNECTED IN SOME WAY.
YES. I SEE.
THANK YOU, RAPHAEL. REST AWHILE.
IT'S ONLY APPROPRIATE THAT I FINISH THIS MYSELF.

"DID YOU SEE ME *FALL*, ELAINE? HEAR ME HIT BOTTOM?

"DID YOU KNOW HOW *ALONE* YOU WERE?

"NOT HAUNTED ANYMORE BY ANYONE. NOT EVEN *ME*.

"JUST A TWELVE-YEAR-OLD GIRL, PRETTY MUCH OUT OF OPTIONS.

AH YES. I SEE.
THAT WAS QUITE CLEVER, UNDER THE CIRCUMSTANCES.
TO HIDE AMONG YOUR DAMAGED SIBLINGS.

BUT THEIR SPIRITS ARE MUDDY RAINBOWS, CHILD.
YOURS IS A FLAWLESS DIAMOND.

THERE IS NO CESSPIT ON EARTH THROUGH WHOSE DEPTHS YOU WOULD NOT SHINE.

AAAAH!

LET ME *GO!*
IF YOU TOUCH ME I'LL *SCREAM!* I'LL SCREAM UNTIL SOMEONE COMES.

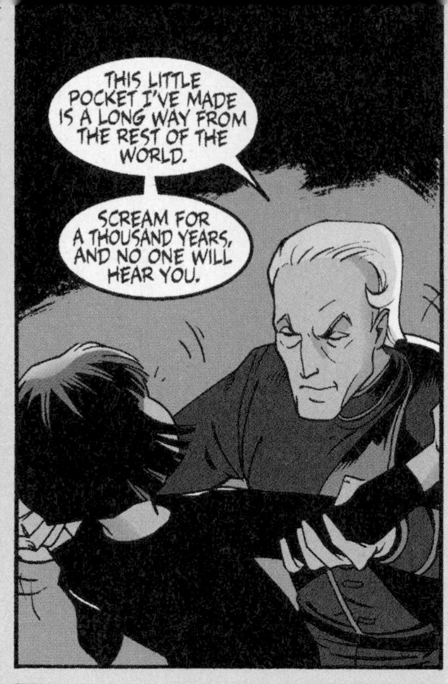
THIS LITTLE POCKET I'VE MADE IS A LONG WAY FROM THE REST OF THE WORLD.
SCREAM FOR A THOUSAND YEARS, AND NO ONE WILL HEAR YOU.

WELL, THAT'S PROBABLY TRUE *NINE* TIMES OUT OF TEN --

-- BUT THERE'S MORE THAN *ONE* WAY TO SKIN A CAT, SANDALPHON.
ESPECIALLY IF YOU HAVE THE RIGHT *MOUSE.*

COME FOR ME THEN, CREATURE.
YOU MADE SHORT ENOUGH WORK OF MY ARMY.
YOU FEAR THIS VESSEL, DON'T YOU?
NOW WHY WOULD THAT BE?
YES, OF COURSE.
NEVER IGNORE THE OBVIOUS.

HELP ME, LUCIFER! HE'S GOING TO CUT BITS OUT OF ME AND THEN KILL ME! HELP ME, PLEASE!

YOU SHOULD NOT INTERFERE HERE, MORNINGSTAR.

OH? AND WHY IS THAT?

BECAUSE THE FIGHT I CONTINUE HERE IS THE ONE THAT YOU BEGAN. I AM RAISING SOLDIERS.

INDEED? TO WHAT PURPOSE?

TO STORM THE GATES OF HEAVEN!

LET ME GO! THE DEVIL'S ON MY SIDE.

HE'LL KILL YOU IF YOU HURT ME!

YOUR ARMY SEEMS RATHER SMALL, SANDALPHON. AND RATHER MUTINOUS.

I DON'T UNDERSTAND WHY YOU'RE HERE AT THIS TIME. HOW YOU EVEN KNEW --
REALLY? YOU THINK YOUR TRAIL WAS WELL-HIDDEN?
I ASSURE YOU IT WASN'T.
I MET THE GIRL A SHORT WHILE AGO, AND I INFERRED MOST OF WHAT YOU'VE DONE JUST FROM ONE GOOD LOOK AT HER.
IT'S TRUE THAT YOUR POCKET WORLD WAS HARD TO FIND. AT LEAST AT FIRST.
LUCIFER!
LOOK OUMMMPHH!
FLOOOMP

LUCIFER, I'VE LABORED TOO LONG AND TOO HARD.
MY PLANS ARE TOO FAR ADVANCED. I WARN YOU --
I CARE NOTHING FOR YOUR LABOR, OR YOUR PLANS. BUT I REQUIRE BOTH MICHAEL AND THIS CHILD INTACT.
NOW YIELD, OR FIGHT ME -- BUT WASTE NO MORE OF MY TIME.
I... I HAVE NO DESIRE TO FIGHT YOU.
I CONSIDER US TO BE ON THE SAME SIDE.
THAT'S A POINT OF VIEW, CERTAINLY. IN ANY CASE, I'M OVERLOOKING THE SENTENCE THAT BEGAN "I WARN YOU."
BUT ONLY BECAUSE YOU DIDN'T GET TO FINISH IT.

MICHAEL.
IT'S BEEN A LONG TIME.
SO IT HAS, MORNINGSTAR.
LONGER FOR ME THAN YOU, PERHAPS.
I HAVE A PROPOSITION FOR YOU. A SIMPLE ONE.
IT CONCERNS DEATH AND REBIRTH.
I MUST RESPECTFULLY DECLINE. YOU KNOW THE POWER THAT IS IN ME.
YOU KNOW WHAT IT WILL DO WHEN IT'S RELEASED.
I HAVE A PLEASANT SURPRISE FOR YOU, BROTHER.
BUT I'LL NEED YOU TO BE IN A MORE PORTABLE SIZE.

UHH!
RRUMBLE

U... UNCLE SANDALPHON. WE HAVE TO G... G... GO.
EVERYTHING'S F... FALLING APART!
I KNOW. IT WAS ONLY MICHAEL'S POWER THAT WAS HOLDING IT TOGETHER.

YOU GO AHEAD, CAL.
I HAVE A LOT TO THINK ABOUT -- A LOT TO DO BEFORE WE CAN START THE PROGRAM UP AGAIN.

B... B... BUT --

LOS ANGELES.
REST EASY, RAPHAEL.
THE CREATURE IS BACK INSIDE ITS BOTTLE, AND ALL IS --
GOOD DAY TO YOU, AMENADIEL OF THE THRONES.
NO DOUBT YOU RECOGNIZE THE ARCHANGEL MICHAEL, EVEN IN THIS DAMAGED AND FRAGILE STATE.
NOW, IF THIS BRICK DUST WE'RE TREADING IN IS WHAT I THINK IT IS --
-- THEN I'D LIKE YOU TO EXPLAIN WHAT YOU'RE DOING ON MY PROPERTY.

THE EXPLANATION IS GLARINGLY OBVIOUS, LUCIFER.
THIS CITY BELONGS TO HEAVEN NOW. AS DOES YOUR GATE.
DISPUTE IT WITH THESE SERAPHS IF YOU WISH.
AMENADIEL, YOU DON'T UNDERSTAND.
LUCIFER HAS WON. WE HAVE TO LEAVE. NOW.
WHAT?
REFLECT A MOMENT. MICHAEL IS A VESSEL FOR THE DIVINE POWER. IF HE DIES -- IF THAT VESSEL CRACKS --
-- THE WORLDS WILL BE SCOURED CLEAN OF LIFE. THERE WILL BE NOTHING LEFT.
EXACTLY SO. AND I HAVE PROMISED HIM DEATH. THE ONLY QUESTION IS WHERE.
IF THE GATE IS YOURS, I'LL HAVE TO DROP THE AXE RIGHT HERE.
THIS IS NOT OVER, MORNINGSTAR. AND IT MUST BE OVER. WHILE YOU LIVE, THERE IS NO JOY FOR ME.
I CHALLENGE YOU TO FACE ME -- ALONE. WHEREVER AND WHENEVER YOU LIKE.
VERY WELL. IN EFFRUL, A YEAR FROM NOW. THAT WILL GIVE YOU TIME TO PUT YOUR AFFAIRS IN ORDER.
PUT THE BOTTLE DOWN BEFORE YOU LEAVE.
THAT'S MINE TOO.

WAIT HERE FOR US. WE'RE UNLIKELY TO BE LONG.
A DOORWAY TO ANOTHER REALM, LUCIFER?
NOT EXACTLY. YOU'LL SEE.
AH! THE VOID. NOW I UNDERSTAND.
YOU HAVE TAKEN ME OUTSIDE OF CREATION. A CONTROLLED DETONATION, THEN.
SOMETHING LIKE THAT.
READY?
FOR EIGHTY THOUSAND YEARS, AT LEAST.
STRIKE CLEAN, BROTHER.

AND THIS IS... WHAT, EXACTLY?
THE CULMINATION OF ALL MY EFFORTS. THE END OF PREDESTINATION. THE END OF TYRANNY.
I HAVE ESCAPED FROM PROVIDENCE, MICHAEL. I'VE GONE INTO THE GOD BUSINESS.
YOU COULD JOIN ME, IF YOU WANTED TO. YOU'D BE WELCOME.
I WILL CONSIDER IT. BUT I THINK NOT.
GO WELL, BROTHER.
"THE DEVIL STAYED AWHILE AND WATCHED. EPHEMERAL PARTICLES DID THEIR DANCE AND THEN DIED.
"GAS CLOUDS BEGAN TO DRAW IMPERCEPTIBLY TOGETHER, AND WEAVE THEMSELVES INTO STARS.
"I WOULDN'T LIKE TO GUESS WHAT HE WAS FEELING."

HE MAY LINGER A WHILE.
I'LL TAKE YOU HOME, IF YOU WISH.
NO, THANKS. I'LL WAIT FOR LUCIFER.

BE WARY OF HIM, ELAINE. YOU HAVE A LONG WAY TO GO, AND HE IS NOT THE SAFEST OF TRAVELING COMPANIONS.
HE SAVED MY LIFE TWICE.

HE'S THE ONLY GROWN-UP I KNOW WHO KEEPS HIS PROMISES.

YES. IT IS A POINT OF PRIDE FOR HIM. BUT PLEASE -- DON'T MISTAKE IT FOR A VIRTUE.
OPEN YOUR HAND. I HAVE A GIFT FOR YOU.

THANK YOU. WHAT IS IT?
AN ANOMALY. WHEN SANDALPHON'S POCKET WORLD COLLAPSED, IT SPAT THIS OUT. AND I CAUGHT IT.

IT IS YOUR GRANDMOTHERS.
TAKE CARE... MY DAUGHTER.

"AND THAT'S IT, MORE OR LESS. HIS STORY, LIKE I SAID, NOT MINE. DESTROYING ME WAS A VERY MINOR SIDE EFFECT.
"I WAS JUST THE HAT ON A STICK YOU WAVE AROUND TO SEE WHERE THE ENEMY'S SHOTS ARE COMING FROM."
AND IT'S NOT EVEN LIKE HE WEIGHED UP THE COST AND WENT AHEAD ANYWAY.
HE JUST TAKES WHAT HE WANTS AND COST DOESN'T COME INTO IT.
HE'D DO THE SAME TO YOU. YOU DON'T BELIEVE THAT, BUT HE WOULD.
YOU LOOK DIFFERENT FROM THIS SIDE. YOU SHINE LIKE A LIGHT SHOW. IT'S SO BEAUTIFUL, BUT IT TAKES SOME GETTING USED TO.
YOU KNOW, THIS IS FUCKED UP BEYOND ALL UNFUCKING. I WANT TO FACE HIM DOWN. I WANT TO PROTECT YOU FROM HIM.
I WANT TO BEAT HIM INTO A SMEAR WITH YOU WATCHING.
I WANT YOU TO LOVE ME AS MUCH AS YOU LOVE HIM.
The End

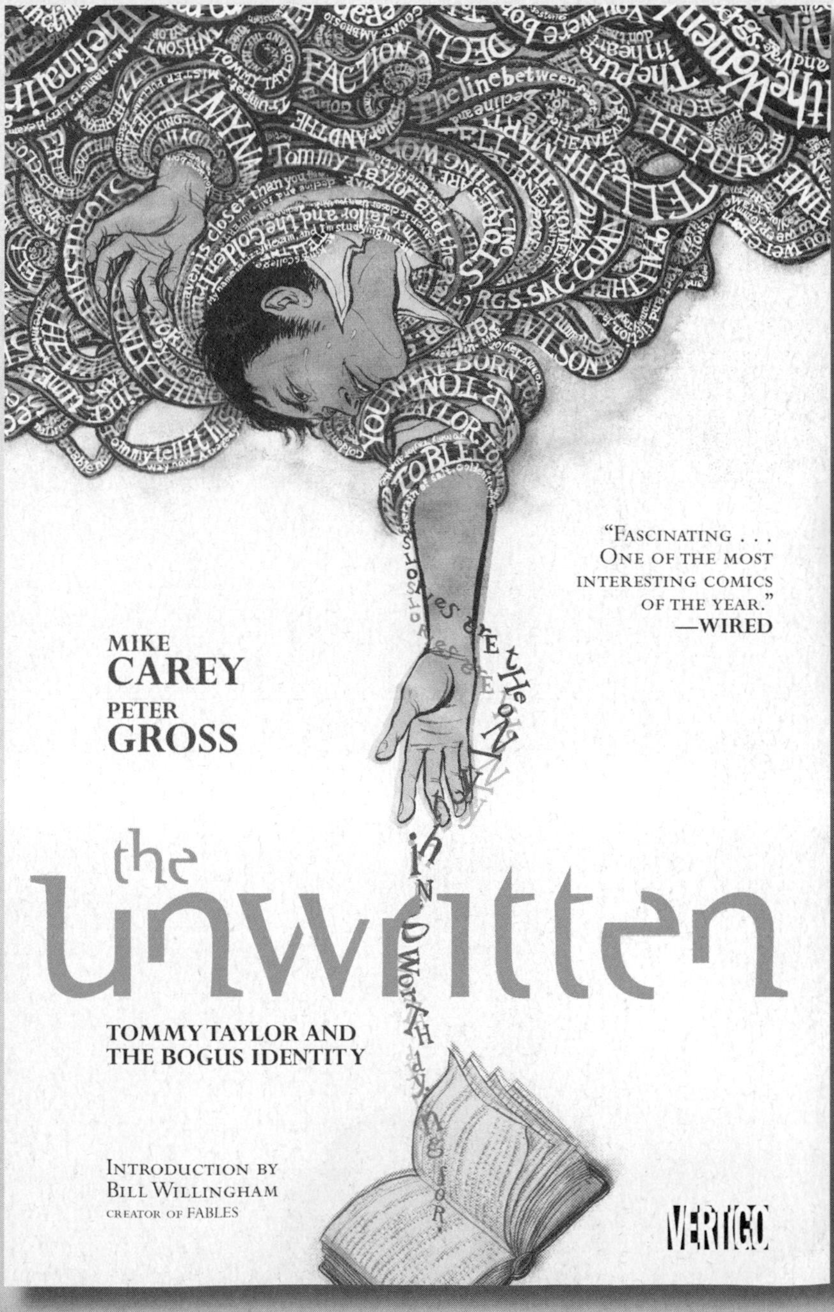

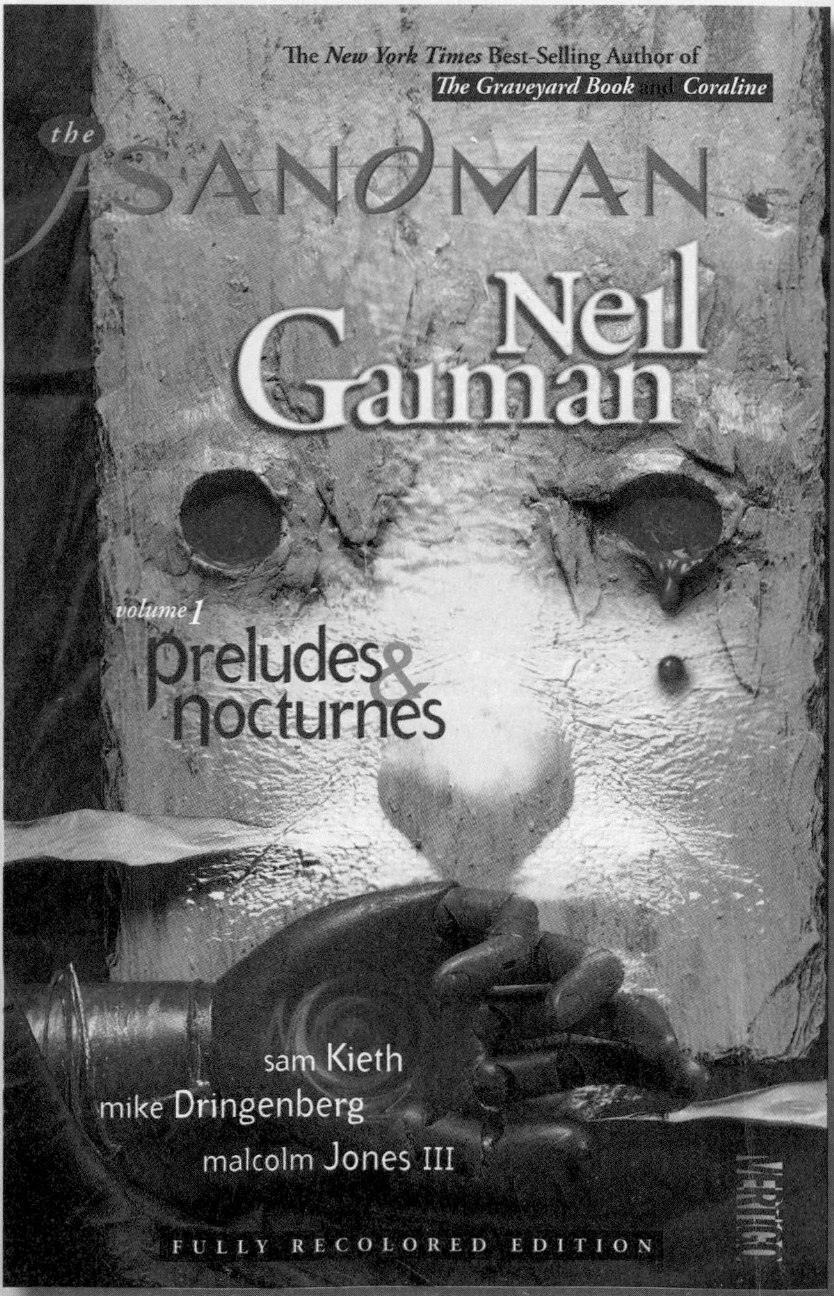